IBERIAN VILLAGES

NORMAN F CARVER JR

IBERIAN VILLAGES

PORTUGAL & SPAIN

NORMAN F CARVER JR

DOCUMAN PRESS

ACKNOWLEDGEMENTS

This work has extended over more than a decade and during that time many persons have given me assistance and advice. I cannot remember them all. My deepest gratitude must go to the many Portugese and Spaniards who never resented my intrusions, and were always friendly and helpful. I should especially like to thank, in Lisbon, Tama, Milu, and Carl who not only directed me to some outstanding villages in Portugal, but took me in when I returned exhausted from my travels. At various times, my son Norman III, my daughter Cristina, and my wife all accompanied me. My thanks to them for their companionship and their patience while I climbed a hill for a long view or waited hours for the right light or went without meals in the desire to use every minute of a fading sun. In the preparation of the book, Harry Randall again gave much invaluable advice and editorial help. Roger Hansen skillfully made hundreds of proof prints. The printers, and especially Rolf Hammer worked diligently and skillfully under a difficult schedule to achieve the desired results.

Again my wife, Joan, contributed endlessly to the project at every stage and without her help it could never have been completed.

Documan Press, Ltd.
Post Office Box 387
Kalamazoo, Michigan 49005

ISBN: 0-932976-02-5 cloth
ISBN: 0-932976-02-3 paper

Designed by Norman F. Carver, Jr.
Printed by EPI, Inc.
Battle Creek, Michigan
Printed in the United States

For my mother and father, whose high creative standards were an inspiration.

CONTENTS

PREFACE

Almost from the beginning, man has made two kinds of architecture. Foremost has always been the architecture of the monuments, temples, and palaces. Built in one of the recognized styles such as Greek, Roman, Gothic, or Modern, this high-style architecture had its own refined aesthetic and palette of acceptable forms. These are the structures so thoroughly documented in the authoritative histories of architecture (whose comprehensiveness may be judged by their failure to include any building east of Egypt). But, as influential as these buildings have been, they are only a tiny fraction of the built environment.

It is the second kind of architecture, those plain, unassuming dwellings in which man has lived over the centuries, that comprises the overwhelming mass of buildings. This is folk or vernacular architecture. In contrast with the pretensions, heroics, and esoteric aesthetics of high-style architecture, its primary motivation was practical, economical shelter. Anonymous craftsmen, disregarding the dominant historical styles, developed forms reflecting the local climate, sites, materials, and needs. Hence vernacular aesthetics sprang from the materials and the construction process itself rather than from imposed abstract concepts. Until very recently, these common and unpretentious structures were largely dismissed as unsophisticated and unimportant.

What is their importance? In ITALIAN HILLTOWNS, the first book in this series, I discussed vernacular architecture's significance as well as its general characteristics in some detail. I will not repeat that discussion here except to stress that indigenous architecture is perhaps our only chance to see some of the fundamental connections between man, society, the natural environment, and architecture. Simpler societies ignored these relationships at their peril. But, shielded by modern technology and obscured by complex functional needs as well as by centuries of stylistic indulgence, these fundamental relationships are now often ignored. The result is a contemporary architecture that is often ecologically unsound and remote from reality.

IBERIAN VILLAGES presents an architecture that not only reflects many of these relationships but does it with elan. It is an architecture that re-affirms the universality of certain vernacular characteristics first outlined in ITALIAN HILLTOWNS. Such characteristics are by their very universality "a basis for a language of form and the means by which we can retain our continuity with the past and enrich our future". The characteristics of vernacular are:

1. Forms are functionally motivated in the fullest sense --that is, physically and psychologically.

2. They are precisely adapted to climate and environment.

3. They reflect the building process and local skills, materials, and technology.

4. They are produced by the whole community and share a common tradition.

5. They vary in detail but seldom in type.

6. Ornamentation, if it is used, generally grows out of the solution to some functional problem.

7. The repetitive individual house form is transcended by the vivid and unique overall form of the whole village.

8. Growth is slow, open-ended, and always in human scale.

6

ORIGINS OF IBERIAN FORMS

There is an underlying similarity to much of the architecture in the Mediterranean basin, reflecting not only a fairly uniform environment but thousands of years of cultural interchange fostered by this convenient sea road. In fact, Mediterranean vernacular can be seen as variations on one main theme --dense hilltowns of stone sheltered against the sun and marauders from the sea.

Iberia --wild and remote at the uncharted end of the Sea -- had little contact with the rest of the civilized world until late Roman times. This remoteness, together with extremes of climate and geography within Iberia and the settlement by culturally diverse groups over the centuries, has produced an astonishing variety of dwellings and village forms.

As in many cultures, the immediate demands of site, climate and available materials, rather than subtler social needs, had the most obvious influence on folk forms. Iberian vernacular confirms this by the many examples where one group evolved various solutions to cope with different environments -- and conversely by the development of similar forms in similar environments by unrelated groups. Such clear reflection of environmental forces does not deny cultural influence, but it does confirm their usually more subtle effects.

One of these forces, climate, influenced the shape and orientation not only of individual houses but of whole villages. The grouping, orientation, number and size of openings, and the location of sleeping, cooking, and animal quarters were the only available means to moderate the climate --whether it was the baking heat of summer or the damp cold of winter.

The Land

Iberian climate is both benevolent and cruel. The peninsula roughly divides into four geographic-climatic regions, ranging from the Alpine to the tropical. The northern region, tempered by the Atlantic, is cool and rainy with high, lush mountains in the interior reminiscent of Switzerland. Because of its remoteness and inaccessibility this region remained free of the Moslem conquest and it is from this enclave the reconquest of the south began. Galacia, in the very northwest corner of Spain, and northern Portugal, though less mountainous, have a similar climate.

In the central part of the peninsula lies the most typical and most influential region -- the high, arid plateaus and mountains of Castile and Extremadura. It is a land of bitterly cold winters and hot dry summers where, despite the impression of vast plains, one is never far from the mountains.

The eastern and southeastern coastal areas are a third region, semi-tropical and typically Mediterranean in feeling. Unfortunately it is the most corrupted by modernization, so little original architecture remains. Fourth is the southwest, stretching from Granada in Spain to the Portugese Atlantic Coast --a relatively hot, dry region of rugged terrain and also huge plains.

Tourist brochures to the contrary, the climate can be extreme in all areas. As the Spanish proverb says, "Nine months of winter and three months of hell".

Iberian Origins

In coping with these extremes early settlers used construction techniques which they brought with them. These were as basic as

AN INTRODUCTION TO IBERIA

Centuries of strife on the Iberian peninsula caused
widespread building of fortified hilltowns — towns
where the houses clustered around a castle on some
strategic peak. Such towns were built by Moslems
defending their shrinking frontier or by Christian
lords resisting attacks from Moors or rival lords.

Almansa's (9) Moorish citadel emerges from a rock
that rises abruptly out of the plains of La Mancha.
Alcala (10) is a northern town in the high mountains
near Teruel. The southern town of Monte Frio,
dominated by its fortress-like church, is built around a
defendable rock to which the inhabitants could retire
when under attack (11, 178-183).

*The dispersed, sun-seeking houses of Carmona
(12, 49-51), a northern mountain village, contrast
with the densely packed sun-shielding houses in the
southern hilltown of Casares. (13, 152-161).*

Compact towns with narrow streets occur in both the north and south but the atmosphere is entirely different. The southern streets are clean, bright, inviting and an integral part of the town's structure. On the other hand, some northern streets, nearly sealed off by projecting upper stories, seem merely left-over, utilitarian passages.

La Alberca a northern mountain town (14, 78-91). Vejer de la Frontera (15, 144-145).

Frequent features of northern towns are the
arcaded streets or plazas. The porticos shade
inhabitants from the hot sun, shelter them from rain,
and expand their main floor work spaces. Porticos also
permit expansion of the upper stories and are the
location for weekly markets in many towns. The
portico is a different kind of space, neither indoors
nor out, but a transition between.

La Alberca's medieval main square has arcades
on three sides (16, 78-91). This stepped portico leads
off the square at Penaranda de Duero (17, 66-67).

The casual blending of column styles with slightly
irregular arches introduces variety within the portico's
ordered rhythms. A disadvantage — the darkening of
the lower floor — is mitigated in Garovillas (19, 94-96)
by the use of thin columns and whitewash that reflects
the light deep inside, unlike the somber porticos
around the plaza in Horta de San Juan (18).

One of the southern village's most appealing aspects is the wave-like pattern of tiled roofs seen from above. The traditional tile roofs are a rich texture of variegated earthtones that combine handsomely with the white walls beneath. This stunning complex at Castellar near Algeciras incorporates subtle curves and the patina of great age. Unfortunately, these roofs are being replaced with modern tiles of a uniform and harsh orange color.

A building form that appears unique to Iberia (but occurs elsewhere in Europe and Asia) is the raised storage house, called in Spanish 'horrero'. Raising the building on pillars with flat stone caps protects the contents from rats and moisture. Stone horreros, such as these at Lindoso (24, 33-34), are common in the northwest of Spain and Portugal. The wooden types are found throughout the northern mountains of the peninsula. This (22-23) is near Cangas de Onis.

24

the Visigoth's north European wooden huts, as structurally advanced as the Roman arch, and as environmentally sound as the Moorish courtyard --though sometimes adapted to conditions inconsistent with their origins. Little remains of the earliest Iberian and later Celtic or Visigoth settlements. Evidently they lived in archetypal hilltop *castros*, collections of stone or wood huts and animal pens ringed with moats and rubble walls.

The Romans were the first to attempt to unify the unruly tribes of the peninsula. During the first to the fifth centuries they attempted to break up the clan system by moving people from small remote, hilltop hamlets into valley towns connected by an extensive system of roads. The road network was an effective means of unification that lasted for centuries. But it also permanently by-passed many places, leaving them more isolated and forgotten than ever. Beyond roads, bridges, and aqueducts, the Romans also left their mark in the characteristic grid plans of their civic centers, many of which still exist as the cores of modern cities.

Roman colonists devised the pattern of large estates under absentee owners who lived in the towns off the profits of their land holdings. The pattern persists to this day especially in the south. With the collapse of the Roman Empire and the subsequent invasions of the Visigoths and Vandals in the fifth century, A.D. an Iberian 'dark age' began. It was a a period of stagnation that, except for a few primitive churches, left little behind.

Islam

In the first half of the eighth century southern and central Iberia was rapidly occupied by Moslem invaders from North Africa. Since Spain and Portugal did not exist as political entities, but as a collection of independent kingdoms whose only common tie was their Christianity, the Moslems were able to occupy most of the peninsula within forty years and set up a strong central government for the first time since the Romans. The Moslem occupation initiated a decisive period in Iberian history, unleashing forces of accord and divisiveness that have racked the peninsula ever since.

The Moors never conquered all, however. In the far north the fierce mountain people held out in their ancient *castros* and from here the re-conquest began --slowly but inexorably moving south until the last Moslem ruler retreated from Granada to a small enclave in the Sierra Nevada. They were finally expelled by King Ferdinand and Queen Isabella in the same year that Columbus discovered America. Moslem control, though diminishing in extent, lasted 700 years.

The centuries of struggle that began in the remote mountains of the north no doubt added to that region's especially strong separatist attitudes. Such attitudes spread as various sections of the peninsula were reconquered and emerged as small independent kingdoms. In Spain the reconquest proceeded slowly and erratically, creating stubborn pockets of resistance and liberation often separated from each other for centuries, and reinforcing a regional rivalry that still plagues Spain today. On the other hand, most of what is now Portugal gained a measure of freedom from Moslem rule as early as 1143, and, except for a brief period, has remained independent ever since.

Since the Christians fought among themselves as much as against the Moslems,

central and southern Spain has literally hundreds of castles --from which the province of Castile derives its name. The effect of this rivalry was crippling. It hindered free trade and sapped manpower and energy away from maintaining the increased agricultural productivity that had developed under the Moors --"the battle against the Moors was won but the battle against nature was lost"[1].

Counteracting separatism was the unifying effect of the early Roman road network, the spread of Christianity, and the foreign influences along the coasts and along the great pilgrimage route to the shrine church at Santiago de Campostela. The *camino de Santiago* was the route for hundreds of thousands of pilgrims from all parts of Europe. It extended across northern Spain from the Pyrenees to the Atlantic coast. Entire villages along it were devoted to the pilgrims' needs (42-45).

The correlation between a society's built forms and its environment are especially evident in Iberia and specific examples will be examined in more detail in the discussion of each region. In general, geographically and culturally separated, each group developed its own methods and forms. Any impetus for change was through the normal evolution of needs and skills as well as through an evolving hierarchy of values and beliefs that changed priorities --and only occasionally through an extraordinary event such as outside contact or conquest.

Isolation and the strength of tradition are particularly evident in remote mountain regions of the north, where some very primitive dwellings were still in use until very recently (46-48). These basic, almost prehistoric forms show little effect from even so radical and durable an influence as the 700-year reign of the Moors -- strong evidence that, when the conservative countryside created a viable custom, it was not easily diverted. One reason for abandoning these ancient patterns so readily today is that modern technology and materials offer vast improvements in physical comfort and convenience. The desirability and availability of these conveniences together with the disappearance of traditional skills make radical change inevitable.

Though even in lonely places change was inevitable, the subsistence level of many early societies did not encourage idle experimentation or frivolous embellishments. While discouragement of innovation insured continuity and order in the community by avoiding the arbitrary or merely fashionable, it also prevented needed improvements.

Country versus City

Though change is a constant in any society, it is the rate at which a society is forced to absorb the new that determines whether it can retain its integrity. Small communities regulated their rate of change and their internal order informally through recognized customs. As municipalities grew in size and complexity, a more rigid and formal system of laws was required. This in turn weakened the sense of participation and the shared value system that is the essence of any tradition --hastening its demise.

In the villages it was relatively easy for time-honored rules and an all-powerful aristocracy to control life, but in the city a measure of independence was possible and the customs were more flexible. This undermined the established order and eventually affected rural life as well. Unrestrained by small town mores, the cities quickly adopted the latest fashions, new ideas, and foreign influences, while the countryside remained conservative and suspicious, accepting new ideas grudgingly if at all.

There has always been a love-hate relationship between city and country. It has existed in nearly every culture, ancient or modern. Country folk, even while longing for the riches and freedom of the cities, regarded life there as physically unhealthy and morally corrupting. City dwellers, in turn, secretly longed for the return to the simpler, purer life of the countryside and the village.

But the pure life was a hard life, a constant struggle to survive against the ravages of nature, marauding armies, and overbearing and feuding landlords. For most people the city was the only opportunity for escape to a life of greater ease, prosperity and security. It was an opportunity they seized with eternal regret for the life they, or their ancestors, had left behind.

The Spaniard, particularly, is susceptible to this emotional tug; he feels little loyalty to anyone except his family and his village. Such fierce local pride, bred in centuries of insularity, has been the source of much of the conflict in Spanish history.

Today the problem is how to exploit the very real advantages of new technology and methods while maintaining the equally real but more subtle and ordinary values of the past. Especially in Spain, which is modernizing at a furious pace, little thought has been given to preservation. Portugal's Monsaraz (106-116) is an admirable exception. By contrast, Italy has several examples of the successful integration of ancient forms and modern amenities such as

Siena and San Gimignano.

Image and Meaning

Many Iberian villages are visually compelling --at least for the casual visitor. It might seem that most inhabitants would have become oblivious to the visual attractions of their native place. But it is difficult to believe that a native of Olvera (135-137), for example, as he glanced back at his village from the fields nearby, could fail to be stirred. Olvera's image is brilliant and potent --at once unique, familiar and orderly. Moreover, it was the center of the inhabitant's universe and it symbolized the established order by the intimate scale of the repetitive, anonymous cottages nestled in the natural contours of the site dominated by the hovering mass of the church or castle. It was a geometry at once integrated with and distinct from the landscape which sustained it --a form determined as much by nature as by man and his institutions. Communicated daily to the inhabitants over a lifetime, generation after generation, it is an image of man, nature, and God in consort and conflict.

Mirroring reality the image could not be trivial. The more remote they were, the more important this image was in the inhabitants' view of themselves and their culture. "The environment men create through their wants becomes a mirror that reflects their civilization; more importantly it also constitutes a book in which is written the formula of life that they communicate to others and transmit to succeeding generations. The characteristics of the environment are therefore of importance not only because they affect the comfort and quality of present-day life, but even more because they condition the development of young people and thereby society..."[2]

Order and Form

Except for their central plazas most villages developed without any preconceived plans or deliberate vistas and compositions. In Spain, an excessive individualism -the attitude of *viva yo* (hurray for me) --made nearly impossible the conception, let alone the execution, of grand schemes. Abstract concepts requiring systematic planning were anathema to the Spaniard more concerned with immediate results.

In place of planning the accidental, expedient clustering of structures created ever changing asymmetries full of surprising views, picturesque juxtapositions of forms, and varied spaces. The consistency and order of the village derived, not from abstract concepts, but from a shared value system that insured an underlying consistency at the same time allowing limited variations of the parts to fit individual needs. Conformity to the deep rooted 'way' was expected and required.

Still insular conformity was relatively lax when contrasted with the rigid geometries of high-style planning where concepts were often adopted more for their novelty and elite aesthetics than for their practicality. Vernacular, while it sometimes discouraged needed change, was at least based on the realities of its locale. It was this foundation which enabled a tradition to act as an "invisible hand" guiding the parts towards a unified and ordered whole even as it grew by accretion --adapting to needs and opportunities without any formal overall conception.

Coherence and regularity came from working within the accepted palette of materials, scale, color, and shapes in fashioning individual dwellings. In addition, common sense oriented individual houses into similar directions even on rugged sites --for example, with entrances and windows facing away from cold winds and towards the sun. Hillside sites with streets necessarily parallel to the slope also imposed a uniform orientation --an aesthetic and practical advantage when the town was built on the south slope (13, 158, 172, 180).

Essential to maintaining a sense of order was a limited scale so that the connection of man-made with natural forms was never lost or the irregular pattern of streets and houses did not become endless and overwhelming to the individual. By contrast, the changes now occurring are especially disruptive, since they involve rapid change in scale and unrestrained growth --as well as unfamiliar materials and technology.

Deadly uniformity was prevented by the adaptation of the elemental dwelling to fit varying family needs or irregular sites, and by individual expression in minor and decorative details. The composition was also unbounded; it could be added to without 'spoiling' the conception by extending the underlying functional network of connecting spaces. The only limits were the constraints of enclosing walls or precipitous sites. In any case the edges of the urban areas were clearly defined -- additions were always adjacent to existing structures. Limited means, then, gave the villages an inherent unity, while exploiting these means created practical, complex, and visually rich environments --without destroying that unity.

Reading Forms

The village forms can, of course, be read on several levels. First, especially from a distance, they can be viewed as abstract sculptural forms with their own aesthetic coherence and fit with the landscape.

Then, as one moves into and through a town, the dominant sense is of a functioning organism structured to meet the inhabitants' needs for shelter, work, and social intercourse.

The surface uniformity soon dissolves. As the houses, churches, castles, streets and plazas are examined, one sees that each element is unique --especially the dwellings whose scale, asymmetry, and flexibility allow endless combinations. Churches, on the other hand, as ceremonial spaces and as pervasive symbols of power, are grand in scale, symmetrical and set apart from the mass of anonymous cottages. Similarly, castles, in addition to their defensive function contribute to the distinctive silhouette of each village (9, 147-149).

Village Patterns

While there is little reliable data on the establishment of particular Iberian towns, the general pattern is discernable and familiar. As in Italy and throughout the Mediterranean, compact hilltop sites were chosen for protection against enemies, to preserve agricultural land, and as market centers for the surrounding countryside. Since all land was owned by the nobles, most of the towns were organized by fiat to resettle and defend areas captured from the retreating Moors. The kings issued *fueros* or charters that granted special freedoms to many of them. As these free centers gained in economic importance, their independence attracted increasing numbers escaping from the poverty of the countryside and the oppression of petty local nobility.

Thus the location and growth of municipalities was determined by a complex interrelationship of accident, political and military needs, land ownership, climate, availability of good sites with a plentiful water supply, and agricultural potential. While the totality of forces is complex, the powerful effects of climate, water, and fertility of the land are readily apparent. For example, the wet northern area with its fertile valleys and good water permitted individual land ownership with people living on or close to their small plots. Villages, therefore, are numerous and small -- sometimes mere agglomerations of farm houses (49-51).

The long dry periods in much of the land made water supply a critical factor in the establishment of a town. Lack of water also limited the ability of individual families to survive on remote farms and forced cooperative efforts in agriculture, such as irrigation. As a result, the country towns in dry areas with good soil are typically large and widely dispersed on huge estates.

In dry areas with poorer soil, such as the central plateau, individual plots were also rare and large non-intensive farming, primarily olive groves or sheepherding, was the rule. Here long periods of inactivity alternating with short intensive harvests made the country towns a refuge much of the year and the only source of work at other times. They are rather large, generally poor, and infrequent.

Conditions, then, forced much of the populace into large villages dependent on the vast land holdings of one family. Since the sixteenth century there have been numerous attempts to break this feudal pattern by resettlement on unused agricultural land, but attitudes are so entrenched that the villages rather than independent farms remain the center of rural life.

STREET PATTERN, MEDINA AT CORDOBA

Additional factors were the differences between the Moslem and Christian areas, remnants of which still endure. "....... in Christian Spain local liberties and feudal privileges developed side by side, whilst among the Moslems nothing was permitted to infringe upon the powers of the central government. This history of Spain can thus be interpreted in the light of two different conceptions of land tenure. In the north the possession of land stood for profit and well being. In the former case the feudal idea became in time, through the medium of the free communes and the increase in the number of *mayorazgos* (entailed estates) democratized: even the humblest aspired to power, to nobility, to family permanence, and the result was a society in which the gentlemanly ideal of leisure and authority took precedence over that of material well being. In the latter a much more expansive and hedonistic frame of mind prevailed and work was regarded as the only road to prosperity."[3]

This attitude, often commented on by Spanish writers is reflected in the ideal of "the impoverished knight" who avoids regimentation and physical labor by escape to the city.

While there may not have been the extreme civic pride of the Italian city-states, citizenship in the Christian towns was a privilege. Citizenship in Moslem towns, all of them under a strong central government, was not a unique right.

Moslem towns also developed without any overall plan. Streets were a maze of narrow lanes lined with blank walled houses. The main public spaces around the mosques were the markets. The density and the customary sequestering of women and family from public life turned the houses inwards on their own courtyards and gardens. Even the smallest opened directly off the street into a small court, sometimes with a well or fountain and always with plants --a common feature to this day in the towns of the south (144-145).

Thus in Iberia three main factors influenced the character and siting of both individual houses and the villages: one, the physical realities --climate, water sources, construction materials, defense, and type of agriculture; two, the cultural influences --a feudal system with entrenched regional traditions; and three, perhaps as an outgrowth of the other two, the character of the people themselves --independent, loyal first to family and clan and with a tendency to avoid abstract, cooperative planning.

In addition, the individual's needs and wealth as well as the skills of local craftsmen introduced other variations. The results are an exceptional opportunity to examine the interplay between architecture, culture, and environment.

Spain and Portugal

The differences between Spanish and Portugese vernacular are differences in detail and 'style' not in type. There is, in fact, a remarkable correspondence in the native buildings of the two countries --just as geography and climate ignored the border so, roughly, did the architecture. In the north sections of both countries, for example, there is wide use of the *horrero* (22-24, 34-35), the wood or stone granaries raised on stilts. And proceeding south in both countries, the types and materials change in corresponding fashion --from the massive stone work of the north to the white stuccoed towns of the south.

NORTHERN IBERIA
PHOTOGRAPHS

The classic composition and heroic site of Morella makes it one of the most spectacular of Spain's walled towns. A site occupied since Iberian times, its mile long wall was begun in the early 14th century when it was one of a series of fortified towns on the Christian frontier. Later Morella was an outpost in conflicts between Valencia and Aragon and because of its strategic position has been repeatedly conquered or beseiged — last in 1873. The interior streets are narrow and winding with steep ramps and stairs where they ascend the rock but the original architecture is much changed.

33

At the village of Lindoso in northern Portugal, more than 50 stone graneries are grouped near the castle — for protection and the availability of flat stone outcroppings used as threshing floors (34, 22, 24).

The wooden horrero of northern Spain come in a variety of styles and frequently stand alongside the south-facing, balconied houses. Near Cangas (35).

Monsanto (36b, 37) is a curious town built among huge boulders that form part of the houses. The masonry in this area is a remarkable blend of rough textured walls and large smooth stones used structurally as lintels and jambs of openings or to strengthen corners. The apparently arbitrary shapes tie the stones into the wall and their expressiveness is frequently enhanced with whitewash. It is a splendid example of how ornamentation in vernacular architecture is so often functionally derived.

Windows near Braga (36t).

The twin doorways of a modest barn below Monsanto have the strength and dignity of an entrance to the tomb of some ancient king. Though working within a tradition, the mason was sensitive to the nuances of proportion and form in each stone and inventive in their assembly, thereby subtly transcending and transforming the tradition (38-39).

Country life in northern Portugal has changed little these women are winnowing wheat on a threshing terrace high above a river valley near Guarda, much as they have for centuries. A sheepherder nearby displays his new charges. (40-41).

Penalba de Santiago (42-44). Penalba is a remote mountain village similar to many along the Camino de Santiago pilgrimage route that passed through these mountains. Roofs are of local slate and walls are of slabs of unmortared stone. Wood was sparingly used for roof structures and balconies — heavy snows and muddy streets made the balconies a necessity. Acebo, a tiny, lonely town whose only street was the Camino de Santiago, at one time was thronged with travelers. (45).

44

Penalba de Santiago

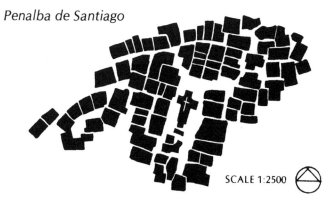

SCALE 1:2500

Huddled on the brow of a hill, sheltered against wind is this group of rare 'pallaza' houses, perhaps descended from prehistoric Iberian round houses, they were in use until a few years ago. They have been recently restored using many of the original furnishings. The simple furniture has carved decoration and a clever bench near the fire uses a tray that flips over the lap like a baby's high chair.

The center cross wall of the houses goes full height and supports the ends of the radiating roof rafters so the round or oval outer wall is a logical form. The interior is divided by this central wall into the animal and family areas with bedrooms sometimes above the animal barn. The interiors are dark, lit only by the open door and a few tiny windows. Cooking was over an open fire pit in the earthen floor and the smoke drifted up through the thatch.

El Cebrero, on the Camino de Santiago in provence of Galacia (46-48).

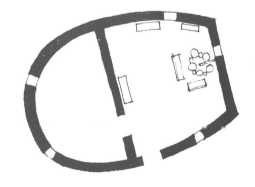

46

In marked contrast with the fortified hilltowns further south, Carmona's site is a lush valley floor adjacent to the terraced fields. This location and Carmona's dispersed plan reflect a history of relative security. Additional evidence of this vernacular architecture's adaptation to its environment are the houses themselves. They are loosely arranged in rows that minimize exposed walls and orient the main openings and balconies to the sun. In the wet, cold climate balconies are essential outdoor space above the mud and snow. Inside the large arches are the stair to the living quarters above, storage for the family cart, and pens for the animals — whose heat helps warm the upper floor (49-51, 12).

Still very much in use, elevated wooden shoes are a necessity in these muddy streets. Working under the balcony of his house, the local shoemaker takes about an hour to hand-carve a pair.

Frias, a hilltown above the beautiful Ebro River valley, guards a Roman bridge. Its castle hangs precariously from an elevated rock at the entrance to the town (52-53).

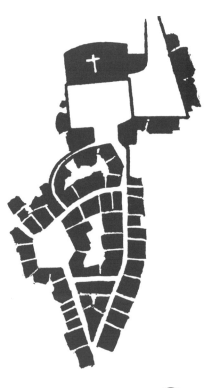

SCALE 1:2500

Its name a contraction of Saint Julliana, Santillana was a pilgrimage center in the Middle Ages, later an important seat of power, and now largely a farm community. Its history explains the rather grand style of some of its houses — mansions really, complete with coat of arms above the doors. Small and well preserved, Santillana is built along the few lanes leading to the monastery. Nearby are the Altamira caves. (54-58).

This entrance is just off the street in one of the larger mansions. The single classical column, an elegant gesture from Santillana's proud past, is remarkably effective in the midst of this rough hewn room and shows that the current fashion of mixing stylistically distant elements is not entirely original (56).

Arcade on Santillana's Plaza Mayor (58).

In compact northern towns the houses usually are without private court yards and so the many tiny plazas serve for leisurely gatherings in the sun. Batea (59).

Moorish arches form arcades and support the
upper floors of houses over the streets in Batea (60-61).

Two strikingly different techniques — half timber and stuccoed masonry are both used in the town of Goizueta and throughout the Basque region. The window treatment, similar to the elemental stonework of northern Portugal (36-39), seems however, more arbitrary and decorative set off by the white stucco that covers the underlying masonry (62-63).

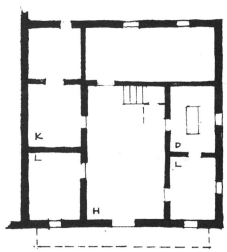

Vinuesa (64-65). This classic northern house has essentially the same layout as the simpler houses at Carmona (49-51) — though the cows and hay have been replaced by living rooms, dining room, and kitchen that open off the grand reception hall. A stairway at the back leads to sleeping rooms on the second floor.

A massive Renaissance palace and a delicate half-timbered house face each other on the Plaza Mayor in Penranda du Duero. This small country town was once an important defensive town along the Duero River that marked the limit of Moslem conquest in the north (66-68, 17).

An early Iberian site on a strategic hill, Segovia
grew into a large walled town and the center of
Castile's wool trade. Its impressive silhouette,
punctuated by the towers of the great cathedral and
the Alcazar, can be seen for great distances across
the plains. Once occupied by Castilian kings, the
castle, both in its form and its site on Segovia's prow
is the most romantic in Spain (69-71).

Entrance to Pedraza, a sleepy, partially deserted Castilian town, is through a tiny gate in the outer wall and then along narrow streets leading to this handsome plaza partially enclosed by a variety of arcaded houses. The fading Arabic patterns of decorated stucco (73) are similar to those found in the mountains of Extremadura (91), a hundred miles to the West.

No matter how poor the village or how primitive its construction it has a kind of order imposed by the unity of materials and house forms and, not least, by the dominance of the omnipresent church. (Valbona 74).

Built over the edge of the cliff, these eight and ten story buildings on Cuenca's outer rim stretch the capability of wall bearing construction to its limits. Entrances are at the middle level on the street side (75).

The pressure for building space on Cuenca's cliff
top forced houses to the very brink and beyond. These
unusual and delicate wooden structures, the hanging
houses of Cuenca have a distinct oriental flavor though
the details are thoroughly Spanish (76-77).

The towns in the mountains of western Spain were long isolated, retaining a medieval flavor unlike any other region in Iberia. Premier among them for the authenticity of its atmosphere is La Alberca (79-90, 14), now protected from change by government controls.

Set in the midst of the wooded uplands, La Alberca has much the same character as its neighbor, Miranda del Castanar (78) whose jubilant roofscape gives little hint of somber streets below.

La Alberca's Plaza Publica (79-84) is surrounded with arcades on three sides off which are shops, the village offices, the tiny jail, and above, important houses. There are other small plazas and a larger space adjacent to the church, but the Plaza Publica is the focus of all activity. Everyone in the village will pass through here at least once a day and usually gather here in the evenings — on rainy evenings standing in groups under the porticos. And on festival days the plaza and the balconies are crowded with townspeople and visitors.

In these dark, confining streets one is always drawn towards the light and openness of the plaza.

The houses follow a timeless pattern — storage and animal quarters on the first floor, sleeping rooms on the second, and the top floor for kitchen and living areas. Sometimes this upper floor has a small balcony opening onto the narrow street or a back yard. On a stone slab in the kitchen is a constantly smoldering fire that blackens the whole upper story before the smoke escapes through the cracks or chimney. Because it has the only access to light and air, the top floor is the most livable in these crowded towns; however, it means all firewood and food must be hauled up the steep stairs (85).

The building method is timber frame with an in-fill of rubble usually plastered over. The floors are framed with logs, covered with twigs and then a thick layer of smooth plaster. The house on page 85 reveals the full range of materials and techniques.

The portico on the east side of the Plaza, (84).

The three and four story houses are tightly packed, not for lack of space since there is no physical restriction to expansion (either natural or man-made), but because of a real or felt need for security and for the benefits of mutual structural support of the multi-story construction.

SCALE 1:2500

In this combination of stone, heavy timber and plaster construction, each material is appropriately used — stone as a massive base on the damp ground, wood to span the longer horizontal spaces, and plaster to seal against rain and drafts. The plaster is occasionally incised with geometric patterns and painted soft colors reminiscent of Arab designs in the Alhambra at Granada. La Alberca (90) and nearby Monforte (91).

Sheep have been both the blessing and the curse of Iberia — even while huge fortunes were made in the valuable wool trade, the over grazing caused irreparable damage to vast stretches of the dry central plateau. Originally grazing rights were granted to orders of knights on the abandoned lands between the Christian and Moslem frontier in exchange for its defense. Developing into the Mesta, the powerful guild of sheep owners extended and maintained absolute grazing rights for over five hundred years.

At its height, more than a million sheep swept across these plateaus in their annual passage from winter pasture in Castile and Extremadura to the summer pasture in the northern mountains. Rights of passage were absolute from which no farm or crop was safe. The sheep picked the land clean along their path, preventing development of a substantial agriculture, devastating the land and perhaps causing a permanent change in the climate by the widespread destruction of vegetation. In many places it has not recovered in the one hundred years since the herds disappeared.

The plaza at Garovillas has a handsome two level portico on three sides, a reminder of the days when the plaza served as the bull ring and the upper story viewing spaces were in demand. It now hosts a small market for several hours every morning. Until a few years ago the well in the center was the only source of water for the neighborhood. A recently installed water system has eased the burden of carrying water and permitted the well to be replaced with an ugly, but 'up to date' terrazzo structure. Much of the cobble paving has also been replaced by concrete. Progress has its price (94-96, 19).

The Portugese gained independence from the Moors in the twelfth century, emerged as a world power in the fifteenth, were eclipsed in the sixteenth but have remained more or less independent, if somewhat impoverished, ever since. While political separation from Spain encouraged the development of a distinctive vernacular architecture, the pervasive influence of Iberian history, geography, and climate determined that it would be a variation on the basic Iberian themes, not a radical departure.

Though the Mediterranean influence is felt throughout the peninsula, the farther removed from the eastern and southern coasts, the less intense it is, until in the far north and northwest it disappears almost entirely (helped, undoubtedly by the cool, wet un-Mediterranean climate). Portugal shares some of this remoteness, though not as conspicuously as the north of Spain. In addition Portugal, like Spain, was a maritime power, with colonies all over the world. This contact with other cultures was felt at home, though little filtered into the remote rural areas.

There are other differences that one senses immediately on entering from Spain into Portugal. Life slows down perceptibly. The towns are quieter and cleaner; the twentieth century is much less in evidence. Compared with Spain's headlong rush to modernize, Portugal is proceeding much more slowly and less destructively --exemplified by the superb preservation of Monsaraz (106-116), one of the most beautiful villages in Iberia.

The photograph on page 93 is of wine caves dug in a low hill near Benavente.

NORTHERN IBERIA

As the photographs reveal, there is considerable justification in dividing so complex a land as Iberia into simply 'north' and 'south'. The logic derives, in part, from the differences in geography and climate (the cool, rainy north versus the hot, dry south), in part, from cultural differences (northern Christianity versus southern Islam), and in part, from architectural antecedents as diverse as the medieval towns of northern Europe and the casbahs of North Africa.

The two regions also share architectural characteristics. Most evident is the Mediterranean influence along the coasts particularly in the south with its more Mediterranean-like climate. In addition, the basic need for accessibility to water and agricultural land, and for defendable sites led to the building of towns on hilltops in both the north and south. And, though by no means uniform in their effect, the periodic dominance of a single culture over most of Iberia, such as the Romans, the Moors, and finally the Catholic Christians, also had a unifying influence.

The line dividing northern and southern vernacular is hardly precise. If I were to define such a line (no Spaniard or Portugese is likely to agree), it would begin at a point just above Valencia on the Mediterranean coast to below Madrid and Toledo in the center and end south of Lisbon on the Atlantic.

Naturally, a different physical environment leads to alternate house forms and construction techniques and general layout of the villages. Man does not merely adapt to a given environment; he changes it, principly through his buildings which moderate the given conditions into something suitable and comfortable. Out of these efforts, through imagination and reason, and the capacity to exchange ideas, man forges a building tradition --a language of form communicable to the whole society.

Materials

Iberian building materials are the same ones used throughout the Mediterranean --cut or rubble stone, rammed earth and adobe, wood for the walls and structure, and with tile, thatch, and slate for the roof. The most plentiful materials in a particular locality are the ones most likely to predominate but they are seldom used to the exclusion of all others. In fact one characteristic of Iberian vernacular is the easy combination of stone, adobe, and wood in a single structure.

Wood with its unique structural capabilities is nearly universal --sparingly used in the dry central and southern areas where it was scarce and the only fuel, but extensively in the forested northern mountains. Only wooden beams could easily span floors and roofs (65). Between the beams were laid small planks and twigs which were plastered over for floors or covered with thatch, tile, or slate for roofing. Wood framed walls, usually in the half-timber technique had larger vertical and horizontal members with an infill of stone rubble or 'wattle and daub' --a woven lattice of twigs plastered on both sides (85).

Perhaps the most typical material and the one that most frequently comes to mind in connection with this land is *pise de terre* - rammed earth and adobe. It is the one material readily at hand on every building site though its appropriateness in the rainy areas is questionable. Rammed earth walls are constructed on a foundation of stone from 6 inches to 2 feet in height to keep moisture out of the wall. Then, in a movable wooden form, dampened earth scooped up from nearby and mixed with straw, is packed in layers from 18 to 24 inches thick. The form slides along at each level and the process is repeated to the desired height. To protect the surface a thin layer of durable plaster is applied and over this frequent coats of whitewash provide a tough weatherproof surface. Though a torrential downpour of long duration can melt it away, such construction endures for generations with occasional surface renewal. In any case it is relatively easy to rebuild or extend.

A variation is adobe; blocks of mud mixed with straw hand molded or cast in a form and set in the sun to dry. The adobe is then piled up and plastered over in shapes similar to the rammed earth. Usually in these earthen buildings, the door and window frames and other areas subject to high wear or requiring precise fit are of stone or wood.

A similar variation is brick. Most often associated with the Mudejar or Muslim style, it may have been introdced then. To make bricks requires a good source of raw materials, kilns and a plentiful supply of fuel, so they were not as widely available as other materials.

Stone in various forms --rubble from river beds, limestone from surface quarries, and large boulders cleared from the fields --is another basic material. Rubble walls (plain or plastered) and shaped stones were combined in handsome and structurally ingenious ways (36-39, 43, 63). Advantage was taken even of huge boulders to form parts of houses or barns especially around Portugal's Monsanto (37).

Occasionally the choice of material, technique or form went beyond the established norms. Innovations were introduced by some exceptionally skilled craftsman or requested by an owner who wished to build a little grander, more distinctive home (64-65, 76-77), such as the home for a wealthy sheep rancher whose migratory herds brought him to a remote village. The changes were not extreme --a slight increase in scale, greater use of an expensive material, and perhaps more lavish decorative elements, but the tradition was changed and expanded nevertheless.

Ancient Round Houses

While most houses are rectangular in plan, one of the most unusual northern houses is circular or oval. The type may be descended from the round houses discovered in the ancient *castros* of the Iberians and Celtics.

Simple, but effective shelter, the *pallaza*, as they are known, appear to have changed little over the centuries (46-48). The oval shape, efficient to build and heat, was divided into two sections by a central masonry wall with the stable usually on the north, and the family living quarters on the other side. The center of family life during the long winters was a large open hearth surrounded by benches. Hanging above the fire was a chain from which were hung cooking pots or meat for smoking. The natural earth floor, packed hard from use and sealed with dung, sloped gradually towards the stable. There was only one door for both the family and the animals --it plus a few tiny windows were the only source of light so the interior was dark even at midday.

Villages composed of *pallazas* were small with only a few houses scattered over a hilltop.

The round shape did not lend itself to compact grouping and there was always the danger of fire spreading in the thatched roofs.

The sharing of living space by man and his animals was common in early societies. The animals contributed needed heat to the living space and as the family's most valuable possessions were kept secure. The lack of ventilation, must have been oppressive, however. A later solution with animals on the lower floor and the living space above, while it had some inconveniences, was a decided improvement (49-51).

Some of the best examples of this advanced house type are in the village of Carmona (49-51). Built primarily of stone, they are a common type in the north. Set between jutting stone walls in row-house fashion, the two-story houses invariably feature a sun gallery the full width of the upper living level. A cantilevered tiled roof shelters the balcony. Decoration is confined to carvings on the balcony railings, balustrades, and window frames. Recently these balconies, particularly in the towns, have been totally glassed in to make private solaria.

The lower floor, which houses the work, storage, and animal spaces, has a large arched opening into which the family cart can be driven. Rows of these houses with their arches and balconies begin to resemble the arcaded streets so numerous in northern towns.

Medieval Towns

In the western mountains of Spain is a group of villages unlike any others. Reminiscent of the busy medieval towns of northern Europe, their development in these remote wooded mountains is strange indeed. Premier among

them, and now proclaimed a national treasure, is La Alberca (78-91). Built on a gentle slope unrestricted by walls or site, the extreme piling up of La Alberca's houses seems to have no practical foundation. More likely, it derives from an instinctive desire for mutual support and security so prevalent elsewhere in folk cultures and in the Mediterranean particularly. Surrounded by oak groves, La Alberca is an agricultural village and was once important for charcoal production.

The typical La Alberca house, similar to those in nearby villages, has some unusual characteristics. The house is narrow, deep front to back and several stories high. The ground floor contains an entrance hall, staircase to the upper floors and storage or stables. Sleeping rooms are on the intermediate floors with only tiny windows front and rear, and the upper floor (which might be the second to the fifth level) is the main living space. The kitchen is here, with a constantly smoldering fire on a huge stone slab set in the floor. Smoke drifts up through the chinks in the roof or through the huge hood with a horizontal grill on which are placed chestnuts for drying or meat to be smoked. The years of smoke blacken the whole ceilng -though the hoods, made of wood covered with clay, may be freshly white washed.

Small front windows look out over the street or at the neighbor's house a few feet away. In the early days, garbage was tossed down into the streets to be consumed by roaming pigs or goats or swept away by the rains. When the houses open onto an interior court at the rear, there is often a small balcony --the only light and airy space in the whole house. Though the upper floor is the most pleasant space in the

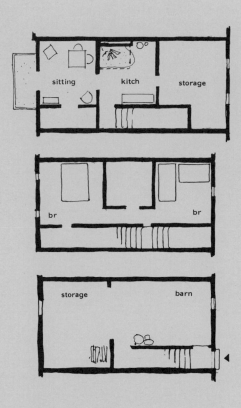

HOUSE, LA ALBERCA

house it was unending toil to haul up all the fuel, food, and water.

The houses of the La Alberca region combine stone, wood, and plaster. The lower walls and pillars are of massive stone -- sometimes with stone lintels --the upper floors are half-timber framing sealed with plaster.

In the narrow streets the projecting upper stories nearly shut out the light giving the towns a closed-in feeling with little sense of the sky above and the landscape beyond. The only large open spaces are plazas. Here and along major streets the houses incorporate porticos which join together in arcades for the gathering of the townspeople, for market stalls, and as extensions to the shops and work spaces.

Porticoed streets (66-67, 72-73, 94-96), a prominent feature in many northern towns, even though they darken the ground floor interiors (60-61), provide useful public spaces. The effect of a whole arcaded street or square is quite extraordinary and goes a long way to humanize the space. The portico is a relatively late development in Iberian vernacular, perhaps as recent as the fifteenth century. If true, the idea spread rapidly and widely. Considering the desirability of shade in southern towns, it seems strange the portico is seldom found.

With the few exceptions discussed above, northern villages when compared with southern villages tend to be more regular in their layout and less densely built-up. Streets are normally wider for more access to light and sun. However, when constricted by encircling walls or cliffs the towns grew vertically with multi-story houses (53, 75) and the streets became dark tunnels.

One of the few examples of pure decoration is patterned plaster known as sgraffito (73, 91). Used mainly in the Segovia region the geometric designs remind us of arabic patterns in the Alhambra of Granada. The technique consists of covering a colored layer of plaster with a light-colored layer, then with the aid of a stencil the top layer is scratched away to expose the colors. Finally the whole surface is burnished smooth.

A technical innovation in heating found in northern Castile is the gloria. It is based on a network of ducts beneath the floor through which passes the heat and smoke from a fire at one side of the house, warming the tiled floor in the process. Only the kitchen and living room floors are warmed. Firewood is scarce so straw is burned in a closed firepit so that it smolders through the night while the adobe and tile mass retains the heat for hours. In the summer a natural draft cools the floors.

Whether handed down from Roman times or developed by a local craftsman to please a wealthy client, the gloria system spread, as its advantages became known, and became a part of the local building tradition. It is an example of how climate, human need, and available materials can be integrated into architectural form.

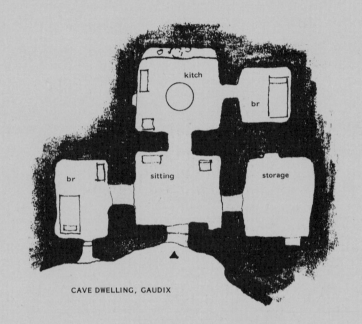

CAVE DWELLING, GAUDIX

SOUTHERN IBERIA

The most ancient houses still in use are southern cave dwellings. It is astounding to think that some of these caves may have been lived in continuously for thousands of years -- perhaps since the first Iberians 20,000 years ago. Natural caves or rock strata in which men carved out habitations for themselves are frequent in the south.

Cave Dwellings

Today we are rediscovering advantages in underground living, such as the constant temperature of the surrounding earth that keeps the interiors cool in summer and warm in winter. Since wood as fuel became scarce long ago, this advantage was not lost on the early cave dwellers. An obvious disadvantage, the lack of light and air, was minimized by ingenious light and ventilation shafts plus generous use of whitewash inside and out to reflect the light deep into the interiors.

Set in a surreal landscape punctuated with white chimneys, the most dramatic cave community is Gaudix (126-129). Chimneys and whitewashed doorways are the only clues to the maze of rooms that honeycombs the soft, eroded stone.

More typical are underground dwellings similar to those at La Guardia pass. Here the earth has been dug out to form rooms and the hill side carved into a flat facade and patio. Every surface is whitewashed to seal and preserve it. A superb integration of man-made and natural forms, it is also an example of man's need, even though he makes his home in the ground, to define a personal space that contrasts with nature. Here the demarcation is through the abstract clarity of the severe, white surfaces.

Compare the grass-roofed cave of La Guardia with the rare example of a thatched roof house (24) -- the relation of roof to wall is remarkably similar. In fact the La Guardia caves can, on first glance, be mistaken for thatched houses.

The cave dwellings at Setenil (130-134) go a step further by up-to-date additions of conventional facades covering the original caves set in the cliffs of the river bank. Situated high, dry and secure, the spectacular cliff dwelling near Monte Frio (177) is another cave that probably has been occupied for eons.

In all of these cave houses the layouts are limited by the sheer labor of making the spaces and the decreasing light and air as one penetrates further into the ground. Typical cave dwellings open initially into a large room which is the main living space with subsidiary spaces branching off in petal fashion. The cooking usually is done in a separate space with its own chimney or outside in good weather.

A more conventional southern house is one of simple stone and adobe blocks found all over in the country towns. The shapes are elemental but in combination they achieve wondrously complex forms and spaces (138, 160). Despite the south's Islamic traditions, these houses seldom have interior courts. They are too small and in the country towns there is less need to escape the press of urban life. Instead the streets, tiny plazas or walled-in yards provide the outdoor living spaces.

Patio Houses

The most elaborate and best known type, the patio house, is based on Islamic concepts. It is the typical house in the larger more sophisticated towns where there was a stronger Islamic influence and a greater need for privacy.

SOUTHERN IBERIA
PHOTOGRAPHS

The southern Portugese village of Monsaraz
(106-116) is one of the most attractive villages in Iberia
and seems destined to remain so as it is now under
government protection. Despite this control it is filled
with the normal activities of a living town. As such it is
an example of how the Iberian traditional village can
incorporate new standards of living and new
technology without destroying its very fabric.

The site, on a hill overlooking the Spanish border,
explains the need for walls and castle.

A composition of traditional forms. Albufeira (105).

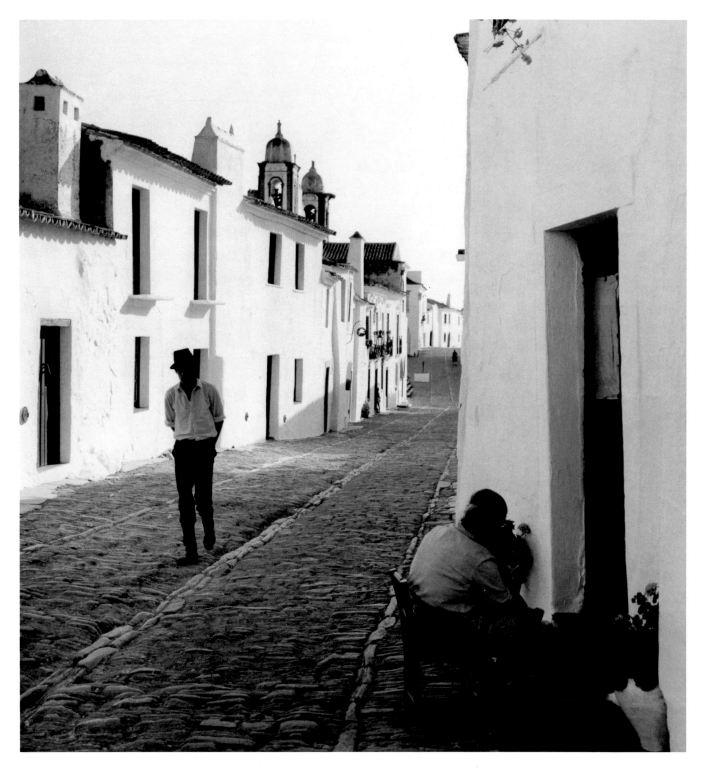

Monsaraz´s main street and plaza (108-109).

In this view (110) we look from the front door on the street through the main living space, with its slate floor and simple furniture, into the private patio in the rear. The few possessions are stored in several niches in the walls.

Monsaraz epitomizes the differences between Portugese and Spanish villages. In Portugal the pace is slower, the towns seem cleaner, and, if it is possible, more freshly whitewashed. And everywhere much less evidence of a frantic modernization.

This room is just inside the front door. A sitting room is off to the left, kitchen through the door at the rear, and sleeping rooms are up the stair. It is spotlessly clean, beautifully simple and elegant. Difficult though it may be to believe, this house, like the one on page 110, is typical Portugese vernacular in daily use by a family, not a room set up in a museum (115).

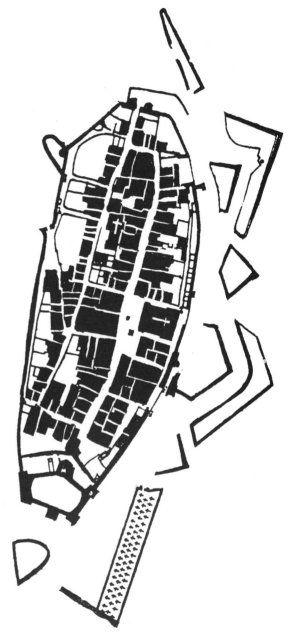

SCALE 1:2500

114

Textures of Monsaraz roofs and paving set off by the white walls (116).

Mertola, Portugal (117). Comparing this town and Monsaraz with the Spanish towns of Casares (152) and Monte Frio (178) demonstrates the related but differing character in both the individual buildings and the townscape of Portugese and Spanish towns.

Calcadinha, outside Elvas, is a one street town centered on the gate of the landowner's estate (118). The row houses with their imposing chimneys and sculpted terraces are at Terrugem (119, 121t).

One of the fascinations in traveling through southern Portugal is the study of the inventive chimney forms — no two are alike. These are in the Loule area (120, 121b).

120

Evocative symbols of La Mancha, these windmills on a ridge above Consuegra face the constant winds of the waterless plains (manxa is the arabic word for parched earth). The castle was a 12th century outpost between the Islamic and Christian territories manned by knights who were rewarded with grazing rights over this vast region. Windmills testify to its later transformation into a grain producing area.

Equally symbolic of the south are the whitewashed wall and tile roof. The detail shows traditional roof tiles and the ridge capped with layered tiles, mortared in place and sealed with whitewash.

The south has some unexpected building types
— thatched roofs and underground houses. The soft
earth, hollowed out and whitewashed, makes efficient
living spaces — warm in winter and cool in summer.
Though windows are small, the whitewash inside and
out reflects light deep inside. Near Utrera (124). La
Guardia (125).

This surreal scene of moonscape pierced by strange white forms is Guadix, a large community of underground houses near Granada (126-128).

Marked only by their whitewashed chimneys and entrances, these houses extend under the whole area in a warren of spaces carved out of the earth. This place has been occupied since pre-historic times probably in much the same way. Cave house with red peppers hung to dry near Baza (129).

Setenil began as a series of ancient cave dwellings burrowed into the cliffs along the river. A conventional town has since grown up around and the caves, still very much in use, have been expanded with conventional fronts (130-134).

Olvera's image sticks in the mind long after leaving. It is uncommonly beautiful, whether when first seen from many miles away gleaming on its hill top in the midst of great rolling plains of olive groves, or more closely, with its houses rippling down between the rocks like a giant glacier issuing from the cathedral. It is a wedding of townscape and landscape that enobles each — and easy to imagine the inhabitants' pride in such a place (135-137).

Of the many tranquil villages near Ronda, several just south of the town are especially beautiful. Small country towns set in wooded hills, their modest houses, churches and winding streets are immaculate with every wall freshly whitewashed. As in most southern towns, during the day the streets are deserted except for an occasional solitary figure venturing into the hot sun. *Alpandere (138-143).*

Composed of simple elements and materials, Alpandere shows how a rich environment may be unconsciously created in a small village. The dwellings are strung along the spines and gentle slopes of the low hills connected by a complex network of streets and tiny plazas — spaces enhanced by changing, contrapuntal patterns of light and shade. And always, just beyond, is the green unspoiled landscape.

142

Vejer de la Frontera is a compact hilltown whose narrow winding streets invite wandering — especially in the cool evening when doorways are left ajar for intriguing glimpses of flower-adorned interior patios. A legacy of the Moslem period, these private spaces on which most rooms open, give each house access to sun and air despite the narrow streets (144-145, 15).

A southern landscape with olive groves near Bednar (146) and the castle town of Biar (147).

One of Spain's most impressive castles soars above this white but dusty town. Velez Blanco's unpaved streets and rows of simple houses are typical of this barren area (148-150).

The random assembly of these austere forms delineated by the dark tile can create striking rhythms — patterns that are at once simple yet complex, clear yet ambiguous. Torre Alhaquime — a name of obvious Arabic antecedence (151).

Casares, the most spectacular of the white towns, has remained so because it was nearly inaccessible until recently and merited no mention in Baedekers. Perhaps inspired by the horrible example of other coastal towns such as Mijas now totally destroyed by rampant tourism, Casares will retain its fragile beauty (152-161).

*At the very top is the town cemetary — above-
ground vaults piled high in the limited space (153-154).*

These spellbinding views of Casares compel reflection that alternates between the abstract geometry enhanced by the contrasting roofs, the sensuous textures of the weathered walls and tile, and the reality — suddenly verified by tiny figures who appear in their midst.

Ardales is a small Andalusian farming community, out of the way and little corrupted by too rapid change. Despite a fairly regular street layout, the random adaptation of the standard house form to the variations of the site has produced an exceedingly complex series of stepped rhythms up the hillside. The practical need to seal the ridges and exposed end walls with whitewashed tile emphasizes the pattern by outlining each roof plane in white. The underlying purpose may be practical but the inhabitants are not unaware of its aesthetic effects (162-167).

Ardales is another example, if one is needed, of how a village composed of simple elements can, by the uniqueness of its site and scale, achieve a distinctive character, and how practical solutions to construction details can add integral, even exuberant, decoration. These villages are composed of the same fundamental building types but the details and the relationships of the parts are infinitely variable so that each village, each street, each plaza is unique yet familiar.

Ardales is in many ways the archetypal Andalusian village — white houses on a hillside beneath a ruined castle, surrounded by olive trees as far as the eye can see.

Problems of security, scarcity of water, and the system of land ownership have limited isolated farms to only a few areas. These compounds of houses and barns are in the exceptionally green and beautiful Valle de Abdalgis between Alora and Antequera (168-169).

In the middle of fragrant orange and lemon groves is this large farm compound near Alora — complete with its own chapel (170-171). The owner now lives in town and the manager's family occupies a portion of the house. Included in the compound are stables, a giant olive press and a large kitchen (171b) with a huge hood over the former cooking area.

To keep the interiors cool in summer and warm in winter the windows are few and small; however, the combination of shutters, splayed walls, and whitewash softens the glare from the sun outside and diffuses its light throughout the interior.

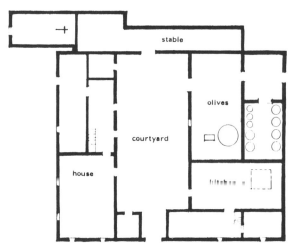

The village of Atajate near Ronda steps down the
south slope so each house catches the sun and view. It
is unusual because, except for the tower, its church is
built in the same style as the houses. The result is a
tiny village of unified composition that sits elegantly
in the unspoiled landscape unmarred even by the, at
times oppressive, mass of a church (172-173).

El Burgo, whose roof patterns are another and distinctive variation on the Andalusian theme (174).

In the towns projecting window bays allow discrete views up and down the street yet maintain privacy for the women of the house — similar to the shuttered balconies in the old Moslem towns in Africa. Their irregular repetition along the facades accented by the black grill work adds a striking sculptural effect to these plain walls in Ronda (175).

In the mountains near Granada where the last Arabs held out, a unique style persists that is remarkably similar to houses in the Atlas mountains of Morocco. The roofs are flat, made of layers of mud, and used for food and clothes drying. The upper stories often incorporate loggias — outdoor living spaces oriented to the sun and view. Near Orjiva (176t). Capileira (176b).

This cliff dwelling near Monte Frio undoubtedly has an ancient history, for such places were the first homes of man in this area. The upper entrance is the house — whitewashed and terraced to lend it a certain dignity — the other entrances are to storage rooms (177).

Through this cleft in the hills the first glimpse of
Monte Frio´s jewel white forms against the olive
green backdrop is breathtaking. The combination of
natural and man-made forms culminates in the
perfectly sited fortress church. Walled off at the lower
end, this central rock around which wrap the older
sections of the town was Monte Frio's natural castle to
which the townspeople could retreat in times of crisis.

Like Monsaraz and Casares, Monte Frio is a vital
place demonstrating how people cling to village life if
they are able to enjoy minimal modern conveniences
and find work nearby. Thankfully bypassed by the
crass tourism that has destroyed so many Iberian
towns, Monte Frio, not only in its overall aspects but in
many of its details, remains an authentic and inspiring
example of Iberian vernacular.

The desire for privacy and the need to both shade the summer sun and embrace it during the colder months led to exterior walls with small openings and rooms that opened onto interior patios. For ample sunlight most houses are not more than one or two stories especially if the court is small. The patio is filled with plants and flowers and may include a well or pool. It is the center of family life in good weather --a play space for children, the laundry and kitchen, a work space, and a gathering spot for evening relaxation. Despite the extremely narrow streets and the solidly packed houses, the low patio house kept the overall density to less than some medieval towns of the north.

One reason the smaller villages lacked the sophisticated patio house is that Islam is an urban phenomenon. Towns grew up around the markets surrounding the main mosque. The market or suq, held weekly, was essential to the economy of a large area and sometimes the very reason for a towns's existence. One still finds these weekly markets in rural Spain, Portugal, Mexico and most of the Arab world. Country folk came from miles around to buy and sell their goods and attend the Friday mosque, --one reason the markets were often held on that day.

Markets may have originated in the town center but the need for larger and larger areas as the town grew caused their shift to the outskirts --just inside or outside the walls near the main gates. The site for festivals and even bull fights, many plaza mayors owe their existence to those early markets.

Most smaller towns have changed little since the reconquest. They are still a maze of streets, lined with introverted houses, interspersed with tiny plazas, all without apparent order. Unhindered by central planning and with little sense of community responsibility (the streets were merely a path to the tranquility of one's own home), the towns reflect adaptation to the interior forces of town life --a life of multiplicity as opposed to the renaissance ideal of centralized hierarchical order.

Gardens and Patios

I would like to comment on Iberian and Islamic gardens. In the grander, more formal gardens, the combined influence of Islam and the later infusion of a renaissance desire for order have resulted in an extraordinary insensitivity to plant forms. It is not at all unusual to see a scraggly tree set forlornly in the midst of a hard tile floor, or rigid rows of slowly dying shrubs, or discordant collections of ungainly plants as the main features of patios and court yards. The apparent desire for total geometric order created an unsympathetic, artificial environment for man or plants. In contrast, the intimate scale of the private patios and the casual arrangements of abundant flowers and shrubs in pots on the floors, steps, sills or hung on the walls creates a humane and inviting atmosphere.(141, 144-145).

The insensitivity to domesticated plants may stem from a background in the waterless environment of the Arabian Peninsula and North Africa. One gets the sense that the survival of any growing thing, no matter how pathetic, is a triumph of man over environment. The sympathetic relation of plants and architecture of Japan, for example, would be incomprehensible. The walled garden represents the control of man over nature -- perhaps in response to the harsh realities of the world outside that space.

Nearly every patio or court includes a fountain, well, or pool. The water was present not only for daily use but also for its psychological effects -the sense of coolness and movement in the enervating heat.

The White Towns

The most spectacular southern villages are, of course, the white hilltowns. Most have now disappeared, buried under tourist hotels and condominiums that litter the Iberian coasts. It is safe to say, that from the French border to the Algarve in Portugal any village within a few miles of the coast is no longer worth visiting and the whole coast so dreary as to make one wonder why anyone still bothers.

Thankfully, some outstanding hilltowns remain in the interior, though one hesitates to identify their locations. Ardales, Olvera, Monte Frio, and especially Casares in Spain and Monsaraz in Portugal. After the desecration of the coast, to visit these brilliant towns is a reminder that man at one time was capable of making an environment of great beauty, sympathetic to nature and himself --and that he may still do so again.

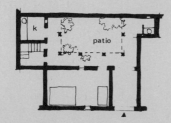

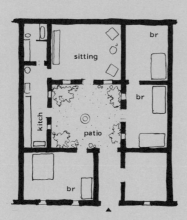

PATIO HOUSES

...the vernacular architecture of farms and inns and the narrow streets of little villages, that is not really architecture at all from an academic point of view, but just the straight forward instinctive building of grave and kindly men behind whom lies the creative tradition of two thousand years.

...here is the art of building reduced to its simplest and plainest forms, and ...is a wholesome lesson for architects of small things (actually more vital and important than the big things) and is a stimulus and inspiration as well.

Consider the simplicity of the materials and forms. Rough rubble, either left grey and silvery or washed a thousand times with white...brown natural wood, and rough tiles of every possible shade...There is little brick and less cut stone, while ornament is most sparingly used; a roughly carved capital here and there, a door architrave, a coat of arms, there is little more, and the effect comes from instinctively good proportions, a perfect designing and placing of windows, and a picturesqueness of composition that is so good it could not be premeditated. The Spaniard understands the wall and roof as no one else: he can build up his flat wall of rubble, cover it with a toned white wash, pierce it with a door and a few windows, add a balcony and two 'rijas', crown the whole with a sweeping roof of tawny tiles, plant two cypress and an almond nearby, and produce a composition that is the despair of the trained and cultured architect...

Pictures such as these are for students and creators of the real architecture of a people; not for copying, but for mental and spiritual illumination...

Ralph Adams Cram, Architect
Boston, 1923

BIBLIOGRAPHY AND NOTES

Architectura popular em Portugal. (2 vols). Lisbon:
National Union of Architects, 1961.

Baedeker, K. *Spain and Portugal.* Stuttgart, 1959.

3   Brennan, G. *The Spanish Labyrinth.* London 1943.

2   Dubos, Rene. *So Human an Animal.* New York:
Scribners, 1968.

Echague, Jose Oritz. *Pueblos Y Paisajes.* Madrid 1966.

Feduchi, Luis. *Arquitectura Popular Espanola.*
Barcelona: Editorial Blume, 1975 (5 vols).

Flores, Carlos. *Arquitectura Popular Espanola.* Madrid:
Aguilar, 1973.

1   Gutkind, E. A. *Urban development in Southern Europe:
Spain and Portugal. International History of City
Development, Vol III.* New York: The Free Press,
1967.

Michener, James A. *Iberia.* New York: Random House,
1968.

Mumford, Lewis. *The City in History.* New York:
Harcourt, Brace and World, 1961.

Morris, James. *The Presence of Spain.* New York:
Harcourt, Brace, and World, 1964.

INDEX

References to photographs are in ( ).

IBERIA

CANGAS
SANTILLANA
CARMONA
GOIZUETA

SANTIAGO DE C
EL CEBRERO
PENALBA DE SANTIAGO
ACEBO
FRIAS
VINUESA

LINDOSO
BÉNEVENTE
PENARANDA DE DUERO
BARCELONA
BRAGA
VILLAFUERTE
BATEA
HORTA

PEDRAZA
SEGOVIA
MORELLA

GUARDA
LA ALBERCA
MIRANDA
MONSANTO
MADRID
ALCALA
VALBONA

CUENCA
LA GUARDIA

GAROVILLAS
VALENCIA

CONSUEGRA

ALMANSA
LISBON
TERRUGEM
BIAR
CALCADINHA
MONSARAZ
BEDNAR

VELEZ BLANCO
MERTOLA
BAZA
SEVILLA
MONTE FRIO
GAUDIX
LOULE
UTRERA
GRANADA
CAPILEIRA
ALBUFEIRA
OLVERA
ARDALES
ABDALGIS
TORRE
ALORA
ORJIVA
SETENIL
EL BURGO
RONDA
ALPANDERE
ATAJATE
VEJER
CASARES
CASTELLAR
ESTEPONA

191

PHOTOGRAPHIC NOTES

The photographs are the result of seven trips to Spain and Portugal since 1970. Because of the tremendous variety in the photographs it was difficult to make the final selection. The book could easily have been twice the size --but alas, twice the price.

There is always a let-down when I finish my travels in a country. I no longer have the excuse to return to some unexplored corner or to re-photograph a favorite village under different light. Some places give one a feeling of relief when you have quit them, but Spain and Portugal still fascinate and I am sure I will return.

The photographs were made with Hasselblad cameras using lenses from 38 to 500mm. Also used were 35mm Nikon and Olympus cameras with lenses from 21 to 200mm. Most of the photographs were duplicated in color. The black and white, however, always took precedence. For me they are the most compelling and being the most abstract, are the strongest images.

AVAILABILITY OF PRINTS:
Archival prints made by Norman F. Carver,Jr. are available of any photograph in the book. A portfolio of 10 prints is also available. Prices as of 1981 range from $50 to $200 per print depending on size. For current prices please contact the photographer in care of the publisher, Documan Press, Box 387, Kalamazoo, Michigan 49005, USA.

S0-AXO-270

CROSSWORDS WORD SEARCHES
LOGIC PUZZLES & SURPRISES!

mind STRETCHERS

TANGERINE EDITION

EDITED BY STANLEY NEWMAN

Reader's Digest

The Reader's Digest Association, Inc.
Pleasantville, NY / Montreal

Project Staff

EDITORS
Neil Wertheimer, Sandy Fein

PUZZLE EDITOR
Stanley Newman

PRINCIPAL PUZZLE AUTHORS
George Bredehorn, Stanley
Newman, Dave Phillips,
Peter Ritmeester

SERIES ART DIRECTOR
Rich Kershner

DESIGNERS
Tara Long, Erick Swindell

ILLUSTRATIONS
©Norm Bendel

COPY EDITOR
Diane Aronson

Reader's Digest Home & Health Books

PRESIDENT, HOME & GARDEN AND HEALTH & WELLNESS
Alyce Alston

EDITOR IN CHIEF
Neil Wertheimer

CREATIVE DIRECTOR
Michele Laseau

EXECUTIVE MANAGING EDITOR
Donna Ruvituso

ASSOCIATE DIRECTOR, NORTH AMERICA PREPRESS
Douglas A. Croll

MANUFACTURING MANAGER
John L. Cassidy

MARKETING DIRECTOR
Dawn Nelson

The Reader's Digest Association, Inc.

PRESIDENT AND CHIEF EXECUTIVE OFFICER
Mary Berner

PRESIDENT, GLOBAL CONSUMER MARKETING
Dawn Zier

VICE PRESIDENT, CONSUMER MARKETING
Kathryn Bennett

ISBN 978-0-7621-0563-2

Address any comments about *Mind Stretchers*, *Tangerine Edition* to:

The Reader's Digest Association, Inc.
Editor in Chief, Books
Reader's Digest Road
Pleasantville, NY 10570-7000

To order copies of this or other editions of the *Mind Stretchers* book series,
call 1-800-846-2100.

Visit our online store at **rdstore.com**

For many more fun games and puzzles, visit www.rd.com/games.

Printed in the United States of America

1 3 5 7 9 10 8 6 4 2

US 4967/L-9

Contents

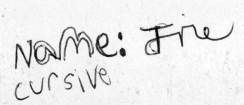

Dear Puzzler,

In these superfast times, video games and puzzles routinely fall in and out of fashion. Then there is the crossword puzzle. Handsome in design, challenging in content, crosswords are the elder statesmen of the puzzle world, respected, cherished, and endless in their variety and personality.

The first crossword ever published was in the December 21, 1913, edition of the New York World. Since that time, crossword puzzles have changed little in structure. Only one issue has challenged the puzzle over the decades—whether to use just "dictionary" words in puzzles, or to include proper nouns and references to classical or popular culture. While the early days of crosswords featured mostly dictionary words, even that first puzzle in 1913 featured a proper noun. The clue was "A river in Russia," with the answer NEVA. (St. Petersburg's Neva River still shows up now and then in crosswords.)

The first crossword puzzle authors certainly didn't show much mercy towards their audience. Looking over the Cross Word Puzzle Book, First Series, the very first crossword book ever published and a New York Times bestseller in 1924, I wonder how many people were actually able to complete all 50 of its puzzles. Those crosswords included such head-scratcher clues as "Albumin from castor-oil bean" (RICIN) and "The bow of Vishnu" (SARAN); and the answer word LARCH was clued by the single word "Tree."

The first Sunday crosswords that appeared in the New York Times in 1942 were filled with proper names, mostly surnames and geographic locations related to World War II. Today's solver would surely not know many of them, such as "Former head of the World Bank" (FRASER), "Commander of Allied Air Forces" (BRETT), and "Important base in New Guinea" (GONA).

I got into the puzzle business in the early 1980s, just in time to meet Margaret Farrar, the first New York Times crossword editor. Mrs. Farrar once advised me to edit puzzles in a way that avoids "here today, gone tomorrow" answers. Sage advice, which I have always tried to follow.

While Mind Stretchers has its share of delightful new puzzle forms, we're proud of our crosswords. Each is fresh and contemporary, made to challenge your brain in just the right way for our times. Whichever puzzles you take on, we hope you find them fun, rewarding, and mind-stretching!

Stanley Newman
Mind Stretchers Puzzle Editor

■ Foreword

Meet the Puzzles!

Mind Stretchers is filled with a delightful mix of classic and new puzzle types. To help you get started, here are instructions, tips, and examples for each.

Crossword Puzzles

Edited by Stanley Newman

Crosswords are arguably America's most popular puzzles. As presented in this book, the one- and two-star puzzles test your ability to solve straightforward clues to everyday words. "More-star" puzzles have a somewhat broader vocabulary, but most of the added challenge in these comes from less obvious and trickier clues. These days, you'll be glad to know, uninteresting obscurities such as "Genus of fruit flies" and "Famed seventeenth-century soprano" don't appear in crosswords anymore.

Our 60 crosswords were authored by more than a dozen different puzzle makers, all nationally known for their skill and creativity.

Clueless Crosswords

by George Bredehorn

A unique crossword variation invented by George, these 7-by-7 grids primarily test your vocabulary and reasoning skills. There is one simple task: Complete the crossword with common uncapitalized seven-letter words, based entirely on the letters already filled in for you.

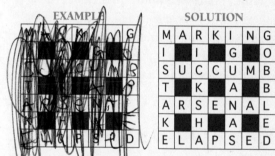

Hints: *Focusing on the last letter of a word, when given, often helps. For example, a last letter of G often suggests that IN are the previous two letters. When the solutions aren't coming quickly, focus on the shared spaces that are blank—you can often figure out whether it has to be a vowel or a consonant, helping you solve both words that cross it.*

Split Decisions

by George Bredehorn

Crossword puzzle lovers also enjoy this variation. Once again, no clues are provided except within the diagram. Each answer consists of two words whose spellings are the same, except for two consecutive letters. For each pair of words, the two sets of different letters are already filled in for you. All answers are common words; no phrases or hyphenated or capitalized words are used. Certain missing words may have more than one possible solution, but there is only one solution for each word that will correctly link up with all the other words.

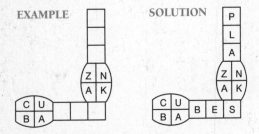

EXAMPLE　　　　SOLUTION

Hints: *Start with the shorter (three- and four-letter) words, because there will be fewer possibilities that spell words. In each puzzle, there will always be a few such word pairs that have only one solution. You may have to search a little to find them, since they may be anywhere in the grid, but it's always a good idea to fill in the answers to these first.*

Triad Split Decisions
by George Bredehorn

This puzzle is solved the same way as Split Decisions, except you are given three letters for each word instead of two.

EXAMPLE　　　SOLUTION

Word Searches

Kids love 'em, and so do grownups, making word searches perhaps the most widely appealing puzzle type. In a word search, the challenge is to find hidden words within a grid of letters. In the typical puzzle, words can be found in vertical columns, horizontal rows, or along diagonals, with the letters of the words running either forward or backward. Usually, a list of words to search for is given to you. But

ANSWERS!

Answers to all the puzzles are found beginning on page 233, and are organized by the page number on which the puzzle appears.

to make word searches harder, puzzle writers sometimes just point you in the right direction, such as telling you to find 25 foods. Other twists include allowing words to take right turns, or leaving letters out of the grid.

Hints: *One of the most reliable and efficient searching methods is to scan each row from top to bottom for the first letter of the word. So if you are looking for "violin" you would look for the letter "v." When you find one, look at all the letters that surround it for the second letter of the word (in this case, "i"). Each time you find a correct two-letter combination (in this case, "vi"), you then scan either for the correct three-letter combination ("vio") or the whole word.*

NUMBER GAMES

Sudoku
by Conceptis Ltd.

Sudoku puzzles have become massively popular in the past few years, thanks to their simplicity and test of pure reasoning. The basic Sudoku puzzle is a 9-by-9 square grid, split into 9 square regions, each containing 9 cells. Each puzzle starts off with roughly 20 to 35 of the squares filled in with the numbers 1 to 9. There is just one rule: Fill in the rest of the squares

EXAMPLE

8	4					7	1	
3			7	1	8			9
		5	9		3	6		
	9	7	8		1	2	3	
	6						9	
	3	1	2		9	7	6	
		4	3		2	9		
1			5	9	4			6
9	8						5	3

SOLUTION

8	4	9	6	2	5	3	7	1
3	2	6	7	1	8	5	4	9
7	1	5	9	4	3	6	8	2
5	9	7	8	6	1	2	3	4
2	6	8	4	3	7	1	9	5
4	3	1	2	5	9	7	6	8
6	5	4	3	8	2	9	1	7
1	7	3	5	9	4	8	2	6
9	8	2	1	7	6	4	5	3

with the numbers 1 to 9 so that no number appears twice in any row, column, or region.

Hints: Use the numbers provided to rule out where else the same number can appear. For example, if there is a 1 in a cell, a 1 cannot appear in the same row, column, or region. By scanning all the cells that the various 1 values rule out, you often can find where the remaining 1 values must go.

Hyper-Sudoku
by Peter Ritmeester

Peter is the inventor of this unique Sudoku variation. In addition to the numbers 1 to 9 appearing in each row and column, Hyper-Sudoku also has four 3-by-3 regions to work with, indicated by gray shading.

EXAMPLE   **SOLUTION**

1	4	5	9			7		
		7	5	8	4	1		
3				7	2		5	
5	9		4	2	7			
	6		8					7
	7	4				2	9	5
	1						8	
	5		2			6		
6			7			5		

1	4	5	9	3	6	7	2	8
9	2	7	5	8	4	1	3	6
3	8	6	1	7	2	9	5	4
5	9	3	4	2	7	8	6	1
2	6	1	8	5	9	3	4	7
8	7	4	6	1	3	2	9	5
7	1	9	3	6	5	4	8	2
4	5	8	2	9	1	6	7	3
6	3	2	7	4	8	5	1	9

LOGIC PUZZLES

Find the Ships
by Conceptis Ltd.

If you love playing the board game Battleship, you'll enjoy this pencil-and-paper variation! In each puzzle, a group of ships of varying sizes is provided on the right. Your job: Properly place the ships in the grid. A handful of ship "parts" are put on the board to get you started. The placement rules:

1. Ships must be oriented horizontally or vertically. No diagonals!

2. A ship can't go in a square with wavy lines; that indicates water.

3. The numbers on the left and bottom of the grid tell you how many squares in that row or column contain part of ships.

4. No two ships can touch each other, even diagonally.

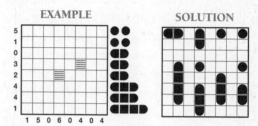

EXAMPLE   **SOLUTION**

Hints: The solving process involves both finding those squares where a ship must go and eliminating those squares where a ship cannot go. The numbers provided should give you a head start with the latter, the number 0 clearly implying that every square in that row or column can be eliminated. If you know that a square will be occupied by a ship, but don't yet know what kind of ship, mark that square, then cross out all the squares that are diagonal to it—all of these must contain water.

ABC
by Peter Ritmeester

This innovative new puzzle challenges your logic much in the way a Sudoku puzzle does. Each row and column in an ABC puzzle contains exactly one A, one B, and one C, plus one blank (or two, in harder puzzles). Your task is to figure out where the three letters go in each row. The clues outside the puzzle frame tell you the first letter encountered when moving in the direction of an arrow.

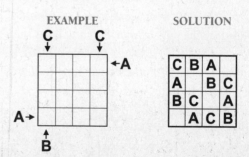

EXAMPLE   **SOLUTION**

Hints: *If a clue says a letter is first in a row or column, don't assume that it must go in the first square. It could go in either of the first two squares (or first three, in the harder puzzles). A good way to start is to look for where column and row clues intersect (for example, when two clues look like they are pointing at the same square). These intersecting clues often give you the most information about where the first letter of a row or column must go. At times, it's also possible to figure out where a certain letter goes by eliminating every other square as a possibility for that letter in a particular row or column.*

Fences

by Conceptis Ltd.

Lovers of mazes will enjoy these challenges. Connect the dots with vertical or horizontal lines, so that a single loop is formed with no crossings or branches. Each number indicates how many lines surround it; squares with no number may be surrounded by any number of lines.

EXAMPLE   SOLUTION

Hints: *Don't try to solve the puzzle by making one continuous line—instead, fill in the links (that is, spaces between two dots) you are certain about, and then figure out how to connect those links. To start the puzzle, mark off any links that can't be connected. That would include all four links around each 0. Another good starting step is to look for any 3 values next or adjacent to a 0; solving those links is easy. In time, you will see that rules and patterns emerge, particularly in the puzzle corners, and when two numbers are adjacent to each other.*

Number-Out

by Conceptis Ltd.

This innovative new puzzle challenges your logic in much the same way a Sudoku puzzle does. Your task is to shade squares so that no number appears in any row or column more than once. Shaded squares may not touch each other horizontally or vertically, and all unshaded squares must form a single continuous area.

EXAMPLE   SOLUTION

Hints: *First look for all the numbers that are unduplicated in their row and column. Those squares will never be shaded, so we suggest that you circle them as a reminder to yourself. When there are three of the same number consecutively in a row or column, the one in the middle must always be unshaded, so you can shade the other two. Also, any square that is between a pair of the same numbers must always be unshaded. Once a square is shaded, you know that the squares adjacent to it, both horizontally and vertically, must be unshaded.*

Star Search

by Peter Ritmeester

Another fun game in the same style of Minesweeper. Your task: find the stars that are hidden among the blank squares. The numbered squares indicate how many stars are hidden in squares adjacent to them (including diagonally). There is never more than one star in any square.

EXAMPLE SOLUTION

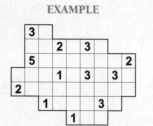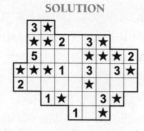

Hint: If, for example, a 3 is surrounded by four empty squares, but two of those squares are adjacent to the same square with a 1, the other two empty squares around the 3 must contain stars.

123

by Peter Ritmeester

Each grid in this puzzle has pieces that look like dominoes. You must fill in the blank squares so that each "domino" contains one each of the numbers 1, 2, and 3, according to these two rules:

EXAMPLE

				1	
		3			
3				2	
	2				
		1		1	

SOLUTION

2	1	2	3	1	3
3	2	3	1	2	1
1	3	1	2	3	2
3	1	2	3	2	1
1	2	3	1	3	2
2	3	1	2	1	3

1. No two adjacent squares, horizontally or vertically, can have the same number.

2. Each completed row and column of the diagram will have an equal number of 1s, 2s, and 3s.

Hints: Look first for any blank square that is adjacent to two different numbers. By rule 1 above, the "missing" number of 1-2-3 must go in that blank square. Rule 2 becomes important to use later in the solving process., For example, knowing that a 9-by-9 diagram must have three 1s, three 2s, and three 3s in each row and column allows you to use the process of elimination to deduce what blank squares in nearly filled rows and columns must be.

Throughout *Mind Stretchers* you will find unique mazes, visual conundrums, and other colorful challenges, each developed by maze master Dave Phillips. Each comes under a new name and has unique instructions. Our best advice? Patience and perseverance. Your eyes will need time to unravel the visual secrets.

In addition, you will also discover these visual puzzles:

Line Drawings

by George Bredehorn

George loves to create never-before-seen puzzle types, and here is another unique Bredehorn game. Each Line Drawing puzzle is different in its design, but the task is the same: Figure out where to place the prescribed number of lines to partition the space in the instructed way.

Hint: Use a pencil and a straightedge as you work. Some lines come very close to the items within the region, so being straight and accurate with your line-drawing is crucial.

One-Way Streets

by Peter Ritmeester

Another fun variation on the maze. The diagram represents a pattern of streets. A and B are parking spaces, and the black squares are stores. Find a route that starts at A, passes through all the stores exactly once, and ends at B. (Harder puzzles use P's to indicate parking spaces instead of A's and B's, and don't tell you the starting and ending places.) Arrows indicate one-way traffic for that block only. No

EXAMPLE SOLUTION

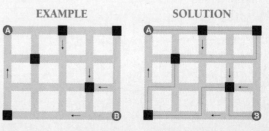

block or intersection may be entered more than once.

Hints: The particular arrangement of stores and arrows will always limit the possibilities for the first store passed through from the starting point A and the last store passed through before reaching ending point B. So try to work both from the start and the end of the route. Also, the placement of an arrow on a block doesn't necessarily mean that your route will pass through that block. You can also use arrows to eliminate blocks where your path will not go.

BRAIN TEASERS

To round out the more involved puzzles are more than 150 short brain teasers, most written by our puzzle editor, Stanley Newman. Stan is famous in the puzzle world for his inventive brain games. An example of how to solve each puzzle appears in the puzzle's first occurrence (the page number is noted below). You'll find the following types scattered throughout the pages.

* Invented by and cowritten with George Bredehorn

** By George Bredehorn

But wait...there's more!

At the top of many of the pages in this book are additional brain teasers, organized into three categories:

• **QUICK!:** These tests challenge your ability to instantly calculate numbers or recall well-known facts.

• **DO YOU KNOW ...:** These more demanding questions probe the depth of your knowledge of facts and trivia.

• **HAVE YOU ...:** These reminders reveal the many things you can do each day to benefit your brain.

For the record, we have deliberately left out answers to the **QUICK!** and **DO YOU KNOW...** features. Our hope is that if you don't know an answer, you'll be intrigued enough to open a book or search the Internet for it!

■ Meet the Authors

STANLEY NEWMAN (puzzle editor and author) is crossword editor for *Newsday,* the major newspaper of Long Island, New York. He is the author/editor of over 125 books, including the autobiography and instructional manual *Cruciverbalism* and the best-selling *Million Word Crossword Dictionary.* Winner of the First U.S. Open Crossword Championship in 1982, he holds the world's record for the fastest completion of a *New York Times* crossword— 2 minutes, 14 seconds. Stan operates the website www.StanXwords.com and also conducts an annual Crossword University skill-building program on a luxury-liner cruise.

GEORGE BREDEHORN is a retired elementary school teacher from Wantagh, New York. His variety word games have appeared in the *New York Times* and many puzzle magazines. Every week for the past 20 years, he and his wife, Dorothy, have hosted a group of Long Island puzzlers who play some of the 80-plus games that George has invented.

CONCEPTIS (www.conceptispuzzles.com) is a leading supplier of logic puzzles to printed, electronic, and other gaming media all over the world. On average, ten million Conceptis puzzles are printed in newspapers, magazines and books each day, while millions more are played online and on mobile phones each month.

DAVE PHILLIPS has designed puzzles for books, magazines, newspapers, PC games, and advertising for more 30 years. In addition, Dave is a renowned creator of walk-through mazes. Each year his corn-maze designs challenge visitors with miles of paths woven into works of art. Dave is also codeveloper of eBrainyGames.com, a website that features puzzles and games for sale.

PETER RITMEESTER is chief executive officer of PZZL.com, which produces many varieties of puzzles for newspapers and websites worldwide. Peter is also general secretary of the World Puzzle Federation. The federation organizes the annual World Puzzle Championship, which includes difficult versions of many of the types of logic puzzles that Peter has created for *Mind Stretchers.*

■ Master Class: **Numbers**

Train Your Mind to Be Better at Mental Arithmetic

In real-life situations, do you think of numbers as useful tools? Or have numbers been your lifelong bugaboos—pesky little annoyances that you try to avoid at all costs?

If it's the latter, this Master Class will put you on the road toward "numerical literacy," by introducing you to some tips and tricks that will jump-start your abilities in the wonderful world of numbers. Even if numbers and you are already getting along smashingly, I suspect there will be some things here that'll be new and useful to you.

And, as a bonus, we'll go through a step-by-step solution of an Addition Switch puzzle, several of which can be found in each edition of *Mind Stretchers*.

Remembering Numbers

There's no getting around it—our lives are all filled with important numbers, of all kinds, that need to be remembered. They might be short—like your ATM code or the number in a friend's address—or more troublesomely long—like seven- or 10-digit (with area code)

telephone numbers, and the multi-digit monstrosities on your credit cards.

If you have difficulty remembering numbers, no matter how long or short they might be, it's not your fault. It's the numbers' fault! What do I mean by that? Let's face it—numbers don't have personalities, and they're highly unlikely to evoke sharp images in your memory. But what if you could somehow magically change a number you wanted to remember into something else—something that you would have no trouble at all keeping in mind? Well, you can. Here are three methods that many people have successfully used. And there's nothing "magical" about them.

1. Your Own Rhyme Scheme
Remember this old nursery rhyme, which has been recited by moms and dads seemingly forever to teach numbers to tots?

> *One, two, buckle my shoe.*
> *Three, four, shut the door.*
> *Five, six, pick up sticks.*
> *Seven, eight, don't be late.*
> *Nine, ten, a big fat hen.*

Well, you can create your own scheme of "number rhymes" to help you remember a series of numbers. Here's how:

Select your favorite rhyming word for each of the digits from 0 to 9 from this list, or some other rhyming word if you prefer, such as:

0 – *crow, doe, snow*
1 – *bun, run, son*
2 – *glue, shoe, zoo*
3 – *bee, knee, tree*
4 – *door, floor, store*
5 – *dive, drive, hive*
6 – *bricks, mix, sticks*
7 – *heaven (sorry, not a lot of choices available here!)*
8 – *crate, gate, skate*
9 – *line, sign, wine*

Then, create a "mini-story" from the number you want to remember, using each of your rhyming words for each digit in the number, from left to right.

Let's say the number you want to remember is 40593 (a number I picked at random, though it happens to be a zip code in Lexington, Kentucky), and you're using the first word listed above as a rhyme for each number. Your task therefore is to create your story from these words: door, crow, dive, line, bee. And it might look something like this:

Open the door, and watch the crow dive into the clothes line and get stung by a bee.

Once you've created your story, you have two choices as to how to commit it to memory. You can either memorize the sentence as is, or create a "mental movie" for yourself that contains all the images of the door, crow, etc., in the correct order. If you're an imaginative person by nature, you may find it easier to remember your "movie" than the sentence.

Does it matter that your story might never happen in real life? Absolutely not! It doesn't

matter how "wild and crazy" your story is. In fact, some experts say that the more outlandish it is, the more you're likely to remember it. What's important for you to remember is this— remembering your story will be easier than remembering the number.

2. The "Symbolic System"

If rhymes aren't your thing, there's a similar method that, instead of rhymes, uses familiar items whose shapes resemble each of the digits. Such as:

0 – an egg
1 – a pencil
2 – a swan
3 – a pair of glasses
4 – a boat's sail
5 – a sea horse
6 – a cherry (with stem attached)
7 – a cane
8 – an hourglass
9 – a balloon (held by a string)

So, to remember 40593 in this system, you'd create a story using (in order) a sail, an egg, a sea horse, a balloon and a pair of glasses.

3. "Numbers to Letters to Words"

Numbers 1 and 2 above work best with numbers that aren't too long. For longer numbers, say a nine-digit Social Security number or a 16-digit credit card number, try this approach.

First, you'll need to create and memorize your own personal "consonant letter code" for each of the nine digits. To work best, your letters should all be common consonants (I'll explain why in a minute).

The code I use for the numbers 0-9, in order, is: T N S H R D L M C W, because they are the 10 most commonly used consonants in English, in their approximate order.

For your system to work for you, you'll need

to memorize your code. The way I remember the order of the letters in my code just happens to be the method I use (and which you will use) to remember any long string of numbers: Create a sentence using those consonants in order (and no other consonants), separating them into words and adding vowels wherever it's convenient. So, my code of T N S H R D L M C W became "Ten shared a lime cow." I can promise you that, from the time I created that very strange sentence long ago, I've never forgotten it!

Of course, you're free to use any ten different consonants you like. But you will want them to be as common as possible, because the more common they are, the easier it will be for you to create sentences from them.

Here's one more example, where, using my code, I turn a random nine-digit number into a sentence.

Addition Switch Solving Tips

This quick, popular *Mind Stretchers* puzzle is primarily a test of your logic skills, with no math required beyond addition.

Just in case you've been puzzled as to how to get started with *Addition Switch,* let's go through the step-by-step solution of one puzzle. In doing so, we'll reveal some tips that should unlock all its mysteries for you.

In *Addition Switch,* you're given an incorrect three-digit sum, and are told to find the two digits whose positions must be switched to get a correct sum. For example:

$$
\begin{array}{r}
6\ 7\ 9 \\
+\ 1\ 7\ 8 \\
\hline
1\ 5\ 0
\end{array}
$$

The key in getting started with any *Addition Switch* is realizing that there will always be one column of three digits (the two digits above the horizontal line, and the one below it) that is completely correct and will have no digits switched. Do you see why this is so? Since only two digits are being switched, they can't be in more than two of the three columns.

In this example, look closely at the three columns, one at a time, and you'll find that only the middle column can possibly be correct as is (with a carried "1"). So the two digits to be switched must be somewhere in the leftmost and rightmost columns.

Once a column is eliminated from consideration, there are two ways to proceed. One is the "try them all" method, which will always work. If you try to switch each of the six remaining digits (one at a time) with each of the other five, you're sure to find the right pair to switch eventually. An additional hint if you go this route: the two numbers "above" the line in the same column will never be switched, because switching them won't change the sum.

The second way is a shorter way that requires more logic. Examine the two remaining columns, and you can often find a digit that must be switched, due to the basics of arithmetic. In this puzzle, the "1" in "150" can't be correct, because the sum of the digits above it (which have to be a 1 and a 1 at minimum) can't be any less than 2. Trying the remaining five digits in turn, you'll find that switching the "1" in "150" with the "8" in "178" produces the correct sum:

$$
\begin{array}{r}
6\ 7\ 9 \\
+\ 1\ 7\ 1 \\
\hline
8\ 5\ 0
\end{array}
$$

905837204 becomes the consonants W T D C H M S T R, which I turned into the sentence "I awaited chum's try." Not a very profound statement, I agree, but, as with the previous two number-learning aids, it's much easier to remember that four-word sentence than the nine digits of a number.

By the way, any number of sentences can be formed from these consonants, so why don't you try making up a couple of your own for practice.

Calculation Made Easy

Unlike high-school math exams, everyday life will find you in many "calculational situations" where you don't really need an exact answer, only a reasonable estimate. So I'd like to share with you a few arithmetic tricks I use to get fast, "close-enough" answers; you should be able to do these in your head with just a little practice.

For the purposes of this section, imagine yourself in your favorite local restaurant.

Adding a Long List of Numbers

Let's say that it's your turn to pay for dinner for your group of friends, and your server presents you with this hand-calculated check:

$8.95
$4.75
$6.25
$12.00
$7.95
$7.95
$13.25
—————
$61.10
$4.40 (6¾% sales tax)
—————
$65.50

Before you pay, you'd like to verify the server's calculations—at least so you'll know that they're not far off. Here's how you can do a quick "approximate" addition.

Rather than working with the three-digit numbers of dollars and cents, round off each amount to the nearest dollar. That is, if an amount ends in .50 or higher, increase it to the next highest dollar. If it's .49 or less, decrease it to the next lowest dollar. So, adding those seven dollar-and-cents amounts becomes: 9 + 5 + 6 + 12 + 8 + 8 + 13, which, adding one number a time, totals 61. Much easier than adding four columns of dollars and cents, right?

Quick Percentages

Now that you've verified that the $61.10 subtotal seems correct, you'd like to check the sales tax also. Even though there's a lot less money involved, of course, the total has come out to an "even" $65.50, which you're just a little suspicious about. (I must admit that this particular example is based on my own personal experience with restaurant bills.)

Once again, you can get an approximate answer by rounding. Round the 6¾% sales tax rate up to 7%, and round the total bill down to $61.00. Remembering "percent" means "per hundred," that means a sales tax of seven cents per dollar. So seven percent of $60 is $4.20, plus another seven cents for the additional dollar, gives you a $4.27 estimate, less than the $4.40 tax that's been added on to your bill.

So it would be perfectly acceptable to call your server back to your table and discreetly suggest a recalculation of the sales tax, since it doesn't look right to you. If the server returns a couple of minutes later with a new bill that includes sales tax of $4.12 (the correct amount) and apologizes for the error, by all means congratulate yourself (silently) for discovering it!

Calculating the appropriate tip for the server is another opportunity to use your estimation skills. Whether you'd like to tip 15%, 20%, or any other percentage, you can estimate it quickly by using multiples of 10%, or one-tenth of the bill before taxes. To find 10% of any number, just move the decimal point one place to the left. To do this most easily in your head, I suggest rounding the bill total to the nearest $10. So 10% of $60 in this instance is $6.00; 20% is twice that, or $12.00. To estimate 15%, add the 10% to one-half of itself, or $6.00 to $3.00, to get $9.00.

Additional Resources

If you have Internet access, you can find much good reading online by typing "how to remember numbers" and "improve mental arithmetic" in your favorite search engine. If not, your local library or bookstore is sure to have books on these subjects.

Good luck, and remember: Numbers are your friends!

—Stan Newman

★ Instructive by Gail Grabowski

ACROSS

1 Essayist __ Waldo Emerson
6 Con game
10 Rescue
14 Texas landmark
15 Flag holder
16 Yoked animals
17 Pricey plane section
19 Sit down with a book
20 Kennedy or Koppel
21 Kite attachment
22 Seashore finds
24 Hatchling's home
25 Fruity desserts
26 Attempted to rip
29 Money-back offers
33 Declare openly
34 Rams' mates
36 Fisherman's lure
37 Cincinnati baseballers
38 Group of ships
39 Rock guitarist Hendrix
40 Get ready, for short
41 Bakery appliance
42 At any time
43 Warehouse's purpose
45 Means of approach
47 Lubricates
48 Thin board
49 Puzzle
52 Adolescent
53 Swampy ground
56 Shakespearean king
57 Entrée
60 Long story
61 Baking utensils
62 Sacred song
63 Molecule part
64 Fully satisfy
65 Toys on strings

DOWN

1 Huck Finn's transport
2 "I cannot tell __"
3 Frying medium
4 Evening hours: Abbr.
5 Chinese restaurant beverage
6 Divide, with "up"
7 Snowman's eye material
8 Pacino et al.
9 Most untidy
10 Sensitive topic
11 Skater's leap
12 Cutlet meat
13 Concludes
18 Stage group
23 Magazine founder, informally
24 11 p.m. TV offering
25 Dress smartly
26 Waterproof covers
27 Out in the open
28 Bronco-riding show
30 Gullible
31 Small coins
32 Uses a spoon
34 Santa's helpers
35 Very small
38 Auto headlight accessories
44 Prepare to shoot
45 Actor Baldwin
46 Awning
48 Sight or smell
49 Born Free feline
50 Tidy
51 Othello villain
52 Add some color to
53 Donkey's sound
54 Capital of Norway
55 Precious stones
58 Motorists' org.
59 GI show sponsor

★ Five Squares

Enter the maze at left, pass through all the yellow squares exactly once, and then exit at right. You may not retrace your path.

COUNT UP

Inserting plus signs and minus signs, as many as necessary, in between the digits from 1 to 9 below, create a series of additions and subtractions whose final answer is 47. Any digits without a sign between them are to be grouped together as a single number.

Example: 1 2 + 3 4 + 5 6 - 7 8 + 9 = 33

$$1 \quad 2 \quad 3 \quad 4 \quad 5 \quad 6 \quad 7 \quad 8 \quad 9 \quad = \quad 47$$

★ Puzzle Pieces

Find all these words associated with portions of things that are hidden in the diagram, either across, down, or diagonally.

```
O  V  N  F  L  P  A  R  T  V  E  C
A  T  U  H  D  E  N  O  E  X  W  Y
Q  T  P  C  I  B  S  L  T  I  H  G
L  E  O  N  N  T  B  R  A  X  I  Q
E  C  E  I  P  B  A  M  O  P  T  J
Q  X  A  P  I  C  S  R  W  M  X  H
Z  R  Z  R  T  P  C  H  U  N  K  S
G  A  D  F  E  O  A  B  W  A  O  P
B  U  T  S  L  R  B  S  A  M  O  M
D  U  F  O  P  T  W  B  E  D  N  U
K  O  E  K  M  I  S  T  U  M  P  L
G  J  L  E  A  O  D  D  R  R  Y  D
J  L  T  L  S  N  A  I  E  A  R  H
T  I  B  L  O  R  S  S  C  O  C  P
M  K  G  D  V  P  H  M  P  Y  T  E
```

ATOM
BIT
CHUNK
DAB
DASH
DOLLOP
DRIBBLE
DROP
EXTRACT
GRAIN
IOTA
LUMP
MITE
MORSEL
PART
PIECE
PINCH
PORTION
SAMPLE
SOME
STUB
STUMP
TRACE
WHIT

INITIAL REACTION

Identify the well-known proverb from the first letters in each of its words.
Example: H.M.W. Answer: Haste Makes Waste

T. I. C. _____

★ Sudoku

Fill in the blank boxes so that every row, column, and 3x3 box contains all of the numbers 1 to 9.

4	6	7		4	9			
7		6	9		4	3		4
1	4	1			2		6	5
		8		2			9	
3			5		8			6
	7			3		8		
9	5		3				2	8
2		4			9	5		1
				7				

MIXAGRAMS

Each line contains a five-letter word and a four-letter word that have been mixed together (the order of the letters in each word has not been changed). Unmix the two words on each line and write them in the spaces provided. When you're done, find a two-part answer to the clue by reading down the letter columns in the answers. Example: D A R I U N V E T = DRIVE + AUNT

CLUE: Buffalo pro

P A B R O C I L E = _ _ _ _ _ + _ _ _ _

W I N H O L E A T = _ _ _ _ _ + _ _ _ _

L E R U G I D E T = _ _ _ _ _ + _ _ _ _

L I D A V Y E R S = _ _ _ _ _ + _ _ _ _

★ Falling by Sally R. Stein

ACROSS

1 Utter confusion
6 Highway, for example
10 Two-year-olds
14 Pizazz
15 Poker-hand preliminary
16 "Yikes!"
17 Walk in
18 Store-sign gas
19 Manufactured
20 Great-grandson, for one
22 Actor Pitt
23 Kids' card game
24 Bowling lanes
26 Poorly done
30 Free-for-all
32 Word form for "all"
33 Chimney dust
35 Out of bed
39 Figure out
41 Figured out
42 Jeopardy
43 So far
44 Fishing-line holder
46 Electrified swimmers
47 Sounded like sheep
49 Give the latest news to
51 Saloon seats
54 Alias letters
55 Tenure of office
56 Calculator predecessors
63 *Moby-Dick* captain
64 *Jane __* (Brontë novel)
65 Japanese city
66 Parcel (out)
67 Mouse catcher
68 Not tilting
69 Jury member
70 Shipped, as a package
71 Wipe clean

DOWN

1 Like many dorms
2 Sharpen
3 Quantities: Abbr.
4 Oil cartel
5 Clever
6 Time off, for short
7 Top draft rating
8 Like __ of bricks
9 Of teeth
10 Rolling plant in Westerns
11 Chicago airport
12 NBC morning show
13 Backyard buildings
21 Thumbs-down votes
25 Jump
26 Slugger Sammy
27 Medical-insurance cos.
28 Merely
29 Type of warplane
30 Sounded like cows
31 Diminutive suffix
34 Dictatorial boss
36 Vicinity
37 Bagpiper's wear
38 Otherwise
40 And others: Abbr.
45 Skywalker of *Star Wars*
48 Balance-sheet column
50 Convict's quest
51 Post-office purchase
52 Giggle sound
53 Stand up and speak
54 Well-versed
57 Ancient stringed instrument
58 Persia's current name
59 Consumer
60 Volcanic flow
61 __ out a living (barely manages)
62 Retail-ad headline

★ Fences

Connect the dots with vertical or horizontal lines, so that a single loop is formed with no crossings or branches. Each number indicates how many lines surround it; squares with no number may be surrounded by any number of lines.

```
·   ·   ·   ·   ·   ·   ·   ·   ·
  3   2   2           3   3
·   ·   ·   ·   ·   ·   ·   ·   ·
                  0           2
·   ·   ·   ·   ·   ·   ·   ·   ·
  2   3                   3
·   ·   ·   ·   ·   ·   ·   ·   ·
  0           0       3
·   ·   ·   ·   ·   ·   ·   ·   ·
          3       1           2
·   ·   ·   ·   ·   ·   ·   ·   ·
      3                   1   1
·   ·   ·   ·   ·   ·   ·   ·   ·
  2           3
·   ·   ·   ·   ·   ·   ·   ·   ·
      2   3           2   2   3
·   ·   ·   ·   ·   ·   ·   ·   ·
```

ADDITION SWITCH

Switch the positions of two of the digits in the incorrect sum at right, to get a correct sum.

Example: 955+264 = 411. Switch the second 1 in 411 with the 9 in 955 to get: 155+264 = 419

```
  1 8 3
+ 2 9 5
-------
  8 7 4
```

★★ Line Drawing

Draw two straight lines, each from one edge of the square to another edge, so that the letters in each of the four regions spell rhyming words.

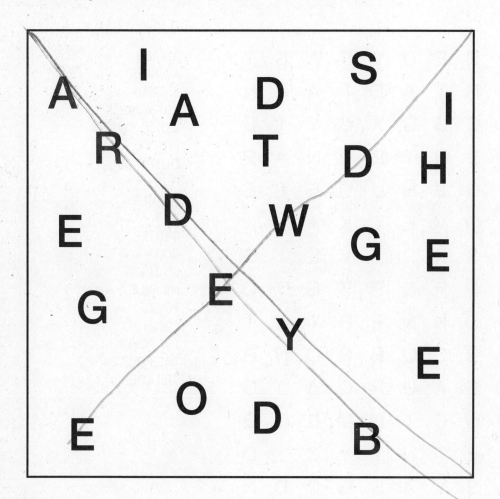

THREE OF A KIND

Find the three hidden words in the sentence that, read in order, go together in some way.
Example: I s̲o̲l̲d̲ No̲r̲ma̲ ̲new screwd̲r̲i̲v̲e̲r̲s̲ (answer: "old man river").

Most Hawaii maps include a shelf, reef, or a valley.

★ The Caped Crusader

Find these words associated with Batman that are hidden in the diagram, either across, down, or diagonally. Slash marks between words indicate that the words are hidden separately.

```
S A L F R E D V R W S T
T U R E H T A E L A N H
E H Z C C G D X C Y I E
G Q E L L N T B L N A P
D I U J O L H U U E L E
A E A W O M E T K A L N
G H Y P S K P L V E I G
N O M R F R E E Z E V U
B A D I C K N R B T W I
R G M F B G G R N Q N R
E O W O E A U R O A J O
G T A R W C I H M B C B
N H Y J E T N T Y C I D
A A N O S Y A R G C D N
D M D Y O B E C I L O P
```

ALFRED
AVENGER
BATMAN
BOY WONDER
BRUCE / WAYNE
BUTLER
CATWOMAN
CLUE
DANGER
DICK / GRAYSON
GADGETS
GOTHAM
LEATHER
MR FREEZE
POLICE
ROBIN
THE JOKER
THE PENGUIN
VILLAINS

WHO'S WHAT WHERE?

The correct term for a resident of Naples, Italy, is:

A) Napulite   B) Neapolitan

C) Napolano   D) Naplian

★ Join the Group by Gail Grabowski

ACROSS

1 *Gone With the Wind* estate
5 Head for the hills
9 Montana city
14 Airline to Israel
15 Marshal Wyatt
16 Radio-studio sign
17 Short skirt
18 Dreadful
19 Author Cather
20 Beast of burden
22 Turnpike charges
23 Clip, as wool
24 Twirl
26 Wide belt
29 Spurn
33 V-shaped cut
37 Horseback game
39 Singer Guthrie
40 Brother of Cain
41 Meal starter, often
42 Pottery material
43 Brazil neighbor
44 Sign of the future
45 Distorts, as data
46 $ or %
48 Usher's offering
50 Mets' former stadium
52 Fills, as a camera
56 Composed a letter
59 Ship-to-pier structure
63 Become ready to eat
64 Creme-filled cookie
65 King of the jungle
66 Wedding site
67 Within reach
68 Succulent houseplant
69 Troublesome
70 Harvard rival
71 Overpublicize

DOWN

1 Short-term worker
2 Assumed name
3 Cattle farm
4 Similarly
5 Soft felt hat
6 Wild animal's home
7 Makes a mistake
8 Fencing blades
9 Tuxedo neckwear
10 British flag
11 Like skyscrapers
12 Cash drawer
13 Chapters of history
21 Corned-beef concoction

25 Nudge
27 Unwanted e-mail
28 Swiss-cheese features
30 __ Stanley Gardner
31 Cat's weapon
32 Yo-yos and kites
33 Afternoon snoozes
34 Do as directed
35 Period of office
36 Beef cut
38 Bowling alley
41 Boot bottom
45 Eight-sided road sign

47 "The Gift of the Magi" author
49 2000 presidential candidate
51 *The __ and the Ecstasy*
53 God of Islam
54 Like many newspapers
55 Nosy one
56 Shawl or stole
57 Annoy
58 Selects, with "for"
60 Neighborhood
61 Patricia of *Hud*
62 Leg joint

★ Number-Out

Shade squares so that no number appears in any row or column more than once. Shaded squares may not touch each other horizontally or vertically, and all unshaded squares must form a single continuous area.

4	2	1	5	1
3	1	3	2	5
5	1	1	2	4
3	4	5	2	2
1	2	4	3	3

OPPOSITE ATTRACTION

Unscramble the letters in the phrase SHORT FAD to form two common words that are opposites of each other. Example: The letters in SLED INFO can be rearranged to spell FIND and LOSE.

_____   _____

★ Stringalong

Which string was laid down in the middle of the pile, having the same number of strings below it as above it?

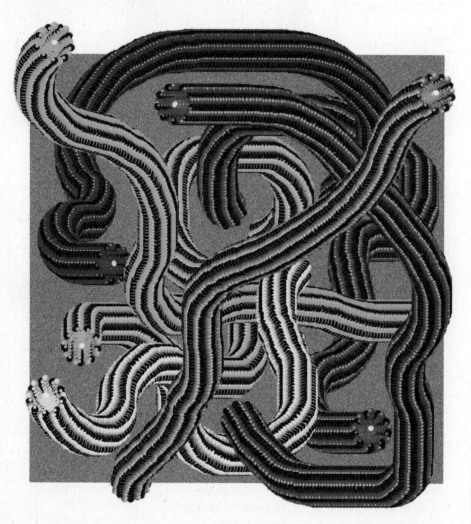

THREE AT A RHYME

Rearrange these letters to form three one-syllable words that rhyme.
Example: A A A B C E K S W X X = AXE, BACKS, WAX

A C E E G H H I L W Y Y

_____ _____ _____

★ Don't 56 Down by Sally R. Stein

ACROSS

1 South Florida city
6 Stars and Stripes
10 Italian wine region
14 Movie award
15 Bell-shaped flower
16 Once __ a time
17 Physicist's fanciful quest
20 Appear to be
21 Gumbo vegetable
22 Mom's sisters
23 Mem. of the bar
25 Real-estate ad abbr.
27 Bike-wheel parts
30 Adversary
31 Astronaut Armstrong
35 Wigwam relative
36 Thanksgiving meal
38 Orange drink
39 Whodunit plot element
42 __ for the course
43 Sedately dignified
44 Hay processing machine
45 Thick piece
47 Dirt + water
48 Like B.B. King's music
49 Supermarket shopper's reference
51 Borscht ingredient
52 Military decoration
55 Tahiti, for one
57 Line on a 49 Across
61 Newlyweds' pledge
64 Go up
65 On the summit of
66 __ Sound (Washington State water)
67 Moose relatives
68 Poisonous snakes
69 In unison

DOWN

1 Floor-washing tools
2 Phrase of understanding
3 Farmland unit
4 Cartographer
5 Anger
6 Happening by accident
7 Fib teller
8 Train conductor's cry
9 Exercise locale
10 Harvest season
11 Rotate
12 Whistle sound
13 Quaint hotels
18 High-chair users
19 Rowboat implement
24 Promgoers
26 Arnaz of early TV
27 Stairway parts
28 Rose leaf
29 The Magic Flute, e.g.
30 Foul-smelling
32 Hawk relative
33 Just hangs around
34 Suspicious
36 Certain woodwind players
37 Dining-room furniture
40 S&L conveniences
41 Captain Nemo's submarine
46 Loud noises
48 Existed
50 Under the weather
51 Radar-screen images
52 Insignificant
53 Diabolical
54 Work station
56 Halt
58 One way to order lunch
59 Equalize
60 Parcel (out)
62 Org. for motorists
63 College student stat.

★ One-Way Streets

The diagram represents a pattern of streets. A and B are parking spaces, and the black squares are stores. Find the route that starts at A, passes through all stores exactly once, and ends at B. Arrows indicate one-way traffic for that block only. No block or intersection may be entered more than once.

SOUND THINKING

The only consonant sounds in what two-word term for a type of person are W, Z, and G (as in "go"), in that order?

_____

★★ Split Decisions

In this clueless crossword puzzle, each answer consists of two words whose spellings are the same, except for the consecutive letters given. All answers are common words; no phrases or hyphenated or capitalized words are used. Some of the clues may have more than one solution, but there is only one word pair that will correctly link up with all the other word pairs.

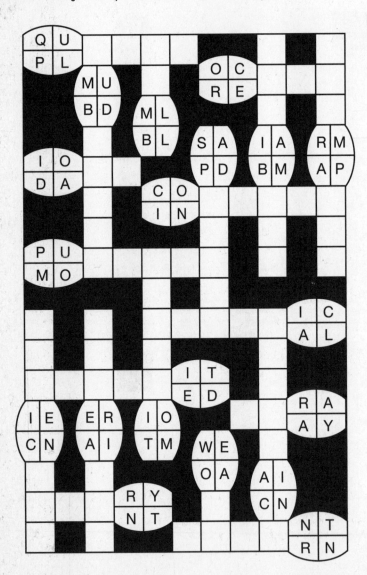

TRANSDELETION

Delete one letter from the word COPILOTS and rearrange the rest, to get a farming term.

★ Star Search

Find the stars that are hidden in some of the blank squares. The numbered squares indicate how many stars are hidden in the squares adjacent to them (including diagonally). There is never more than one star in any square.

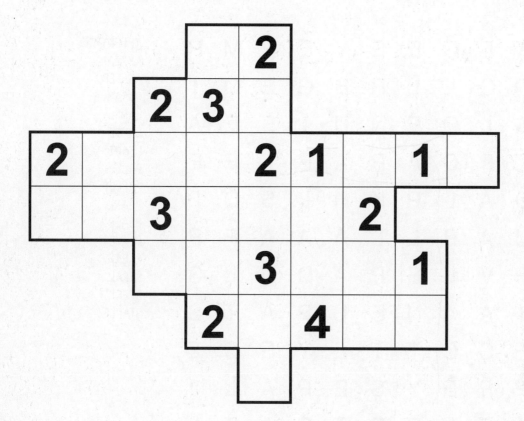

TELEPHONE TRIOS

1	ABC **2**	DEF **3**
GHI **4**	JKL **5**	MNO **6**
PRS **7**	TUV **8**	WXY **9**
*	**0**	**#**

Using the numbers and letters on a standard telephone, what three seven-letter words or phrases from the same category can be formed from these telephone numbers?

333-4268 _ _ _ _ _ _ _

425-5268 _ _ _ _ _ _ _

825-4268 _ _ _ _ _ _ _

★ Leap Day

Find all these words that contain the letters L, E, A, and P that are hidden in the diagram, either across, down, or diagonally. There are two additional words in the category, not listed below, that are also hidden in the diagram. If they're both types of animals, what are they?

```
B L K E C E E Y E P M H
V A O G L L R B G E Q T
Y E W L O E N U I E E A
R P L P C A P A B L E E
J P D A L P K H L S Q L
L A U A P L L A A A F P
T A P V L E P A D N L S
F S I A A N E L P A T S
E A F C C T T L Y E C Z
Z O P P E Y S E P A L J
P E A R L P R T P A E L
X D J N M S S X H T I W
```

APLENTY (crossed out)
APPEAL
ASLEEP
CAPABLE (crossed out)
LAPEL
LAPSE
LEAPT
PALE
PALLET
PEARL
PLACE
PLAYER
PLEAT
SEPAL
SPECIAL
STAPLE
Ear (crossed out)

IN OTHER WORDS

Other than the hyphenated card game ACEY-DEUCY, there is only one common uncapitalized word that contains the consecutive letters UCY. What is it?

_____

★ Watch Your Step by Gail Grabowski

ACROSS

1 Recedes
5 Small piece of paper
10 Search for bargains
14 Genuine
15 Chicago airport
16 Toe the __ (obey)
17 In addition
18 Symptom of 42 Across
19 Creative thought
20 Backwash of an aircraft
22 Classroom furniture
23 Icy precipitation
24 Small or extra-large
26 Roman robe
29 Ripped to shreds
33 Huff and puff
37 Bread with a pocket
39 Hospital employee
40 Sleeper's sound
42 Winter ailment
43 Fudd of cartoons
44 Bacon piece
45 Sharp taste
47 Sunrise direction
48 State of mind
50 "Wait a minute!"
52 Timid
54 In the neighborhood
58 Part of Batman's costume
61 Aster or mum
65 Landed (on)
66 Clear the board
67 Put money in the bank
68 Unaccompanied
69 Plane tracker
70 Peach or beech
71 Look slyly
72 Editors' marks
73 Peddle

DOWN

1 Historical times
2 They ring in churches
3 Pesto herb
4 Mountain incline
5 Convertible car's cover
6 *Moonstruck* actress
7 Speak wildly
8 Neighborhoods
9 Allow
10 Obsolete calculating tool
11 Make oneself scarce
12 Singles
13 Alpine apex

21 Prepare, as a table
25 Sector
27 Birthday present
28 Geographical reference book
30 Author Bombeck
31 Depletes, with "up"
32 Sassy
33 Subtle "Hey!"
34 Poker payment
35 Standard
36 Resettable mileage gauge
38 Female relative
41 Fencing weapon

46 People who putt
49 Alludes (to)
51 Rep. or Sen.
53 Gold measure
55 Purchase prices
56 In the know
57 Not at all bumpy
58 Use the phone
59 Hand-cream ingredient
60 Tree with cones
62 Stow, as cargo
63 Future attorney's exam: Abbr.
64 Fishing-rod attachment

★ Hyper-Sudoku

Fill in the blank boxes so that every row, column, 3x3 box, *and* each of the four 3x3 gray regions contains all of the numbers 1 to 9.

4		7				9		1
			8	1	9		7	4
9	1				6	2	3	
5	9				4	1		
	2		3	5	1		4	
1			2					3
		8	1		2	3		7
2								5
			9					6

MIXAGRAMS

Each line contains a five-letter word and a four-letter word that have been mixed together (the order of the letters in each word has not been changed). Unmix the two words on each line and write them in the spaces provided. When you're done, find a two-part answer to the clue by reading down the letter columns in the answers.

CLUE: A big deal

```
K E N I A F E S Y  =  _ _ _ _ _  +  _ _ _ _

O S C A N I R O N  =  _ _ _ _ _  +  _ _ _ _

A Z E B A L O U T  =  _ _ _ _ _  +  _ _ _ _

A S H I S R E A K  =  _ _ _ _ _  +  _ _ _ _
```

★★ Window Dressing

Which of the numbered stencils has been used to create each of the snowy decorations on the window?

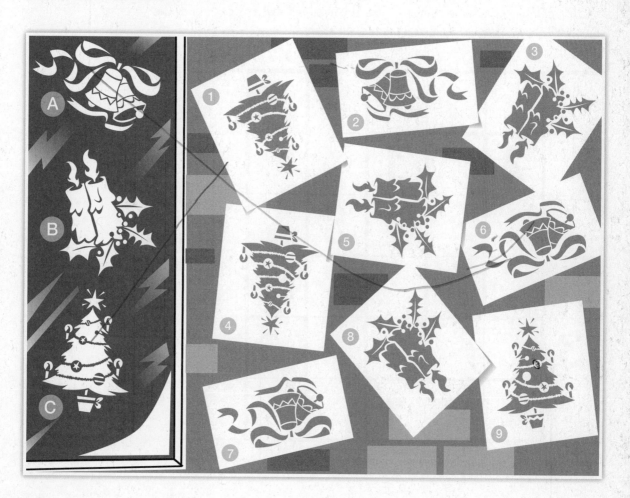

BETWEENER

What three-letter word belongs between the word at left and the word at right, so that the first and second word, and the second and third word, each form a common two-word phrase?

BAT __ __ __ SCOUT

★ 123

Fill in the diagram so that each rectangular piece has one each of the numbers
1, 2, and 3, under these rules: 1) No two adjacent squares, horizontally or
vertically, can have the same number. 2) Each completed row and column of the
diagram will have an equal number of 1s, 2s, and 3s.

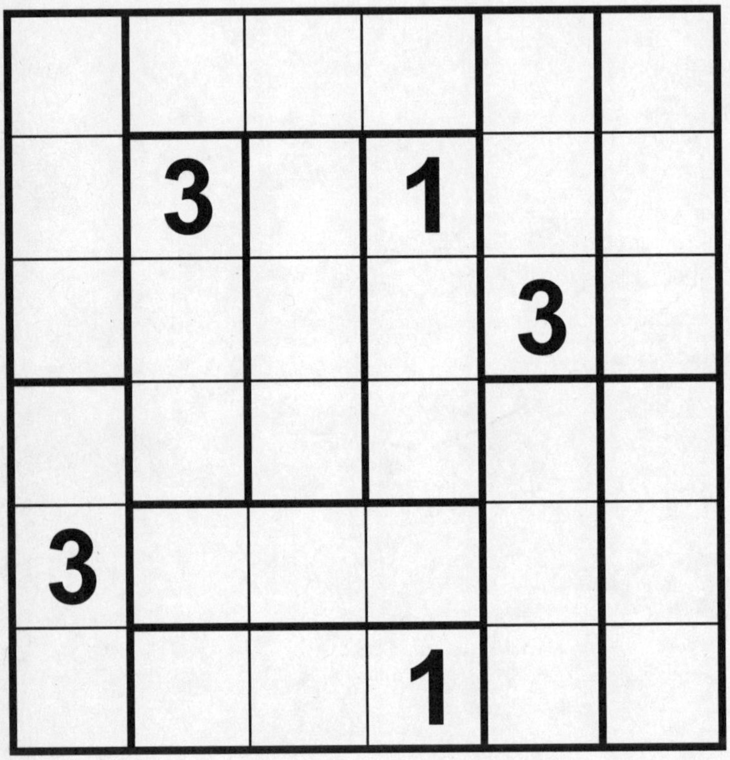

	3		**1**		
				3	
3					
			1		

SUDOKU SUM

Without repeating any digits, complete the sum at right,
by filling one digit in each of the five blanks.

```
    _ _ _
 +  3 9 5
  _ _ 0 _
```

★ "A" in Geography by Sally R. Stein

ACROSS

1 Milky gems
6 Urban-renewal target
10 Add 32 Down to
14 Parcel out
15 Prepare to be photographed
16 Subjective atmosphere
17 Make fun of
18 Needle holes
19 Agitate
20 Silicon Valley city
22 Wide-eyed
23 Breaks in the action
24 Sort of steak
25 Opulent residence
29 Officeholder, for short
30 Attain
31 Places for parking meters
37 __ Antony
38 Film award
39 Playwright Simon
40 Drew, as a crowd
42 Post-office device
43 Industrious insect
44 Grazing ground
45 Loose, as trousers
48 New Orleans cuisine
51 Great Salt Lake state
52 Island off east Africa
57 Molten rock
58 Bettor's concern
59 Brown shade
60 Secluded valley
61 Governor's turndown
62 Fix deeply
63 Singer Fitzgerald
64 English prep school
65 Farmer's plantings

DOWN

1 Horse's meal
2 "Guilty" or "not guilty"
3 Astronaut Shepard
4 "Get __!" ("Scram!")
5 Sneakiness
6 Compete in a bee
7 True-blue
8 Computer owners
9 Elevated flat land
10 Setting for a Bogart/Bergman film
11 Expense
12 Hunter constellation
13 Humongous
21 Billiards stick
24 Pull from behind
25 Humorist Bombeck
26 Chair part
27 Sour-tasting
28 African capital
29 For each
31 Retired fast plane: Abbr.
32 Frozen water
33 "Dear old" relative
34 Heavy metal
35 Metric weight
36 Whole bunch
38 Sept. follower
41 Whichever
42 Legislature divisions
44 Beer holder
45 Protrusion
46 In any way
47 Judge's need
48 West Point student
49 Augment
50 Golden Fleece seeker
52 Go to a new home
53 Identical
54 Sugar shape
55 Imitated
56 Cherry and carmine

★ ABC

Enter the letters A, B, and C into the diagram so that each row and column has exactly one A, one B, and one C. The letters outside the diagram indicate the first letter encountered, moving in the direction of the arrow. Keep in mind that after all the letters have been filled in, there will be one blank box in each row and column.

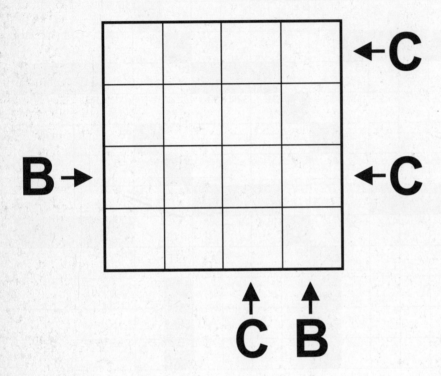

CLUELESS CROSSWORD

Complete the crossword with common uncapitalized seven-letter words, based entirely on the letters already filled in for you.

★ Find the Ships

Determine the position of the 10 ships listed to the right of the diagram. The ships may be oriented either horizontally or vertically. A square with wavy lines indicates water and will not contain a ship. The numbers at the edge of the diagram indicate how many squares in that row or column contain parts of ships. When all 10 ships are correctly placed in the diagram, no two of them will touch each other, not even diagonally.

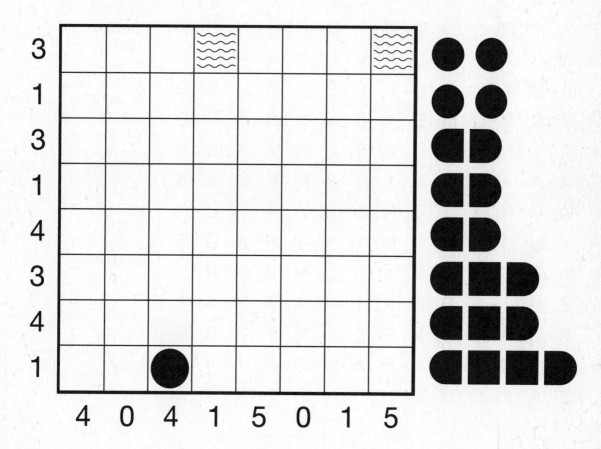

TWO-BY-FOUR

The eight letters in the word ABNORMAL can be rearranged to form a pair of common four-letter words in three different ways, if no four-letter word is repeated. Can you find all three pairs of words?

_ _ _ _ _ _ _ _   _ _ _ _ _ _ _ _

_ _ _ _ _ _ _ _

★ National League

Try to find these world nations that are hidden in the diagram either across, down, or diagonally, and you'll discover that one of them isn't there. What's the missing nation? As indicated by the slash mark below, the words SOUTH and KOREA are hidden separately.

```
Y C L E C E E R G A A B U C Y
T A I W A N T H I M D U N R Z
Q W B A L O L N V E M N A I K
L S E Y C H E L L E S G M E O
F Z R P Q M E I S N N B G C R
Y R I P R K H C S U A A W U E
S A A A D C I F H B M D J A A
U O U N A J R R W B A P R D G
R Y U G C K A E I X I H K O R
P W E T A E M A B B N J G R J
Y Z G I H R N A I N A Z N A T
C R O A T I A F I I M T E S R
V U Z O T F Y P A M O K I V C
O B B X Q U M H D Y R R X T N
```

ARMENIA
BELARUS
CHILE
CROATIA
CUBA
CYPRUS
ECUADOR
FRANCE
GAMBIA
GREECE
HUNGARY
JORDAN
KIRIBATI
LIBERIA
MYANMAR
PARAGUAY
ROMANIA
SEYCHELLES
SOUTH / KOREA
TAIWAN
TANZANIA
ZIMBABWE

INITIAL REACTION

Identify the well-known proverb from the first letters in each of its words.

L. B. Y. L. _____

★ Face Invaders by Sally R. Stein

ACROSS

1 Not quite shut
5 Coconut tree
9 Takes chances
14 Traditional knowledge
15 Margarine
16 Loosen, as shoelaces
17 Courtroom statement
18 Something prohibited
19 Blackboard material
20 Idealistic frame of mind
23 Golf platform
24 Ignited
25 College grounds
29 India's continent
31 Chatter
34 Dined at home
35 Slightly
36 Marching-band instrument
37 Poor judgment
40 __ upon a time
41 Burden
42 Take a sip of
43 Meadow
44 Go after a gnat
45 Apple core, e.g.
46 Fitness center
47 Squeezing snake
48 Result of an embarrassing statement
57 Small songbird
58 Shrivel
59 Land measure
60 Atmospheric layer
61 Environmental sci.
62 Imperfection
63 Is introduced to
64 Moist, as a morning lawn
65 Utters

DOWN

1 Austrian mountains
2 Shake up severely
3 Vicinity
4 Caboose's place
5 Small horses
6 Without company
7 A *Tonight Show* host
8 Project Apollo destination
9 Moscow's country
10 Arm of the sea
11 Remain
12 Toy with a tail
13 Looks at

21 Appalls
22 Privileged group
25 Yuletide song
26 Make up for
27 Tourist draw
28 Toll road
29 Approximately
30 Sermon topics
31 Party attendee
32 Ease up
33 Supreme Court justice Ruth __ Ginsburg
35 Fictional Karenina
36 As compared to

38 Dubuque native
39 Water vapor
44 Parts of books
45 Expensive
46 Tour of duty
47 Underneath
48 Gift-card word
49 Flow slowly
50 Bassoon relative
51 Was indebted to
52 Pleasant
53 Clumsy people
54 West Coast sch.
55 Serving platter
56 Chops down

★ Star Maze

Enter the maze at top, pass through all the stars exactly once, and then exit at bottom. You may not retrace your path.

THREE AT A RHYME

Rearrange these letters to form three one-syllable words that rhyme.

B E N N O O T U

_____   _____   _____

★ Fences

Connect the dots with vertical or horizontal lines, so that a single loop is formed with no crossings or branches. Each number indicates how many lines surround it; squares with no number may be surrounded by any number of lines.

```
1     1 0         2
3   2         1 1
3                 3
      2 0
      3 3
3                 3
2 3         2     1
2     3 3         2
```

ADDITION SWITCH

Switch the positions of two of the digits in the incorrect sum at right, to get a correct sum.

```
  254
+ 367
-----
  801
```

★ Multiple Meanings

Find these words that are hidden in the diagram, either across, down, or diagonally. They may not seem like they're all from the same category, but in fact, one of the answer words, which has several different meanings, is related to all of the others. Which word is the "key" to the list?

```
D R Z P K E S H E R E D I T P
R I I D I B G L I N C L I N W
O D O R I G J N A L S D S V E
P B A C K G R O U N D E D X E
V T N E C S E D Y L T E T Y X
F A L D P G N T C F P R D G N
N O I T A V I R E D A G E O U
L V R E R D G O I C I I C L O
Q L N D E I I A T N F D L A R
S I A R N V R I C A I E I E G
L L E F T U O L L M F P V N K
A H O G A N I N I R O I I E C
N D H P G N F A M I L Y T G A
S L O L E A N C E S T R Y R B
```

ANCESTRY
BACKGROUND
DECLIVITY
DERIVATION
DESCENT
DIP
DIVE
DROP
EXTRACTION
FALL
FAMILY
GENEALOGY
HEREDITY
INCLINE
LINEAGE
ORIGIN
PARENTAGE
PEDIGREE
PLUNGE
SLANT
SLOPE

WHO'S WHAT WHERE?

The correct term for a resident of Suriname is:

A) Surinamer   B) Rinamian

C) Surinite   D) Surinami

★ TV Talk by Gail Grabowski

ACROSS

1 Part of the hand
5 Desert haven
10 A few
14 Director Kazan
15 Squeaky sound
16 Adam's second son
17 High-tech office system
20 Bishop's domain
21 All ready
22 Irrigates
23 Way of doing something
26 Small bouquet
27 Hamburger meat
29 Got out of bed
31 Make watertight
33 601, to Nero
34 Wise one
38 Place for a fill-up
41 Certain government agents
42 Paving material
43 Wore down
44 Place for a cookout
46 Days before holidays
47 Delicate fabric
50 Like a midnight movie
52 In the direction of
54 Twosome
55 Sci-fi transport
58 Advanced course of study
62 Memo phrase
63 Jeweled crown
64 __ spumante
65 Mile fractions
66 Choir section
67 Bygone days

DOWN

1 Bodybuilder's chest muscles
2 Skin-lotion additive
3 Citrus fruit
4 Traveler's guide
5 Musical eightsome
6 Soul singer Franklin
7 Sun. speech
8 Author Fleming
9 Veer off course
10 Took care of
11 Woodwind instruments
12 Full of good cheer
13 Some lodge members
18 Worthwhile
19 Answering-machine insert
23 Breakfast fruit
24 Have lunch delivered
25 Physicians, for short
27 Roof support
28 Make simpler
30 Location
31 Police dept. rank
32 Greek bread
34 Kitchen appliance
35 Office assistant
36 Leaves the premises
37 Outcome
39 Defense grp. since 1949
40 "Am not!" retort
44 Lima's country
45 Seasoned player
47 Greene of *Bonanza*
48 Conscious (of)
49 Military-school student
51 Subtle glows
52 Letters heard end-of-week
53 Statistical info
55 Constellation bear
56 They may be unsaturated or polyunsaturated
57 Forget to include
59 Up to, briefly
60 Have a snack
61 Empty space

★ Sudoku

Fill in the blank boxes so that every row, column, and 3x3 box contains all of the numbers 1 to 9.

	6		9		2		1	
1								5
		5	4		3	6		
8		3	2		7	1		9
				3				
4		7	1		5	2		8
		9	3		1	4		
6								7
	7		6		4		2	

MIXAGRAMS

Each line contains a five-letter word and a four-letter word that have been mixed together (the order of the letters in each word has not been changed). Unmix the two words on each line and write them in the spaces provided. When you're done, find a two-part answer to the clue by reading down the letter columns in the answers.

CLUE: Silver of note

J I B E V E L L Y = _ _ _ _ _ + _ _ _ _

O K A M I Z O T O = _ _ _ _ _ + _ _ _ _

H A R E A N W A K = _ _ _ _ _ + _ _ _ _

N E R O U S G E T = _ _ _ _ _ + _ _ _ _

★ 123

Fill in the diagram so that each rectangular piece has one each of the numbers 1, 2, and 3, under these rules: 1) No two adjacent squares, horizontally or vertically, can have the same number. 2) Each completed row and column of the diagram will have an equal number of 1s, 2s, and 3s.

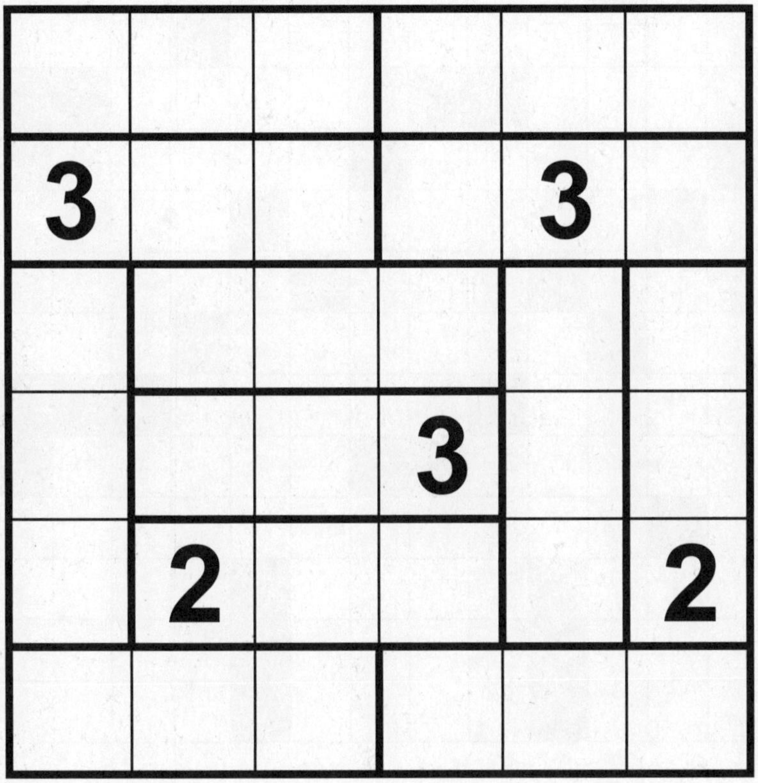

3				**3**	
			3		
	2				**2**

SUDOKU SUM

Without repeating any digits, complete the sum at right, by filling one digit in each of the five blanks.

```
    1 6 9
+   _ _ _
─────────
    4 _ _
```

★ At the Deli by Gail Grabowski

ACROSS

1 Bulletin-board fastener
5 Of unknown authorship: Abbr.
9 Sounds of shock
14 Alda of *M*A*S*H*
15 Volcano outflow
16 Video game name
17 Unaccompanied
18 Seize
19 From the sun
20 Lightweight cotton fabric
23 Sailor's yes
24 Stray from the script
25 Sulk
27 Sandal feature
30 Old-time oaths
32 Ooh and __
35 With little effort
37 Detest
39 Shawls and stoles
41 Debtor's letters
42 Credit-card user
43 Soup bean
44 Showy ornament
46 Health resort
47 Stage whisper
49 Take care of
51 Dog's reward
53 Help for a climber
56 Tavern
58 Less than adequate
62 Martini garnish
64 Store sign
65 Hawaiian feast
66 *Lou Grant* actor
67 Something prohibited
68 Oklahoma city
69 Thesaurus compiler
70 British prep school
71 Matinee days: Abbr.

DOWN

1 Skin-powder ingredient
2 Waikiki welcome
3 Repaired, as wicker
4 Prepares to propose
5 High-school math
6 Drug-fighting cop
7 Egg-shaped
8 Influential person
9 Uneconomical vehicle, slangily
10 From __ Z
11 Times of youthful inexperience
12 Beseech
13 Kingly address
21 Locations
22 Deuce topper
26 Pearl Harbor's island
28 China's continent
29 Devout
31 Dance move
32 Piercing tool
33 Opera solo
34 Leg tendon
36 Garage job
38 Historical period
40 Set of socks
42 Support, as with a wager
44 Boyfriend
45 Beirut locale
48 Gobi or Sahara
50 Lots and lots
52 Steakhouse order
54 Steam bath
55 Characteristic
56 Wild hog
57 In addition
59 Dry cleaner's challenge
60 __ 'clock (coffee-break time)
61 Clothing, informally
63 Neckline shape

★ One-Way Streets

The diagram represents a pattern of streets. A and B are parking spaces, and the black squares are stores. Find the route that starts at A, passes through all stores exactly once, and ends at B. Arrows indicate one-way traffic for that block only. No block or intersection may be entered more than once.

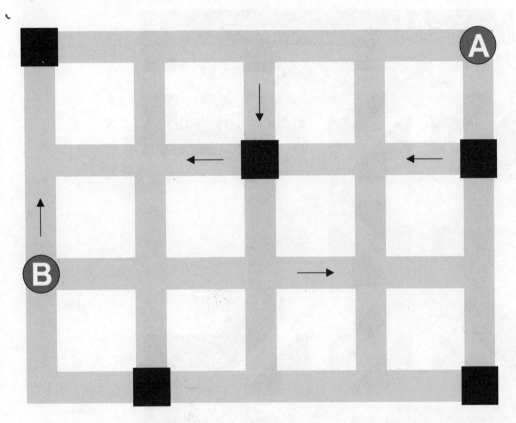

SOUND THINKING

What 11-letter word that means "agitated" has only three consonant sounds: V, R, and T, in that order?

_____

★ No Three in a Row

Enter the maze at bottom, pass through all the squares exactly once, and then exit, all without retracing your path. You may not pass through three squares of the same color consecutively.

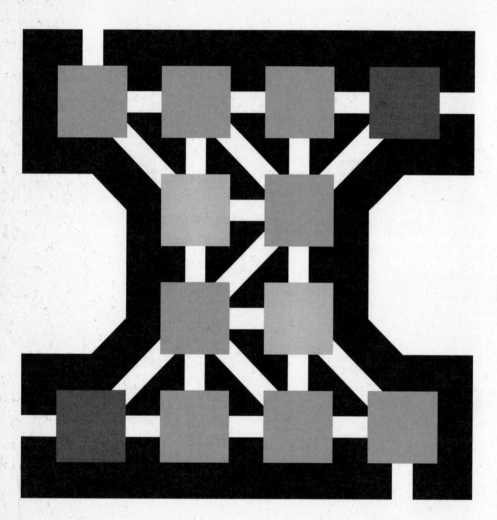

SAY IT AGAIN

What three-letter word for a type of farm animal, when pronounced differently, is also a verb for a farm activity?

_ _ _

★ Star Search

Find the stars that are hidden in some of the blank squares. The numbered squares indicate how many stars are hidden in the squares adjacent to them (including diagonally). There is never more than one star in any square.

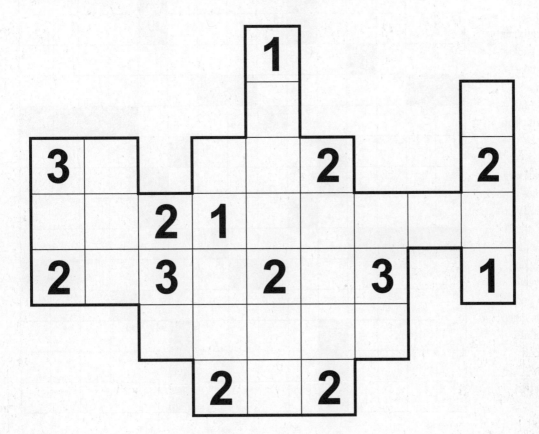

TELEPHONE TRIOS

1	ABC 2	DEF 3
GHI 4	JKL 5	MNO 6
PRS 7	TUV 8	WXY 9
*	O	#

Using the numbers and letters on a standard telephone, what three seven-letter words or phrases from the same category can be formed from these telephone numbers?

532-2666   _ _ _ _ _ _ _

857-2463   _ _ _ _ _ _ _

878-4829   _ _ _ _ _ _ _

★ Lighten Up by Norma Steinberg

ACROSS

1 Paycheck extra
6 Sudden inhalation
10 Industrial storage containers
14 Like Humpty Dumpty
15 Bestselling cookie
16 Cleveland's lake
17 Not as high
18 Having little fat
19 Carnival attraction
20 ___ Moines, IA
21 Gymnastics event
24 Tinkerbell, for one
26 Inconvenience
27 Underground floor
29 Catch sight of
31 Jordanian, e.g.
32 *Beetle Bailey* dog
34 Mine passageway
39 Freelancer's encl.
40 Fabrics from sheep
42 Spherical hairdo
43 Hearth residue
45 Italy's shape
46 Recipe direction
47 Frosted
49 Bear witness
51 Point a finger at
55 Not cloudy
56 *The West Wing* star
59 Certain MDs
62 "What's ___ for me?"
63 Pigeon-___
64 God of Islam
66 A few
67 Fashion mag
68 Nary a soul
69 Crystal-ball user
70 Workout iterations
71 Dragged behind

DOWN

1 Intrepid

2 One of the woodwinds
3 Bulletin
4 ___ only as directed
5 Balkan region
6 "Wow!"
7 Field of expertise
8 Actor Penn
9 Blanketlike cloak
10 Action words
11 Spring zodiac sign
12 Of ocean motion
13 "If they could now ..."
22 Archer's weapon

23 Diner sign
25 Playwright Edward
27 Hernando's home
28 Chapters of history
29 Got out of one's chair
30 Game on horseback
33 One of Hamlet's choices
35 "___ la vista, baby!"
36 Pleasant remembrance
37 TGIF days
38 Legal wrong
41 No longer fresh

44 Emphatic Spanish affirmative
48 Core
50 Apartment renter
51 Not quite right
52 Lake craft
53 Felony or misdemeanor
54 Speak
55 Gives up, as territory
57 Filet fish
58 Give assistance to
60 Window section
61 Lose fur
65 Old card game

★ I At Last

Find these world place names ending with I that are hidden in the diagram, either across, down, or diagonally. There's one additional answer in the category, not listed below, that's also hidden in the diagram. If it gave its name to an article of clothing, what's the word?

```
N  I  A  B  U  D  I  M  O  G  S  A
N  J  E  I  I  A  W  A  H  T  W  S
V  A  L  P  B  C  A  P  R  G  A  T
B  A  I  M  I  S  S  O  U  R  I  I
M  I  U  R  I  A  M  I  I  A  K  T
I  M  K  R  O  B  T  A  E  M  I  I
I  B  P  I  O  B  A  H  N  A  K  L
W  A  O  L  N  I  I  G  U  L  I  O
C  E  I  G  C  I  M  N  R  F  H  V
P  O  M  P  E  I  I  A  B  I  W  I
I  L  O  P  I  R  T  H  I  L  F  T
H  A  I  T  I  R  H  S  U  M  X  O
```

AMALFI
ASTI
BRUNEI
CAPRI
DUBAI
GOBI
HAITI
HAWAII
MALI
MIAMI
MISSOURI
MUMBAI
NAIROBI
POMPEII
SHANGHAI
STROMBOLI
TAIPEI
TIVOLI
TRIPOLI
WAIKIKI

IN OTHER WORDS

There is only one common uncapitalized word that contains the consecutive letters SPB. What is it?

_____

bRain BREAtHer
DUMB AND DUMBER

People say (and do) the most unbelievably idiotic things sometimes. These flubs and fiascos oftentimes become our favorite anecdotes to share with friends and family—that is, as long we weren't the ones being stupid!

On my way to a picnic, I stopped at a fast-food place to order a quart of potato salad.

"We don't sell it by the quart," the clerk snapped.

"Okay, then give me two pints, please," I replied.

I'm proud to say that I held my tongue when she asked, "Do you want it in one container?"

—JULIE GUITERREZ

* * *

It was the standard series of check-in questions that every traveler gets at the airlines counter, including, "Has anyone put anything in your baggage without your knowledge?"

"If it was put there without my knowledge," I asked, "how would I know?"

The agent behind the counter smiled smugly. "That's why we ask."

—KATE VETTER

* * *

On vacation in Hawaii, my stepmom, Sandy, called a café to make reservations for 7 p.m. Checking her book, the cheery young hostess said, "I'm sorry, all we have is 6:45. Would you like that?"

"That's fine," Sandy said.

"Okay," the woman confirmed. Then she added, "Just be advised that you may have to wait 15 minutes for your table."

—KELLY FINNEGAN

* * *

Dining out one evening, I noticed some teenagers celebrating at a nearby table. When one girl pulled out a camera, I offered to take a picture of the group. After one photo, I suggested taking another just in case the first one didn't come out.

"Oh, no, that's okay," she said, as she took back her camera. "I always get double prints."

—DEANNA GUY

* * *

During weekly visits to my allergist, I've noticed a lot of inattentive parents with ill-behaved children in the waiting room. So I was impressed one day to see a mother with her little boy, helping him sound out the words on a sign.

Finally he mastered it and his mother cheered, "That's great! Now sit there. I'll be back in 15 minutes."

What did the sign say? "Children must not be left unattended."

—DARLENE HOVEL

★★ Line Drawing

Draw two straight lines, each from one edge of the square to another edge, so that the first names in each of the four regions have two things in common.

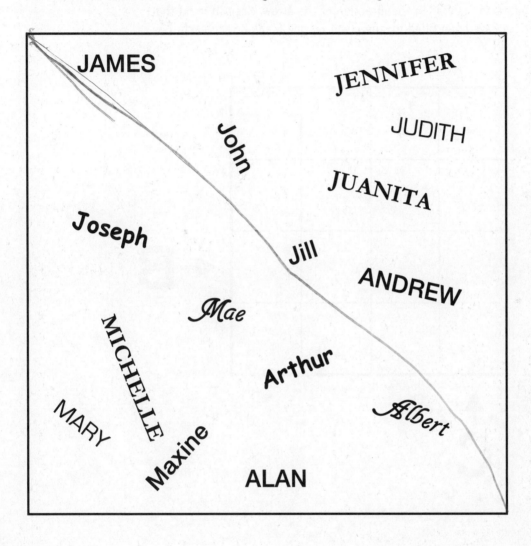

THREE OF A KIND

Find the three hidden words in the sentence that, read in order, go together in some way.

The buffalo steak's tiny width ought to be larger.

★ ABC

Enter the letters A, B, and C into the diagram so that each row and column has exactly one A, one B, and one C. The letters outside the diagram indicate the first letter encountered, moving in the direction of the arrow. Keep in mind that after all the letters have been filled in, there will be one blank box in each row and column.

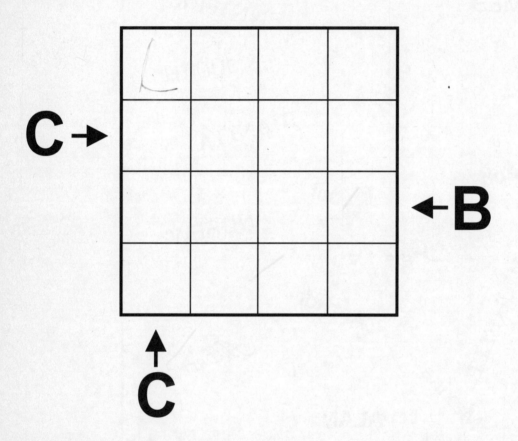

NATIONAL TREASURE

Using the letters in MOZAMBIQUE, we were able to form three common uncapitalized five-letter words. Can you find them?

_ _ _ _ _　　_ _ _ _ _　　_ _ _ _ _

★ Scare Words by Sally R. Stein

ACROSS

1 Fashion designer Donna
6 Mr. Flintstone
10 Shut with force
14 Run off to wed
15 Capital of Italy
16 Window glass
17 "Absolutely!"
20 Complete collection
21 Percussion instrument
22 Parts of eyes
23 Ladder rung
24 Object of adoration
25 After-shave __
28 Biblical garden
29 Floor-cleaning implement
32 Supply-and-demand sci.
33 Computer keyboard key
35 Greek island
37 Places to make calls
40 Raft wood
41 Go on horseback
42 Sandwich cookie
43 Ems' followers
44 Fence entryway
46 Crocs' relatives
48 Residence
49 Greet the villain
50 Take in __ (deal with calmly)
53 Part of the eye
54 Game-show hosts: Abbr.
57 Playful phrase from Mommy
60 A Great Lake
61 Word of regret
62 Hearing or touch
63 Is victorious
64 Mailed away
65 Wood strips

DOWN

1 Door openers
2 Spiny houseplant
3 Defeat decisively
4 PD alert
5 Must
6 Cook, as onion rings
7 Den or kitchen
8 Australian bird
9 Make light of
10 Go bad
11 Thailand neighbor
12 Poker starter
13 Something to clean up
18 Deep ditch
19 Rodeo mount
23 Trig ratios
24 Did nothing
25 Leave alone
26 Large body of water
27 Turnpike fees
28 Bert's *Sesame Street* friend
29 __-Goldwyn-Mayer
30 "None of the above" choice
31 Mexican coins
34 Rich cake
36 Shows team spirit
38 Chinese temple
39 Gets started
45 One-celled creatures
47 Evaluate
48 Boy Scout trips
49 Robbery
50 Cast forth
51 Garr or Hatcher
52 Horse controller
53 Mortgage, e.g.
54 Talking bird
55 Price-tag info
56 Takes to court
58 Cheer for a matador
59 Snakelike fish

★★ Time Out

Which of the reflected images of Father Time can be seen in the puddle?

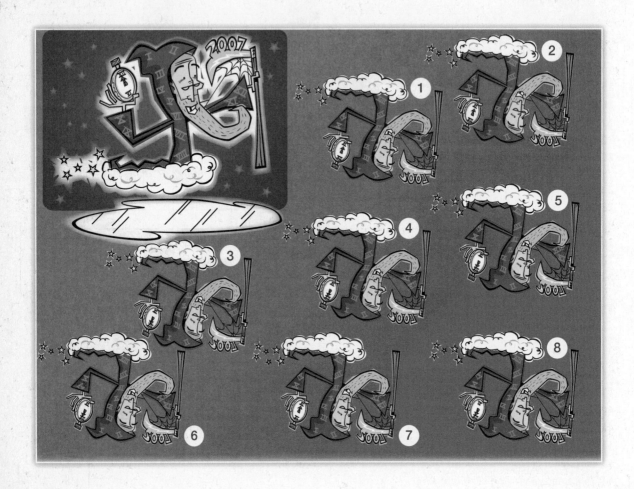

BETWEENER

What three-letter word belongs between the word at left and the word at right, so that the first and second word, and the second and third word, each form a common two-word phrase?

BLACK __ __ __ CLIP

★ Just Marvelous

Find these "topnotch" words that are hidden in the diagram either across, down, or diagonally. As indicated by the slash mark below, the words FIRST and CLASS are hidden separately. There's one additional word in the category, not listed below, that's also hidden in the diagram. What's the word?

```
M T N J H S G S G C W G
F A N U G R U N P I O N
I E G A A O I P L F N I
R R G N I K C Z E I D H
S G D R I L S V P R E S
T C O R A F L K U R R A
Q L T S Y N I I S E F M
G S S E L C M C R T U S
S U O L U B A F E B L F
C I T S A T N A F N D A
I N S P I R E D I T T L
S P L E N D I D O R B C
```

BRILLIANT
FABULOUS
FANTASTIC
FIRST / CLASS
GLORIOUS
GRAND
GREAT
INSPIRED
MAGNIFICENT
SMASHING
STRIKING
SUPER
TERRIFIC
WONDERFUL

INITIAL REACTION

Identify the well-known proverb from the first letters in each of its words.

T. E. I. H. _____

★ Find the Ships

Determine the position of the 10 ships listed to the right of the diagram. The ships may be oriented either horizontally or vertically. A square with wavy lines indicates water and will not contain a ship. The numbers at the edge of the diagram indicate how many squares in that row or column contain parts of ships. When all 10 ships are correctly placed in the diagram, no two of them will touch each other, not even diagonally.

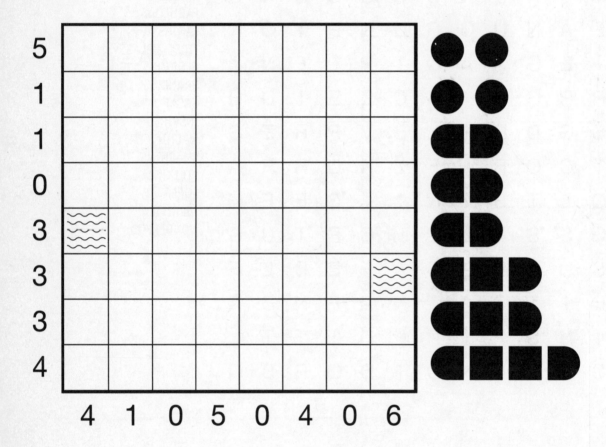

TWO-BY-FOUR

The eight letters in the word BRICKBAT can be rearranged to form a pair of common four-letter words in only one way. Can you find the two words?

— — — —   — — — —

★★ Sudoku

Fill in the blank boxes so that every row, column, and 3x3 box contains all of the numbers 1 to 9.

	2	5		6		3	4	
3								1
4			9		3			8
	8		5		6			
5		6		2				9
	3		4		7			
8			5		4			6
7								3
	4	1		8		9	2	

MIXAGRAMS

Each line contains a five-letter word and a four-letter word that have been mixed together (the order of the letters in each word has not been changed). Unmix the two words on each line and write them in the spaces provided. When you're done, find a two-part answer to the clue by reading down the letter columns in the answers.

CLUE: Off-the-board action

P A B S O D S E Y = _ _ _ _ _ + _ _ _ _

S E X A W I T E D = _ _ _ _ _ + _ _ _ _

B O G I A V E S T = _ _ _ _ _ + _ _ _ _

L U S T E N G E P = _ _ _ _ _ + _ _ _ _

★ Loved Ones by Gail Grabowski

ACROSS

1 Hollywood award
6 Memorable times
10 Sky light
14 Snoozer's sound
15 Opposite of fem.
16 Luau dance
17 Term of endearment
19 Leprechaun land
20 Help a hoodlum
21 Playground reply
22 Playground game
23 Possesses
25 Final tallies
28 Washington Irving character Crane
32 Doily material
33 Deer mom
34 Gives the cold shoulder to
37 Longish skirts
40 Rub out with rubber
42 Actor Gibson
43 Dote on
44 Ohio city
45 Oyster product
47 Delivery vehicle
48 Diplomacy
50 Saturday + Sunday
52 City road
54 Credit application number: Abbr.
55 Cheering word
56 Of high ideals
59 Husband of a British countess
63 French money
65 Term of endearment
67 On the peak of
68 Electrified swimmers
69 Music symbols
70 Something owed
71 "Doggone it!'"
72 Curvy letters

DOWN

1 Workplace safety agcy.
2 Snooty type
3 Ice-cream holder
4 Soul singer Franklin
5 The Bridge of San Luis __
6 Flightless birds
7 Talk wildly
8 Wide tie
9 Instructional institution
10 That girl
11 Term of endearment
12 Fictitious name
13 Called up
18 American buffalo
24 Attendance-book notation
26 Mexican foods
27 Battery fluid
28 Notion
29 Wine-bottle stopper
30 Term of endearment
31 Place for trash
35 Spelling competition
36 Shredded cabbage
38 Turkey neighbor
39 Put in a mailbox
41 Fly high
46 Bowling-alley button
49 Got uptight
51 Prepares to propose
52 Fry lightly
53 Sky-high structure
55 Review one's notes
57 Lugosi of film
58 "__ we forget"
60 Chimps and orang-utans
61 Widespread
62 Subtraction word
64 Make a choice
66 Cola cooler

★ Fences

Connect the dots with vertical or horizontal lines, so that a single loop is formed with no crossings or branches. Each number indicates how many lines surround it; squares with no number may be surrounded by any number of lines.

```
      2           2

  1 3 2

    3           3   3

    2 3         2     1

  0     1       3 3

  2     2         0

                3 1 2

    2           3
```

ADDITION SWITCH

Switch the positions of two of the digits in the incorrect sum at right, to get a correct sum.

```
  3 4 5
+ 2 7 8
-------
  2 6 3
```

★★ Triad Split Decisions

In this clueless crossword puzzle, each answer consists of two words whose spellings are the same, except for the consecutive letters given. All answers are common words; no phrases or hyphenated or capitalized words are used. Some of the clues may have more than one solution, but there is only one word pair that will correctly link up with all the other word pairs.

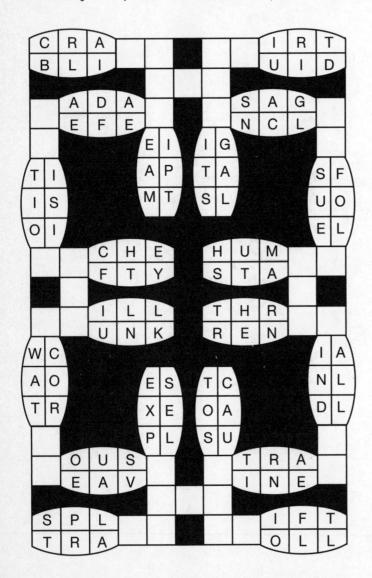

TRANSDELETION

Delete one letter from the word DEPLETES and rearrange the rest, to get something with a point.

_____

★ 123

Fill in the diagram so that each rectangular piece has one each of the numbers 1, 2, and 3, under these rules: 1) No two adjacent squares, horizontally or vertically, can have the same number. 2) Each completed row and column of the diagram will have an equal number of 1s, 2s, and 3s.

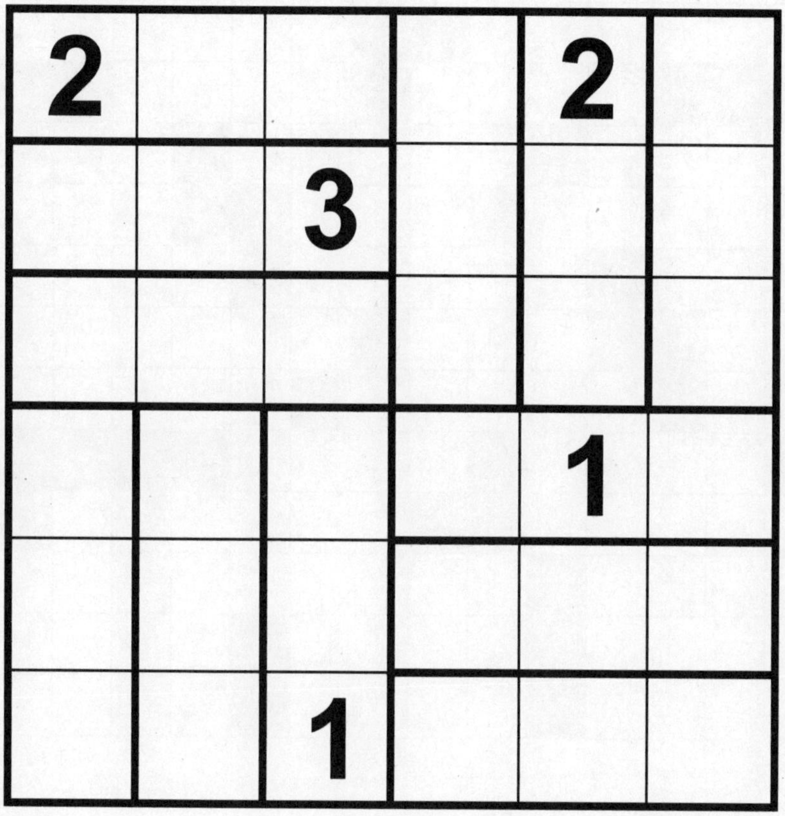

2				2	
		3			
				1	
		1			

SUDOKU SUM

Without repeating any digits, complete the sum at right, by filling one digit in each of the five blanks.

```
    _ _ 9
  + 5 2 _
  ———————
    _ 7 _
```

★ Let's Be Candid by Gail Grabowski

ACROSS

1 Gorillas, for example
5 Shine softly
9 Bus passenger
14 Cooing bird
15 Yard tool
16 Author Jong
17 Real-estate sales technique
19 Fortune-teller's deck
20 Make lovable
21 Discussion groups
22 From scratch
24 *Iliad* or *Odyssey*
25 Cavalry weapon
29 Run out, as a subscription
31 Coffee alternative
34 "Finally!"
36 Speck
37 On the __ (fleeing)
38 Guided vacation
39 Wild West show
41 Traveler's document
42 Rural hotel
43 Night bird
44 Play segments
46 Butterfly catcher
47 Use a broom
49 Shoe parts
50 Winslet of *Titanic*
52 Location
54 Underground passage
56 Cookbook component
60 Stage whisper
61 Kentucky's capital
64 Call attention (to)
65 Mixed-breed dog
66 Song for one person
67 Use an iron
68 Observes
69 Creme-filled cookie

DOWN

1 Fuss
2 Benedict XVI, e.g.
3 Not odd
4 Put in the mail
5 Reaction to a bad joke
6 Hardy's partner
7 Gives the go-ahead
8 Very small
9 Make another recording
10 Teheran native
11 Shortest path
12 Environmental sci.
13 Lab animals
18 Gets wind of
21 Sauces made with basil
23 Walks like a duck
25 Glossy fabric
26 Make amends
27 Flatware needing sharpening
28 Teacup handle
30 "The Raven" author
32 Artist's stand
33 Gather up
35 Bricklayer's tool
40 Have a payment due
41 Neckline shape
45 Restaurant bill
47 Takes the wheel
48 Captain Kidd, for one
51 South American mountains
53 Campsite shelters
54 Waterproof covering
55 Computer operator
57 In that case
58 Unsatisfactory
59 __ Stanley Gardner
61 Some radio bands: Abbr.
62 Feel bad about
63 Also

★ Number-Out

Shade squares so that no number appears in any row or column more than once. Shaded squares may not touch each other horizontally or vertically, and all unshaded squares must form a single continuous area.

5	5	2	1	2
1	5	3	3	2
2	5	5	3	1
1	3	4	3	5
3	4	1	5	4

OPPOSITE ATTRACTION

Unscramble the letters in the phrase TEN DARTS to form two words that are opposites of each other.

_____   _____

★★ Dicey

Group the dice into 18 pairs whose sum is an even number. The dice in each pair must be connected to each other by a common horizontal or vertical side.

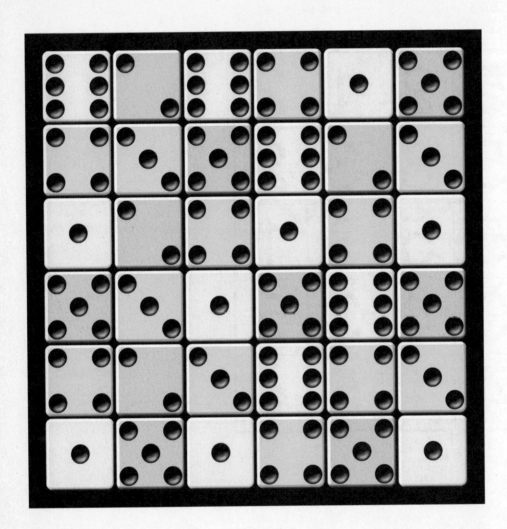

SAY IT AGAIN

What four-letter word for a type of bird, when pronounced differently, is also the past tense of a verb?

__ __ __ __

★ Exotic Vacation

Try to find these words associated with a big-game hunt, and you'll discover that one of them isn't there. What's the word that has run off?

```
E L E P H A N T S E J L
H N S J N A S B I Y U I
S E L E R S J I E T N T
G H A E O E N N Q S G R
O U M T E T R O E U L A
R A I P S U I C I D E C
C S N D O A T U S L S K
I R A J E S F L Q A Y S
R E D R O C M A C S N U
F V S A N D G R R U O U
A I S E K A N S S I T M
K R A F R I C A M E R C
```

AFRICA
ANIMALS
BINOCULARS
CAMCORDER
CAMERA
DUST
ELEPHANTS
GUIDE
HEAT
INSECTS
JEEP
JOURNEY
JUNGLE
LIONS
MOSQUITOES
RHINOS
RIVERS
SAFARI
SAND
SNAKES
SUN
TRACKS

WHO'S WHAT WHERE?

The correct term for a resident of Albany, New York, is:

A) Albaner

B) Albanite

C) Alban

D) Albanian

★ A Day At the Races by Sally R. Stein

ACROSS

1 Artist Salvador
5 Motel employee
9 Wide awake
14 Prayer ending
15 Land measure
16 Wears a hole in the carpet
17 Get free tuition, perhaps
20 Under, poetically
21 City in Oklahoma
22 Daughter's brothers
23 Guns, as an engine
25 Italian farewell
27 Video-game parlor
30 Objectives
31 Life-saving technique: Abbr.
34 Ball-__ hammer
35 *The Wizard of Oz* dog
37 California/Nevada lake
39 Where one works
42 High-tech beam
43 Quickly
44 Sparrow's home
45 Hurricane center
46 Manner of walking
48 Loves
50 Type of pear
51 Angry mood
52 Exxon's ex-name
55 Fourth dimension
57 Western film
61 Display attractively
64 Takes a survey
65 Wedding-cake level
66 Subject for an MBA student
67 Loop in a 10 Down
68 Irish Republic
69 Mediocre

DOWN

1 Daybreak
2 French girlfriend
3 Singer Horne
4 Dazed, as through hypnosis
5 PC alternative
6 __ and pains
7 Remove wrinkles from clothes
8 Very tasty
9 Spring mo.
10 Cowboy rope
11 Repeated sound
12 Horse controller
13 Sugar amts.
18 Backyard structure
19 Take __ view (disapprove)
24 Reject, as legislation
26 __ spumante
27 Pie fruit
28 Four-person team race
29 Stop
30 Facing the pitcher
31 Make happy
32 Sheriff's group
33 Takes a break
36 Act as referee
38 Writes in the margin
40 Therefore
41 Comedian Laurel
47 Regarding
49 Singer Celine
50 Soup holders
51 Cut off
52 Basketball cable network
53 Chasing-away word
54 Individual performance
56 1502, to Caesar
58 Mexican snack
59 Swelled heads
60 City near 37 Across
62 Mao __-tung
63 Form of "to be"

★ One-Way Streets

The diagram represents a pattern of streets. A and B are parking spaces, and the black squares are stores. Find a route that starts at A, passes through all stores exactly once, and ends at B. Arrows indicate one-way traffic for that block only. No block or intersection may be entered more than once.

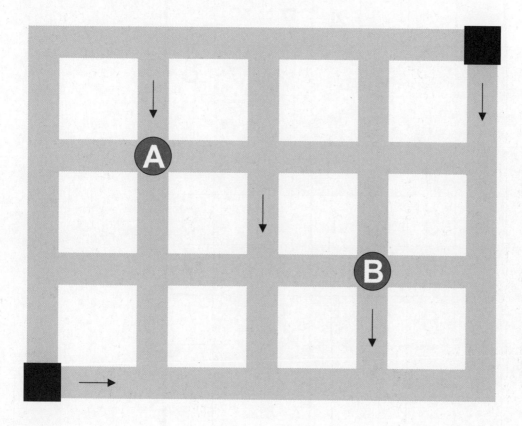

SOUND THINKING

Words whose only consonant sounds are T, R, P, and D include TREPID and TRIPOD. What's the only common three-syllable word with the same consonant sounds in the same order?

_____

★ Hyper-Sudoku

Fill in the blank boxes so that every row, column, 3x3 box, *and* each of the four 3x3 gray regions contains all of the numbers 1 to 9.

					4	7		
		3		5		9	6	8
7			1		8			
	2	8	9				1	
6	7	4	5	8	1			9
	9		2	6			8	7
		8	2	5	1	7		
8	5	7						

COUNT UP

Inserting plus signs and minus signs, as many as necessary, in between the digits from 1 to 9 below, create a series of additions and subtractions whose final answer is 96. Any digits without a sign between them are to be grouped together as a single number.

$$1 \quad 2 \quad 3 \quad 4 \quad 5 \quad 6 \quad 7 \quad 8 \quad 9 \quad = \quad \boxed{96}$$

★ Star Search

Find the stars that are hidden in some of the blank squares. The numbered squares indicate how many stars are hidden in the squares adjacent to them (including diagonally). There is never more than one star in any square.

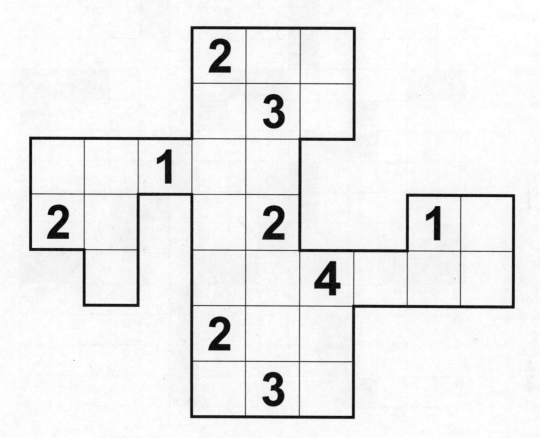

TELEPHONE TRIOS

1	ABC 2	DEF 3
GHI 4	JKL 5	MNO 6
PRS 7	TUV 8	WXY 9
*	o	#

Using the numbers and letters on a standard telephone, what three seven-letter words or phrases from the same category can be formed from these telephone numbers?

269-4687 _ _ _ _ _ _ _

548-8379 _ _ _ _ _ _ _

539-3387 _ _ _ _ _ _ _

★ What's the Holdup? by Gail Grabowski

ACROSS

1 Engaged in a battle
6 Rock-band equipment
10 Complete collection
13 Baggy
14 Come in last
15 Tiresome speaker
16 Casino machines
17 Airline to Tel Aviv
18 China's continent
19 '50s song, e.g.
20 Prison section
22 Historical times
24 Not very bold
25 Skillet
27 The Dalai __
30 Took another chair
33 And so on: Abbr.
34 Veterinary visitors
36 Records on video
38 Plays Pebble Beach
41 Pub beverage
42 Scarecrow filler
43 Prying person
44 Domesticated
46 Lyricist Gershwin
47 Marsh bird
49 Knights' titles
51 St. Louis clock setting
52 Stop running, perhaps
54 Nevada city
56 Auto tune-up item
61 Prudential rival
64 Long-eared hopper
65 Window section
66 Colonel's subordinate
67 Pinnacle
68 Middle East ruler
69 Video-game name
70 Casual greeting
71 See socially
72 Wanderer

DOWN

1 In addition
2 Turnpike charge
3 Traditional Dutch shoe
4 Moving about
5 Close again, as a jar
6 Actor Baldwin
7 Burrowing mammal
8 Sacred song
9 Merchant
10 Run-of-the-mill
11 Guitarist Clapton
12 Ship wood
15 Refuses to go along with
21 Borscht vegetables
23 Maple product
25 Wooden pins
26 Make amends
28 Butcher-shop buy
29 Collection of maps
31 Fruity toast topper
32 Signs of sorrow
35 Prefix for sweet
37 Attack, as a fly
39 At no charge
40 Talk
45 Get it wrong
48 Left 15% on the table
50 Naval recruit
53 Camel's South American cousin
55 "Cool!"
56 Old Iranian ruler
57 Walk back and forth
58 Military force
59 58 Down division
60 Pretty Woman star
62 Director Ephron
63 Dry as a desert

★ ABC

Enter the letters A, B, and C into the diagram so that each row and column has exactly one A, one B, and one C. The letters outside the diagram indicate the first letter encountered, moving in the direction of the arrow. Keep in mind that after all the letters have been filled in, there will be one blank box in each row and column.

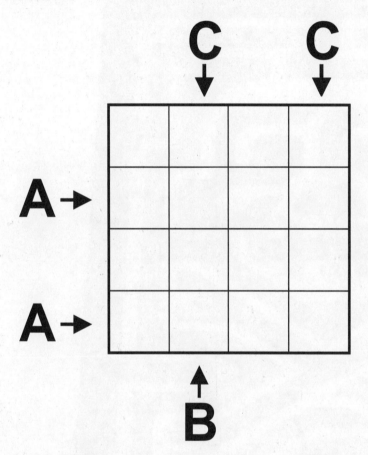

CLUELESS CROSSWORD

Complete the crossword with common uncapitalized seven-letter words, based entirely on the letters already filled in for you.

★★ Jolly Roger Maze

Enter the maze at top, pass through all the stars exactly once, and then exit at bottom. You may not retrace your path.

BETWEENER

What three-letter word belongs between the word at left and the word at right, so that the first and second word, and the second and third word, each form a common two-word phrase?

RED __ __ __ AIR

★★ Sudoku

Fill in the blank boxes so that every row, column, and 3x3 box contains all of the numbers 1 to 9.

9	7					8	4	
8			4			9		1
			2				3	6
	6	8		4				
			5		3			
			1			6	5	
7	5				4			
6		1			9			2
	8	3					9	4

MIXAGRAMS

Each line contains a five-letter word and a four-letter word that have been mixed together (the order of the letters in each word has not been changed). Unmix the two words on each line and write them in the spaces provided. When you're done, find a two-part answer to the clue by reading down the letter columns in the answers.

CLUE: Like microcomputers?

E R A S E H Y A B = _ _ _ _ _ + _ _ _ _

B O T R I O T O Y = _ _ _ _ _ + _ _ _ _

D E R A B Z E U T = _ _ _ _ _ + _ _ _ _

P E D A C R E W E = _ _ _ _ _ + _ _ _ _

★ Hi, Guys by Sally R. Stein

ACROSS

1 Be concerned
5 Competent
9 Watch face
13 Kind of vaccine
14 Gather, as grain
15 Actress Jane or Bridget
16 Points at the target
17 Mean one
18 Parcel out
19 TV interviewee's clip-on
21 Trumpet sound
22 Author Fleming
23 Team member
24 Cold sufferer's sounds
28 "Olé," for example
30 Video-store rental
31 Ill-gotten gains
32 Explosion sound
36 9 Down, in quantity
37 Reveals
38 __ la Douce
39 "Gee!"
40 December 24 and 31
41 Goes on the lam
42 Notions
44 Hair stylists' employers
45 Grade better than a C
48 Collection
49 Big T-shirt size
50 Fax-machine plug
56 Eye-bending painting
57 Smallest of the litter
58 Succulent houseplant
59 Female voices
60 Actor Sharif
61 Femur or fibula
62 Prepared to hit a golf ball
63 Agile
64 Assembly instructions part

DOWN

1 Old furnace fuel
2 Opera solo
3 Freeway exit
4 Otherwise
5 Pleasant smells
6 Get started
7 Carefree escapade
8 Fencing sword
9 Where to see George Washington
10 Dental work
11 Really like
12 In a few hours
15 Story from Aesop
20 Vitality
23 Collies and canaries
24 Urban pollution
25 It's taboo
26 Currier's partner
27 Angler's gear
28 Apple centers
29 Farm implements
31 Molten rock
33 Triple-decker cookie
34 Seer's sighting
35 Church service
37 Honey handlers
41 Destiny
43 Songs for two
44 Military guard
45 Overfill
46 Syrup source
47 Angry
48 Sub tracker
50 __ and cons
51 Camel feature
52 Boxing punches
53 Very much
54 Funnel shape
55 Retain

★★ Line Drawing

Draw three straight lines, each from one edge of the square to another edge, so that the total of the numbers in each of the four regions is the same.

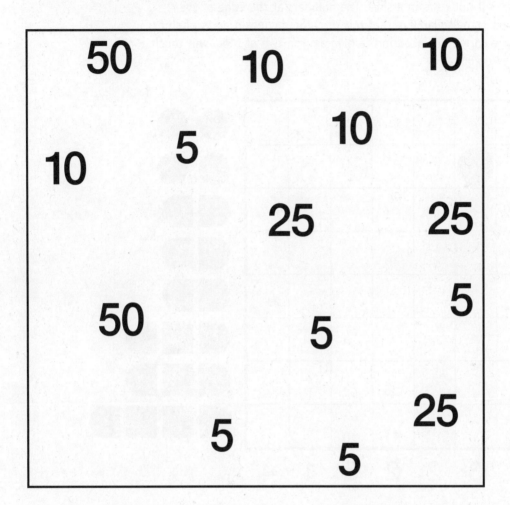

THREE OF A KIND

Find the three hidden words in the sentence that, read in order, go together in some way.

You should read the ad about Tip-Top Potatoes.

★ Find the Ships

Determine the position of the 10 ships listed to the right of the diagram. The ships may be oriented either horizontally or vertically. A square with wavy lines indicates water and will not contain a ship. The numbers at the edge of the diagram indicate how many squares in that row or column contain parts of ships. When all 10 ships are correctly placed in the diagram, no two of them will touch each other, not even diagonally.

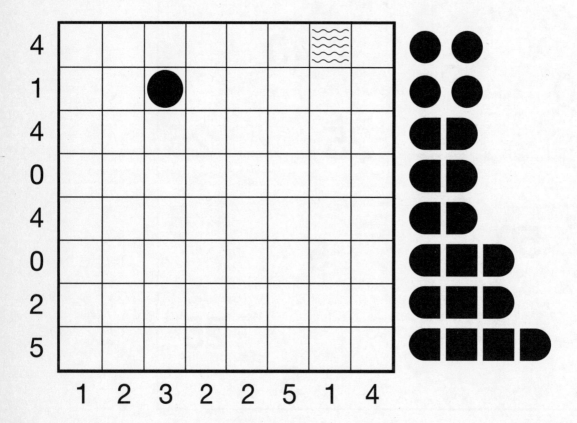

TWO-BY-FOUR

The eight letters in the word YACHTING can be rearranged to form a pair of common four-letter words in three different ways, if no four-letter word is repeated. Can you find all three pairs of words?

— — — — — — — —   — — — — — — — —

— — — — — — — —

★★ Fences

Connect the dots with vertical or horizontal lines, so that a single loop is formed with no crossings or branches. Each number indicates how many lines surround it; squares with no number may be surrounded by any number of lines.

```
1  2  3     2  1  3
      3              2
3              2  2
3        3
            3        0
2  0                 2
2              2
1  3  2        2  3  3
```

ADDITION SWITCH

Switch the positions of two of the digits in the incorrect sum at right, to get a correct sum.

```
  703
+ 196
-----
  845
```

★ Food Money by Gail Grabowski

ACROSS

1 Thin pancake
6 "Woe is me!"
10 Clue
14 "You've got mail" subscriber
15 Bath-powder ingredient
16 Falco of *The Sopranos*
17 Fettuccine recipe need
19 First-class
20 Before, in verse
21 Drop in the mail
22 Lots and lots
24 Autry of oaters
25 Work hard
26 Hollywood awards
29 Save stamps, say
32 Listens to
33 Carpenter's tools
34 Southwest art center
36 Carpenter's fastener
37 Exist
38 Lean slightly
39 Prefix for present
40 Snow glider
41 Blender setting
42 Private matters
44 Author Louisa May
45 Large group
46 Factual
47 Turn suddenly
50 Severely harm
51 Pocketbook
54 Honeybees' home
55 Slaw ingredient
58 Neighborhood
59 In addition
60 Mistake
61 Make repairs to
62 Fibs
63 Kitchen appliance

DOWN

1 Zorro's wrap
2 Lion's warning
3 Otherwise
4 Vet's patient
5 Pencil ends
6 Do penance
7 Praise
8 HS math
9 Educates
10 "Iceberg" produce purchase
11 Fan-mail recipient
12 Workday start for many
13 Golf platforms
18 Family rooms
23 Mideast export
24 Trattoria side order
25 Hauled away, as a car
26 "That's terrible!"
27 Stitched lines
28 Michael of *The Cider House Rules*
29 Is concerned
30 City on the Nile
31 Vacancy sign
33 Like some peanuts
35 Editor's notation
40 Two or three
41 Pipe pro
43 Gun, as an engine
44 Opera highlight
46 Tortillas that are filled
47 Pillow cover
48 Metal thread
49 __-steven (tied)
50 Store inventory: Abbr.
51 Farm building
52 Highly excited
53 Richard of *Chicago*
56 Inventor Whitney
57 Swimsuit part

★★ Out with the Old

Which fragment will correctly complete the tapestry?

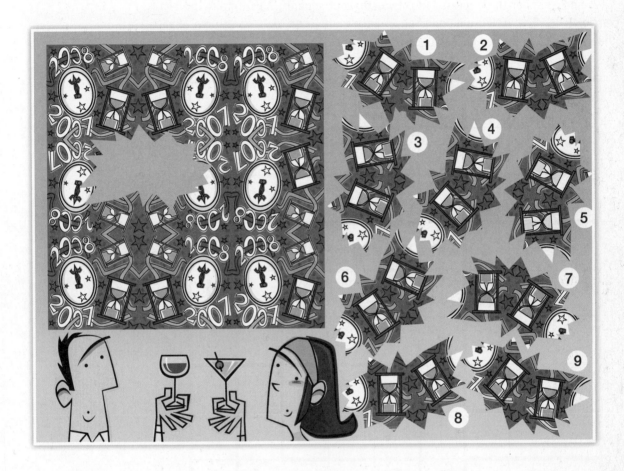

THREE AT A RHYME

Rearrange these letters to form three one-syllable words that rhyme.

A A A D E P P P P R T T T

_____ _____ _____

★★ 123

Fill in the diagram so that each rectangular piece has one each of the numbers
1, 2, and 3, under these rules: 1) No two adjacent squares, horizontally or
vertically, can have the same number. 2) Each completed row and column of the
diagram will have an equal number of 1s, 2s, and 3s.

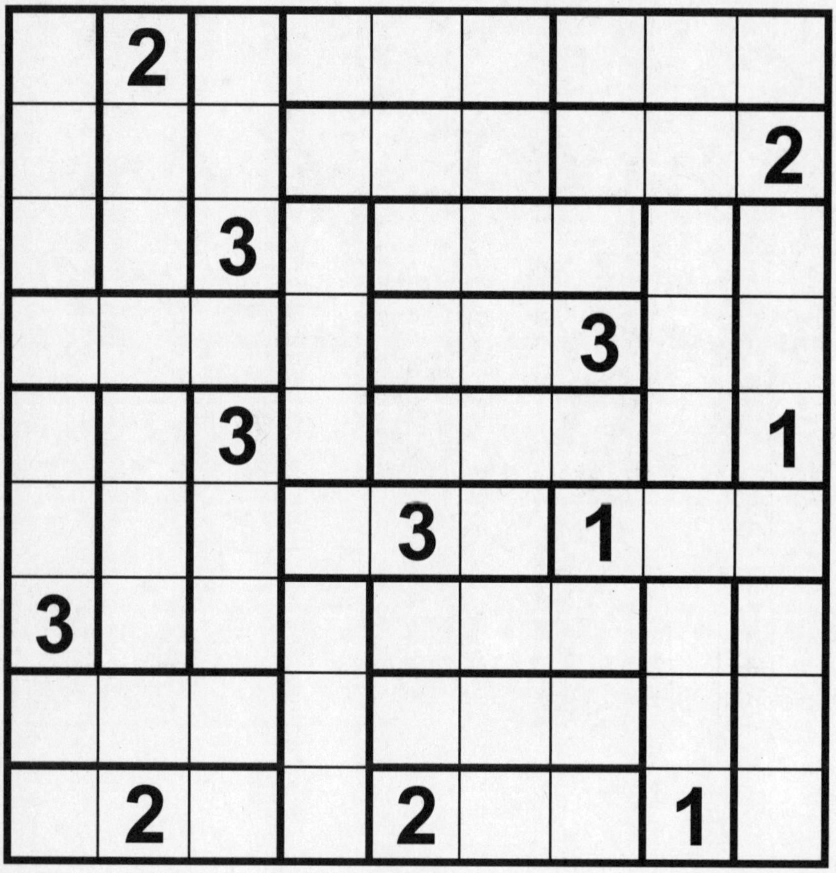

SUDOKU SUM

Without repeating any digits, complete the sum at right,
by filling one digit in each of the five blanks.

```
  _  2  5
+ 6  _  _
─────────
  7  _  _
```

★ Number-Out

Shade squares so that no number appears in any row or column more than once. Shaded squares may not touch each other horizontally or vertically, and all unshaded squares must form a single continuous area.

5	1	1	4	3
5	5	3	1	4
2	4	4	1	5
3	4	2	1	1
4	4	5	2	3

OPPOSITE ATTRACTION

Unscramble the letters in the word GASOLINE to form two common words that are opposites of each other.

_____   _____

★ Reptile House by Shirley Soloway

ACROSS

1 Give an appraisal
5 Map book
10 Jury member
14 Mellowed, as wine
15 Interrogate aggressively
16 Sondheim's __ the Woods
17 Fender blemish
18 Young Montague
19 Datum, for short
20 Avocado
23 Authority defier
24 Senator Kennedy
25 Swiss peak
28 Subterfuges
32 Tennessee __ Ford
34 1200, to Caesar
37 Some sweaters
40 Hawaii's most populous island
42 Paperless letter
43 Podiatrist's concerns
44 Indian ceremonies
47 Dentist's deg.
48 Sultan's pride
49 Clay target
51 Actor Wallach
52 Charged atom
55 Narratives
59 Eyeglass-frame material
64 Send a package
66 "Deck the Halls" plant
67 Not busy
68 "Oh, sure!"
69 Come after
70 Pigeon-__
71 Throw carelessly
72 Paper quantities
73 Travelers' stops

DOWN

1 Airplane tracker
2 Well-coordinated
3 Dumbbell marking
4 Less serene
5 Taj Mahal city
6 Moderate gait
7 VIP's wheels
8 Paying attention
9 Angle of inclination
10 Italian tower town
11 Thoroughly absorbed
12 Greek vowel
13 Go bad
21 Oversupply
22 Biblical garden
26 Was fond of
27 Annoyances
29 Took to court
30 Humorist Bombeck
31 Getz and Laurel
33 Wrestling official
34 Dayan of Israel
35 Suez or Panama
36 Fund-raiser beneficiaries
38 Defeat, so to speak
39 General Robt. __
41 Luau instrument
45 Arab prince
46 Full collections
50 Part of French Polynesia
53 Turn the __ cheek
54 Not a soul
56 Gave a false impression
57 Comic DeGeneres
58 Winter vehicles
60 Selects, with "for"
61 Casablanca heroine
62 Urban blight
63 Mr. Potato Head pieces
64 Command to a dog
65 The Sopranos network

★★ Sequence Maze

Enter the maze at top left, pass through all the squares exactly once, then exit at top right, all without retracing your path. You may not pass through two squares of the same color consecutively.

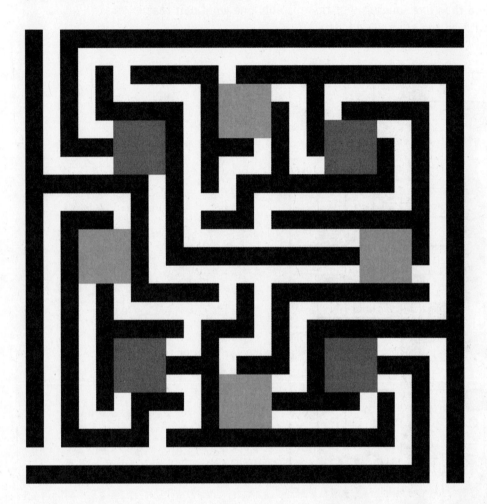

SAY IT AGAIN

What four-letter word for a type of metal, when pronounced differently, is also a verb meaning "to conduct"?

— — — —

★★ Split Decisions

In this clueless crossword puzzle, each answer consists of two words whose spellings are the same, except for the consecutive letters given. All answers are common words; no phrases or hyphenated or capitalized words are used. Some of the clues may have more than one solution, but there is only one word pair that will correctly link up with all the other word pairs.

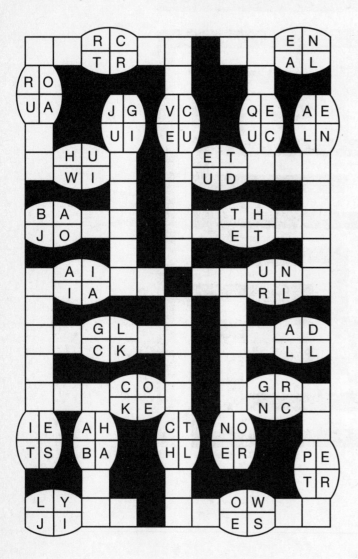

TRANSDELETION

Delete one letter from the word ALTERNATE and rearrange the rest, to get a type of animal.

★ Hyper-Sudoku

Fill in the blank boxes so that every row, column, 3x3 box, *and* each of the four 3x3 gray regions contains all of the numbers 1 to 9.

3				8		7		
7		1			2	6	5	3
5			7		3	8		4
		5	3				7	8
4	3				9			1
6		7	8			5		
		3	2					
	5		9				2	
	7				8			

MIXAGRAMS

Each line contains a five-letter word and a four-letter word that have been mixed together (the order of the letters in each word has not been changed). Unmix the two words on each line and write them in the spaces provided. When you're done, find a two-part answer to the clue by reading down the letter columns in the answers.

CLUE: Driver's needs

V I M A L G O R T = _ _ _ _ _ + _ _ _ _

S A I D O R T E N = _ _ _ _ _ + _ _ _ _

C O M A L C O R E = _ _ _ _ _ + _ _ _ _

L I P F L E U R S = _ _ _ _ _ + _ _ _ _

★ Time For Bed by Gail Grabowski

ACROSS

1 One of the Three Bears
5 Diver's device
10 Campus area
14 Stuntman Knievel
15 Tiny amounts
16 Strongly recommend
17 Princess of India
18 Breakfast bread
19 English nobleman
20 Long-billed diving bird
22 Airline to Israel
23 Stalin's predecessor
24 Elevator direction
26 Spinning toys
29 National bird
33 Stepped heavily
37 Cashews, e.g.
39 Bother
40 Form of jazz
42 Stew vessel
43 Scoundrel
44 Capital of South Korea
45 Fly high
47 Fleecy females
48 West Point freshman
49 Salon tints
51 Scottish girl
54 Piece of celery
58 Strong wind
61 Type of small plane
65 Laundry measure
66 Send out for pizza
67 Cain's brother
68 Prefix for freeze
69 Change, as a law
70 JFK or LBJ
71 Not shallow
72 Citrus fruits
73 Lighten

DOWN

1 Job benefit
2 Be of use
3 Rigatoni relative
4 Make even
5 Audit, as a college course
6 Doves' sounds
7 Western state
8 Stationed
9 Houston baseballer
10 Antique furniture style
11 Russian river
12 Taj Mahal city
13 Wooded valley
21 __ to be tied (angry)
25 Not strong
27 Young dogs
28 Got up
30 Chew like a beaver
31 Valentine card word
32 Needle holes
33 Recipe amount: Abbr.
34 Fishing-rod attachment
35 Slender woodwind
36 Ice-cream cone order
38 Remain
41 "Not guilty," for one
46 Faxes again
50 Greyhound stop: Abbr.
52 Shoplift
53 Hindu guru
55 Open-mouthed
56 Zodiac sign
57 Leg joints
58 Cheerful
59 Top-notch
60 Not on time
62 Thing on a list
63 Prime-time hour
64 "If all __ fails ..."

★★ On the Trail

Beginning with A FISTFUL OF DOLLARS, then moving up, down, left, or right, one letter at a time, trace a path of these 41 westerns and words associated with westerns in the diagram.

```
F T S A C E M U S T A R U L E R S B D E
U L I F N N E K O R N G S T N E H O R R
F O N F A L N B O B U H A O A O S E V R
D O U O R G E A N A K C H D N D A R L I
L L S M I I V N W I T W D O A R S M I V
A B L U N D A Z S W H E F L L A S O S E
R S S E E A N C E O L V A L D D E R E R
O Z T L D I R E H C S E R E A L H T A R
N I E E E D A L I V O F O R T L I N W H
A R N Y R J P U S A R B O I E G A N O I
N A E A H O M R T E S T P A S S R O D
E R O W N I T N O H W E T D N G O I N E
W F N L N M S A L A R T S E A R I G H J
E I T A E V A D S A R S W A G O H S E E
R O R R C F F E H P A O N R C N T A M S
T C I P A T I R O T H C H U A A R J E S
H E R M E T D A K A H I G Z R I H E C I
E V A N E L H C A E G A T S E L T O C S
R I I T S E C H O C O D B U V D I K I L
G I N H E A R E R S R E O F F A L O B L
```

A FISTFUL OF DOLLARS	NEVADA SMITH
ARIZONA	NEW FRONTIER
BLUE STEEL	NORTHWEST PASSAGE
BONANZA	PALE RIDER
BORDER RIVER	RAWHIDE
BROKEN LANCE	RIO BRAVO
BUFFALO BILL	RIO GRANDE
CATTLE EMPIRE	RODEO
CHISUM	RUSTLERS
CHUKA	SHENANDOAH
CORRAL	SHERIFF
DAKOTA	SILVERADO
DANCES WITH WOLVES	STAGECOACH
DENIMS	STETSON
FOR A FEW DOLLARS MORE	TALL IN THE SADDLE
HIGH CHAPARRAL	THE CISCO KID
HIGH NOON	THE SEARCHERS
JESSE JAMES	THE VIRGINIAN
JOHN WAYNE	UNFORGIVEN
MUSTANG	VERA CRUZ
	WAGON TRAIL

IN OTHER WORDS

There is only one common uncapitalized word that contains the consecutive letters OYB. What is it?

_____

bRain BREatHer
I CANNOT TELL A LIE

Polite fibbing is something we all do time to time; flat-out lying is something that few of us will readily admit to. Whether done with good or ill intent, the art of telling mistruths is a subject that some of history's best thinkers have ruminated on for years.

Never trust a person who says "frankly," "candidly," or "to be honest." He probably is none of those things.

—ROGER SIMON

Of course I lie to people. But I lie altruistically—for our mutual good. The lie is the basic building block of good manners. That may seem mildly shocking to a moralist—but then what isn't?

—QUENTIN CRISP

There is nothing as deceptive as an obvious fact.

—ARTHUR CONAN DOYLE

A man always has two reasons for doing anything: A good reason and the real reason.

—J.P. MORGAN

It is hard to believe that a man is telling the truth when you know that you would lie if you were in his place.

—H.L. MENCKEN

THOSE THAT THINK IT PERMISSIBLE TO TELL WHITE LIES SOON GROW COLOR-BLIND.

—AUSTIN O'MALLEY

The best measure of a man's honesty isn't his income tax return. It's the zero adjust on his bathroom scale.

—ARTHUR C. CLARKE

Lying to ourselves is more deeply ingrained than lying to others.

—FYODOR DOSTOYEVSKY

★★ One-Way Streets

The diagram represents a pattern of streets. P's are parking spaces, and the black squares are stores. Find the route that starts at a parking space, passes through all stores exactly once, and ends at the other parking space. Arrows indicate one-way traffic for that block only. No block or intersection may be entered more than once.

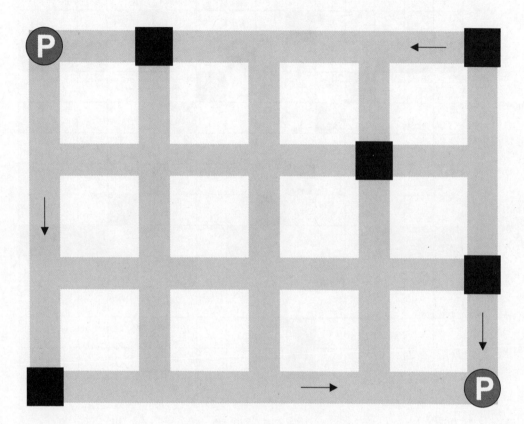

SOUND THINKING

The consonant sounds in the word SWEDE are S, W, and D. What common uncapitalized two-syllable word consists of exactly the same consonant sounds in the same order?

_____

★ Turkey Leftovers by Sally R. Stein

ACROSS

1 Floor-washing tools
5 Writer Ferber
9 Onrush
14 Give off
15 Fairway club
16 Alternatives to potatoes
17 Turkey __ (post-Thanksgiving lunches)
20 Pro hockey venue
21 Clinton's vice president
22 Casino game
23 Uses a shovel
25 Dutch cheese
27 Uppercut alternative
30 H.S. seniors' exams
32 Paint stains
36 Sale condition
38 Garden flower
40 Bach work
41 Ancient Turkey was part of it
44 Built like a wrestler
45 Places (down)
46 Shut loudly
47 Certify
49 Getz of jazz
51 Overhead trains
52 Collarless shirts
54 Waikiki banquet
56 Like some garage floors
59 At any __ (nevertheless)
61 Soda-shop sipper
65 Go cold turkey
68 On the up and up
69 Become unclear
70 Author Wiesel
71 Signs of the future
72 Swiss mountains
73 Sandwich breads

DOWN

1 Arizona city
2 Actor Sharif
3 Heap
4 Get to one's feet
5 __ for Evidence (Grafton book)
6 Car-racing course
7 Forbidden thing
8 Agassi of tennis
9 __ Lanka
10 Tonics
11 Workout result, perhaps
12 Adolescent
13 Exxon's former name
18 Banquet platform
19 Ties the knot
24 Trot or gallop
26 Two-band radio
27 __ the Hutt (Star Wars series villain)
28 So far
29 Composer of Carmen
31 Nasal passage
33 Like gymnasts
34 Of country life
35 Appears to be
37 Diaper fastener
39 Paid one's bills
42 "Big Board" of Wall St.
43 Brother of Isaac
48 Tenure of office
50 Cape Canaveral org.
53 Brazilian dance
55 Speak
56 Scandinavian city
57 Line on a list
58 Theater level
60 Spill the beans
62 Depend
63 "I cannot tell __"
64 Letters before zees
66 Part of TGIF
67 Tax agcy.

★★ Missing Links

Find the six polygons that are linked together, and linked to no other polygons on the page.

THREE AT A RHYME

Rearrange these letters to form three one-syllable words that rhyme.

C C F F F F G H O O O S U

_____ _____ _____

★★ Star Search

Find the stars that are hidden in some of the blank squares. The numbered squares indicate how many stars are hidden in the squares adjacent to them (including diagonally). There is never more than one star in any square.

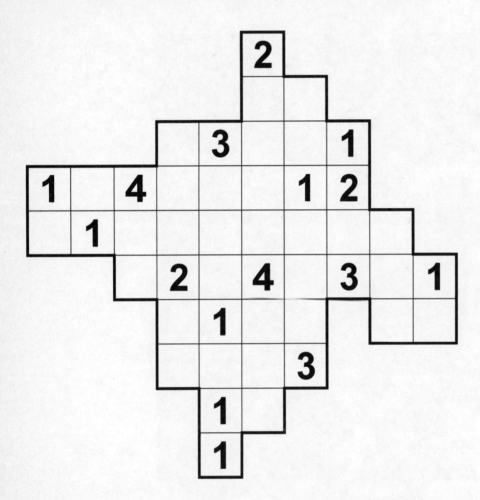

TELEPHONE TRIOS

	ABC	DEF
1	**2**	**3**
GHI **4**	JKL **5**	MNO **6**
PRS **7**	TUV **8**	WXY **9**
*	**0**	**#**

Using the numbers and letters on a standard telephone, what three seven-letter words or phrases from the same category can be formed from these telephone numbers?

472-3866   _ _ _ _ _ _ _

474-7426   _ _ _ _ _ _ _

769-5464   _ _ _ _ _ _ _

★★ Triad Split Decisions

In this clueless crossword puzzle, each answer consists of two words whose spellings are the same, except for the consecutive letters given. All answers are common words; no phrases or hyphenated or capitalized words are used. Some of the clues may have more than one solution, but there is only one word pair that will correctly link up with all the other word pairs.

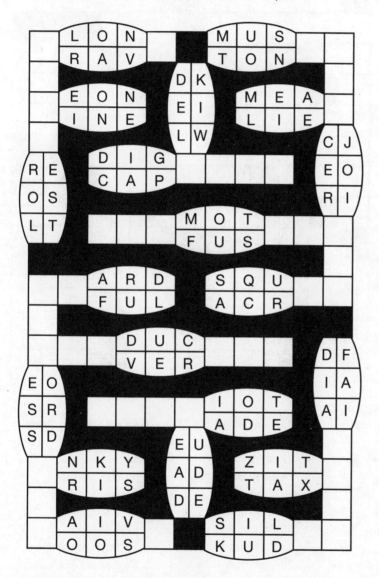

TRANSDELETION

Delete one letter from the word EMIGRANT and rearrange the rest, to get a style of music.

★★ Listen to the Blackbird by Fred Piscop

ACROSS

1 Poodle skirts, once
4 Soft seats
9 Reserve fund
14 St. crosser
15 Preferred invitees
16 Low-budget, in brand names
17 President pro __
18 Oscar de la __
19 Zulu or Swahili
20 Stone Age race
23 Actor John or Sean
24 Metered ride
25 Idler
28 MTV watcher
29 Hole-making tool
32 Put together
33 Pueblo brick
35 Saw into, in a way
37 Plains tribesmen
39 Close behind
41 In need of cleaning
42 Show support
43 Derby town
45 Drops back
49 Punch sound
50 Bikini part
51 Baseball great Hank
52 *Gladiator* star
56 "I dunno" gesture
59 Judge, at times
60 "__ is me!"
61 In the midst of
62 Make amends
63 Big __, CA
64 Daft
65 Faxes, say
66 Sci-fi beings

DOWN

1 Moneybags
2 Strongly opposed
3 Reduce in rank
4 Clear wrap
5 Cassini of fashion
6 Sawyer's pal
7 Regarding
8 Batter's concern
9 Skewered dish
10 Optimistic words
11 Whole bunch
12 Blaster's need
13 "__ rang?"
21 Mosque tower
22 It influenced Lenin
25 Cargo areas
26 Luau strings
27 Shirt tag abbr.
29 Gentlemen's hats
30 Kimono sash
31 Tears apart
32 Project work unit
34 Anonymous John
36 Pied Piper follower
37 Chuck-wagon fare
38 Twosome
39 Dada pioneer
40 As well
44 Rotini and penne
46 Relax at the library
47 Withdraw
48 Unkind looks
50 Horse-drawn vehicle
51 Estate units
52 Pipsqueak
53 Art Deco notable
54 Emerald City visitor
55 Give for a while
56 Feeling blue
57 Medical-coverage grp.
58 Go bad

★★ ABC

Enter the letters A, B, and C into the diagram so that each row and column has exactly one A, one B, and one C. The letters outside the diagram indicate the first letter encountered, moving in the direction of the arrow. Keep in mind that after all the letters have been filled in, there will be two blank boxes in each row and column.

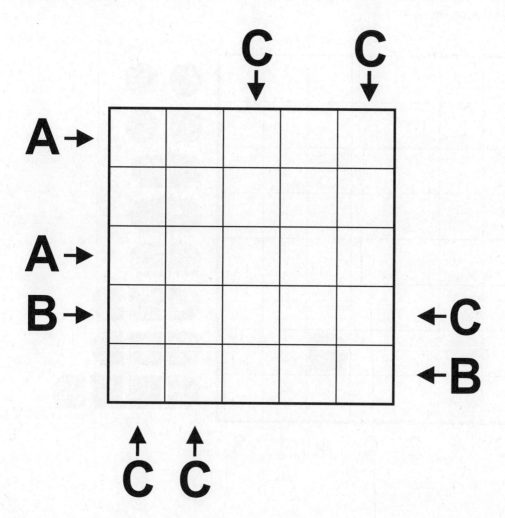

NATIONAL TREASURE

Using the letters in COLOMBIA, we were able to form only one common uncapitalized six-letter word. Can you find it?

_ _ _ _ _ _

★★ Find the Ships

Determine the position of the 10 ships listed to the right of the diagram. The ships may be oriented either horizontally or vertically. A square with wavy lines indicates water and will not contain a ship. The numbers at the edge of the diagram indicate how many squares in that row or column contain parts of ships. When all 10 ships are correctly placed in the diagram, no two of them will touch each other, not even diagonally.

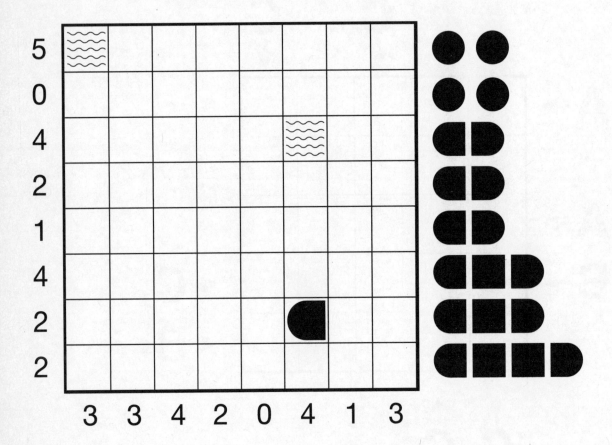

TWO-BY-FOUR

The eight letters in the word UPWARDLY can be rearranged to form a pair of common four-letter words in only one way, if no four-letter word is repeated. Can you find the two words?

— — — —   — — — —

★★ Physical Figures by Doug Peterson

ACROSS

1 "__, Joy of Man's Desiring" (Bach hymn)
5 Sonny ex
9 Concoct, as a plan
14 Introductory material
15 Stadium section
16 D-Day beach
17 Parachute pull
18 Mosque official
19 Early bird's hour, perhaps
20 Las Vegas machines
23 "Later!"
24 Sit-up muscles
25 Baseball card stat
26 Henpecks
28 Small island
29 Expresses disapproval
33 He preceded 9 Down
35 German painter Max
37 Actress Carrere
38 *Braveheart* weapons
41 Mexican metal
42 "Whither thou __ ..."
43 From Limerick
44 Combustible heap
46 Sandwich order
47 Piece of cake
48 Was certain of
50 __ Miss
51 More, to a *señor*
54 Company picnic competition
59 *Wheel of Fortune* purchase choices
60 Kansas town
61 Utah ski resort
62 Transpire again
63 City east of Cairo
64 Supermodel Heidi
65 Student of Socrates
66 Light on one's feet
67 Lay eyes on

DOWN

1 Ebenezer's partner
2 Black-key material
3 Bug blocker
4 Meat inspection org.
5 Tackles K2
6 Real-estate listings
7 "My word!"
8 He has his own Amsterdam museum
9 Mubarak of Egypt
10 Surrounded by
11 Curbside call
12 Make small talk
13 Unlikely Oscar nominees
21 Motley
22 Immeasurable depth
27 Sound of contentment
28 High point
30 Neighborhood shopping spots
31 Grade-schoolers
32 Merit-badge site
33 Discontinue
34 Out of whack
35 *The Sound of Music* song
36 Coiled around
39 Dynamite guy
40 "... man __ mouse?"
45 Barely manage
47 Disreputable
49 Prefix with surgeon
50 Rude viewer
52 Misbehave
53 Disreputable
54 Infield covering
55 Obedience school command
56 Costa __
57 Increase
58 Croupier's tool

★★ What's Next?

Which one of the numbered squares should replace the question mark, to follow the logical pattern in each of these three sequences?

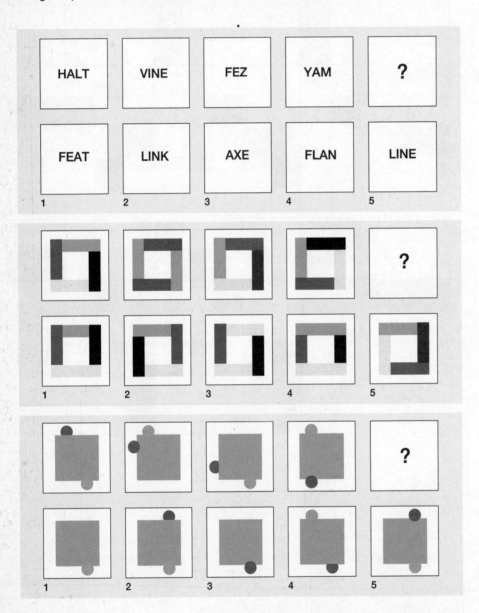

HALT	VINE	FEZ	YAM	?

FEAT	LINK	AXE	FLAN	LINE
1	2	3	4	5

BETWEENER

What four-letter word belongs between the word at left and the word at right, so that the first and second word, and the second and third word, each form a common two-word phrase?

FREE __ __ __ __ GUY

★★ Sudoku

Fill in the blank boxes so that every row, column, and 3x3 box contains all of the numbers 1 to 9.

3	5					2		
6				4				
		4	5		3			1
		3	1			9		
	4						6	
		1			7	3		
9			2		5	4		
			1					6
		6					8	2

MIXAGRAMS

Each line contains a five-letter word and a four-letter word that have been mixed together (the order of the letters in each word has not been changed). Unmix the two words on each line and write them in the spaces provided. When you're done, find a two-part answer to the clue by reading down the letter columns in the answers.

CLUE: Don't be hasty

S O A M O A S T S = _ _ _ _ _ + _ _ _ _

F U R E G V U S E = _ _ _ _ _ + _ _ _ _

G O O L E D S E N = _ _ _ _ _ + _ _ _ _

A L L U G R A K E = _ _ _ _ _ + _ _ _ _

★★ Fences

Connect the dots with vertical or horizontal lines, so that a single loop is formed with no crossings or branches. Each number indicates how many lines surround it; squares with no number may be surrounded by any number of lines.

```
3   3     1 2 1
      0           3
        3       0
  3             2
    0             1
    2     2
  2         3
    2 0 2   3   3
```

ADDITION SWITCH

Switch the positions of two of the digits in the incorrect sum at right, to get a correct sum.

```
  384
+ 257
─────
  661
```

★★ Just Imagine by Daniel R. Stark

ACROSS

1 Director Ephron
5 Wishes undone
9 Tax pros
13 Qatar ruler
14 One of the Brontë sisters
15 Safari sighting
17 Road rally
18 Translucent mineral
19 Pungent
20 Attractive person
22 Pebble's big brother
23 Charged atoms
24 Nightclub renditions
25 Colleague of Byron and Shelley
29 Party to some contracts
32 Van Buren, presidentially
34 __ Paulo, Brazil
35 Gouda cousin
39 Spoke well of
41 Driving hazard
43 Aquatic bird
44 Thieve
46 More tightfisted
47 __ Abdul-Jabbar
50 Frontier transport
51 Gnats and mice
54 Keep going
56 Swears
57 Not in love
62 Magic-lamp occupant
63 European volcano
64 Ready for picking
65 Put into law
66 Abound
67 Up to no good
68 Three, in Tijuana
69 Puts two and two together
70 Gumshoes

DOWN

1 Dweeb
2 "A loaf of bread ..." poet
3 Paddy crop
4 Rug's coverage
5 Stallone role
6 Mergers
7 Crates up
8 Straphanger's lack
9 Clean-living
10 Garden-party attire
11 Protective clothing
12 Book part
16 25 Across works
21 Light fogs
25 Held onto
26 Colleen's home
27 Thickening agent
28 Reconsider
30 Wash against, as waves
31 Appear menacing
33 *Frau*'s spouse
36 Lisbon lady
37 Shake __ (rush)
38 Nothing but
40 Forest mom
42 Easily irritated
45 Overdue
48 Valuable holdings
49 Not run by computer
51 Magazine part
52 Javelin or marathon
53 Treasure hunter's aid
55 Hoaxes
57 Crumbly cheese
58 Guitar-neck bump
59 __ *gauche*
60 DeMille genre
61 Slithery swimmers

★★ Number-Out

Shade squares so that no number appears in any row or column more than once. Shaded squares may not touch each other horizontally or vertically, and all unshaded squares must form a single continuous area.

2	2	6	5	4	3
3	2	3	4	5	5
5	2	1	2	5	4
6	3	4	1	1	2
4	6	2	1	6	6
4	1	5	1	2	6

OPPOSITE ATTRACTION

Unscramble the letters in the phrase DINGY HAT to form two common words that are opposites of each other.

_____   _____

★★ Hyper-Sudoku

Fill in the blank boxes so that every row, column, 3x3 box, *and* each of the four 3x3 gray regions contains all of the numbers 1 to 9.

	9			8			5	7
		4						
7			3	4				
		2	7		3	8	4	
3							7	
		9			2			
		6						
		1	2		4	5		6
		7				3	9	

COUNT UP

Inserting plus signs and minus signs, as many as necessary, in between the digits from 1 to 9 below, create a series of additions and subtractions whose final answer is 84. Any digits without a sign between them are to be grouped together as a single number.

$$1 \quad 2 \quad 3 \quad 4 \quad 5 \quad 6 \quad 7 \quad 8 \quad 9 \quad = \quad 84$$

★★ Grainy by Fred Piscop

ACROSS

1 Toy glider wood
6 Northern Finn
10 Fancy dance
14 Nom de plume
15 Director Kazan
16 Dairy tubful
17 Nebraska collegian
19 MGM cofounder
20 Use the stove
21 Hush-hush org.
22 Dreaded fly
24 Nastase of tennis
26 __-bitty
27 Deli sandwich order
32 Aunt Millie's competitor
33 Freeway access
34 Furniture wood
35 Worth a C
36 Weather, in verse
38 Trig function
39 Propel, as a shot
40 Pupil controller
41 Bubbly bandleader
42 Shows liveliness
46 Otherwise
47 Fourth-down option
48 Shippers' cases
51 Yearbook sect.
52 Shopper's guide
56 Monthly outlay
57 Coin last minted in 1958
60 Pot starter
61 Well-ventilated
62 Italian city
63 Dayan colleague
64 Thumbs-ups
65 Ill will

DOWN

1 Baroque composer
2 Skin soother
3 Former Florentine money
4 South American capital
5 Volcano spew
6 Not as significant
7 __-Seltzer
8 Round food
9 Working afternoons, say
10 Henry VIII's second
11 "Thanks __!"
12 Vintner's dregs
13 Actor Rob or Chad
18 ICU part
23 Go no further
25 Baton Rouge sch.
26 Shi'ite leader
27 Fake jewelry
28 Greet the day
29 Churns up
30 American, to Brits
31 __ out a living
32 Dissolute one
35 Tanning lotion letters
36 Road intersector
37 Place to wait
38 Pay one's debt
40 Land in the sea
41 Hardly ruddy
43 College athlete's award
44 Uses a mister
45 Give the boot to
48 Study hard
49 Actress Russo
50 Pro's foe
51 Blood fluids
53 Crucifix letters
54 Peeved mood
55 Newcastle's river
58 Speed along
59 Qt. halves

★ G Whiz

Beginning with IMPUGN, then moving up, down, left, or right, one letter at a time, trace a path of these 19 words that have a silent G.

```
I  C  M  L  H  G  I  N  G  S  A
M  O  G  E  P  N  E  F  I  S  M
P  N  S  I  C  A  M  G  N  O  G
U  P  O  G  N  A  P  T  E  M  I
G  N  I  S  I  I  G  A  P  A  D
G  I  G  E  G  N  N  N  G  R  A
N  L  N  R  N  G  F  N  E  N  G
D  A  A  N  T  I  O  G  H  C  I
I  N  G  U  O  E  R  A  A  D  E
A  R  A  P  P  A  W  P  M  D  E
P  H  G  M  G  N  G  N  A  R  L
```

ALIGN
ASSIGN
CAMPAIGN
CHAMPAGNE
CONSIGN
DEIGN
DIAPHRAGM
FEIGN
FOREIGN
GNAT
GNARLED
GNAW
GNOME
~~IMPUGN~~
OPPUGN
PARADIGM
PHLEGM
POIGNANT
RESIGN

INITIAL REACTION

Identify the well-known proverb from the first letters in each of its words.

O. O. S. O. O. M. _____

★★ Color Paths

Find the shortest path through the maze from the right to the center, by using paths in this color order: red, blue, yellow, red, blue, etc. Change path colors through the white squares. It is okay to retrace your path.

SAY IT AGAIN

What four-letter weather term, when pronounced differently, is also a verb meaning "turn"?

— — — —

★★ Double-O Four by Fred Piscop

ACROSS

1 Goblet feature
5 Chums
9 Watch sounds
14 Typewriter type
15 Diabolical
16 Layer with a "hole"
17 "This weighs __!"
18 Censor of ancient Rome
19 Scout's job, for short
20 "Tea for Two" musical
23 Mel in Cooperstown
24 Refuses to
25 Rocker Clapton
27 Damon of *Mo' Money*
30 Rainy-day footwear
34 Be wild about
35 Dosage unit
36 Angelic topper
37 Wray of *King Kong*
38 Group of guys, familiarly
41 French diarist
42 Clashers in Hollywood
44 Blunted blade
45 Eta follower
47 Closed up again
49 Bucket-brigade member
50 Spill the beans
51 Touched down
52 Title for Mick Jagger
54 Discotheque employees
60 Chum
62 Limburger quality
63 Flag down
64 Hopeless case
65 Use a dishtowel
66 Art Deco master
67 Hidden agenda
68 They hang from basketball hoops
69 Floored it

DOWN

1 Reach across
2 Onetime leader of Yugoslavia
3 Business-school subj.
4 Legendary racehorse
5 Praline nuts
6 __-garde
7 Lo-cal
8 Coin taker
9 Corrida celebrity
10 Suffix with lion
11 French fashion designer
12 Board flaw
13 Shipped out
21 Trio times three
22 Brit's appliance
26 It means "kind of"
27 Thin cookie
28 Old saw
29 Part of a "sleeping" toy
30 Mocked
31 Natural emollient
32 A-list
33 Sub detector
35 Toon Le Pew
39 Nametag word
40 Wood finish
43 "I told you so!"
46 Thumbs a ride
48 Dick Cheney's predecessor
49 Siren sounds
51 Take as one's own
52 Epic tale
53 "__ a roll!"
55 Formal dress
56 Garfield's pal
57 Wyatt of the West
58 Baptism, e.g.
59 Winter conveyance
61 Hair goo

★★ One-Way Streets

The diagram represents a pattern of streets. P's are parking spaces, and the black squares are stores. Find the route that starts at a parking space, passes through all stores exactly once, and ends at the other parking space. Arrows indicate one-way traffic for that block only. No block or intersection may be entered more than once.

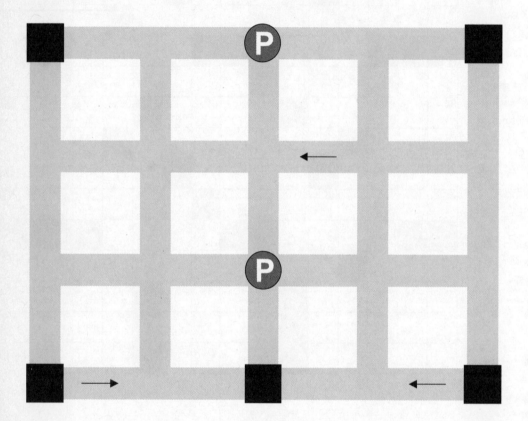

SOUND THINKING

The consonant sounds in the word PUZZLE are P, Z, and L. What other common uncapitalized word, a fashion term, consists of exactly the same consonant sounds in the same order?

_____

★★ 123

Fill in the diagram so that each rectangular piece has one each of the numbers 1, 2, and 3, under these rules: 1) No two adjacent squares, horizontally or vertically, can have the same number. 2) Each completed row and column of the diagram will have an equal number of 1s, 2s, and 3s.

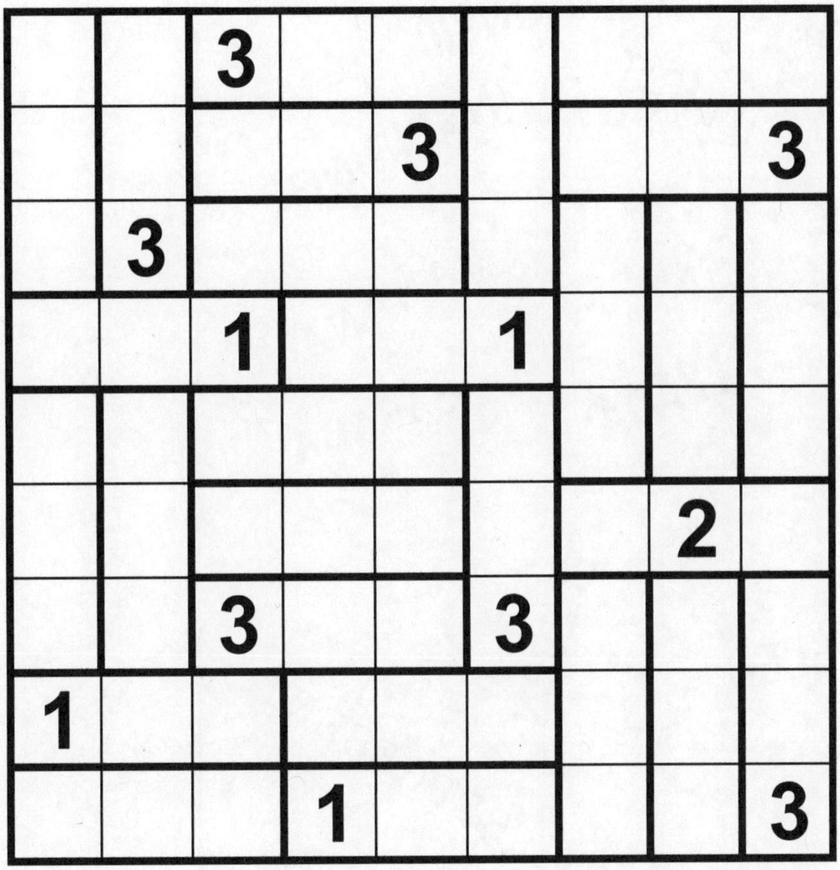

		3						
				3				**3**
	3							
		1			**1**			
							2	
		3			**3**			
1								
			1					**3**

SUDOKU SUM

Without repeating any digits, complete the sum at right, by filling one digit in each of the five blanks.

```
  8 _ _
+ _ 0 5
-------
_ _ 2
```

★★ Line Drawing

Draw two straight lines, each from one edge of the square to another edge, so that the words in each of the three regions have something in common.

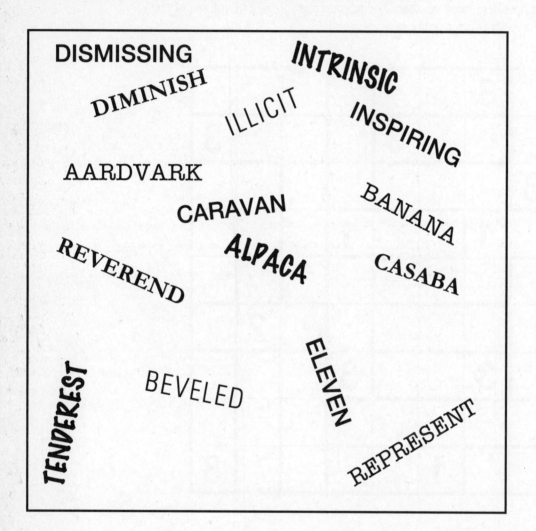

THREE OF A KIND

Find the three hidden words in the sentence that, read in order, go together in some way.

The Maple Avenue Café serves homemade veal on Easter.

★★ Say Cheese by Fred Piscop

ACROSS

1 Molten rock
6 Travelers' aids
10 Wild guess
14 Imam's faith
15 Coup d'__
16 Game with mallets
17 Future fern
18 Big bash
19 Unnamed auth.
20 Multipurpose tool
23 Bite like a pup
24 "Got it!"
25 Midpoint: Abbr.
26 Barbecue bit
29 "... man __ mouse?"
31 Oater challenge
33 Post-ER place
34 Goes limp
37 Check datum
40 Home-based business
44 Detractor
45 Show disdain for
46 Musical gift
47 Former spouses
50 Cut short
51 Deli loaf
52 Guffaw syllable
54 Bonkers
57 Vintner's vessel
59 Veterans' organization
64 "Veni, __, vici"
65 Passionate about
66 Xbox enthusiast
68 Burden of proof
69 Commotions
70 Wipe clean
71 Manage somehow
72 Bound along
73 Blowgun ammo

DOWN

1 Wrong: Pref.
2 Nile reptiles
3 Healthy look
4 Sausalito's county
5 Hawkeye State city
6 Prefix with bucks
7 Video game pioneer
8 Where lifelines are
9 Hung around
10 Reach across
11 Bar mixer
12 In the air
13 Embarrassing error

21 Parsley bit
22 Prefix with plunk
26 Costa __
27 Clickable symbol
28 Flattered excessively
30 Brewpub wares
32 Web pop-ups, e.g.
35 __-tac-toe
36 Nose-in-the-air sort
38 Carhop's load
39 Brontë governess
41 Theater passes, slangily
42 Teed off

43 Put away, as groceries
48 Inventor Whitney
49 Church party
52 It's wreaked
53 Acid in proteins
55 "No problemo"
56 In command
58 Pageant topper
60 Heed the alarm
61 Get whupped
62 Actor Epps
63 Hatchling's home
67 Scale notes

★★ Star Search

Find the stars that are hidden in some of the blank squares. The numbered squares indicate how many stars are hidden in the squares adjacent to them (including diagonally). There is never more than one star in any square.

TELEPHONE TRIOS

1	ABC 2	DEF 3
GHI 4	JKL 5	MNO 6
PRS 7	TUV 8	WXY 9
*	o	#

Using the numbers and letters on a standard telephone, what three seven-letter words or phrases from the same category can be formed from these telephone numbers?

225-4279   _ _ _ _ _ _ _

425-4329   _ _ _ _ _ _ _

867-6686   _ _ _ _ _ _ _

★★ Cat and Mouse Maze

Enter the maze at bottom, pass through all the stars exactly once, and then exit at right. You may not retrace your path.

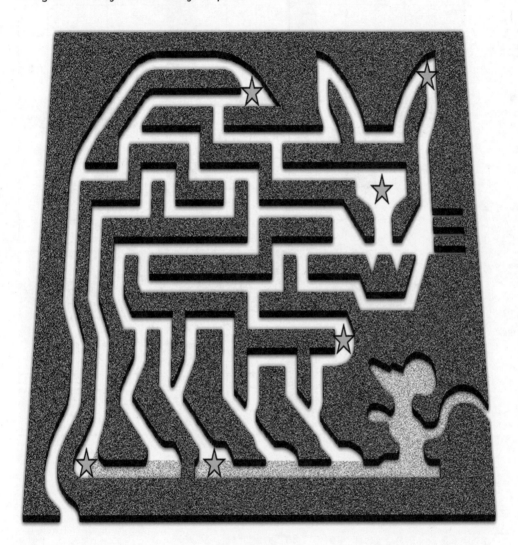

THREE AT A RHYME

Rearrange these letters to form three one-syllable words that rhyme.

A A A B D D D E G H R R R U

_____ _____ _____

★★ Snack-Time Pairs by Fred Piscop

ACROSS

1 Basketball position
6 Jazz genre
9 Chocolate substitute
14 Ear or tube preceder
15 Big brute
16 State one's view
17 Slight trace
18 Court do-over
19 *Philadelphia* or *Chicago*
20 British snack pair
23 Altar avowal
24 Wall St. debut
25 Chess piece
28 Sly sort
31 Stir up
36 Lawyers' org.
37 Conical home
39 Corday's victim
40 Mid-morning snack pair
43 Civil-rights leader Medgar
44 Go online
45 __ Jeanne d'Arc
46 Add a star to, perhaps
48 Court divider
49 *Mask* star
50 Dove sound
52 Roofer's need
54 After-school snack pair
62 Theater awards
63 Wall Street index, with "the"
64 Mullah's faith
66 Tubular pasta
67 Preceding period
68 Señor's squiggle
69 Leaves in, editorially
70 Embarrassed
71 Useful quality

DOWN

1 "Scoot!"
2 Condo division
3 Comic Meara
4 Take back
5 Intense fear
6 Lacking tread
7 Crude cartel
8 __ dish (lab item)
9 Average Joe
10 Each, informally
11 Tear apart
12 "Don't bet __!"
13 Nectar collectors
21 Free

22 AP counterpart
25 Expectant dad, perhaps
26 Superior to
27 Thin cookie
29 October birthstone
30 Inert gas
32 Preserve, in a way
33 From Waterford
34 Take a sip of
35 Old anesthetic
37 Precedent setters
38 Upper hand
41 Lobster __ Diavolo
42 "Same here!"

47 Very long time
49 Emergency situation
51 More off-the-wall
53 Japanese dog
54 Unruly hairdos
55 "Yeah, right!"
56 It's one-dimensional
57 *Daily Planet* reporter
58 Place to moor
59 Was in the red
60 Pipe bends
61 Marquis de __
65 Bumped into

★★ Hyper-Sudoku

Fill in the blank boxes so that every row, column, 3x3 box, *and* each of the four 3x3 gray regions contains all of the numbers 1 to 9.

						2		4
	8	4		3		5		7
		7						
	6		3					
			6		7	4		2
7								
			1	2		6		
	4		9					8
9		8				1	5	

MIXAGRAMS

Each line contains a five-letter word and a four-letter word that have been mixed together (the order of the letters in each word has not been changed). Unmix the two words on each line and write them in the spaces provided. When you're done, find a two-part answer to the clue by reading down the letter columns in the answers.

CLUE: King-size alternative

G A S T R O B O D = _ _ _ _ _ + _ _ _ _

A W A P I K E K E = _ _ _ _ _ + _ _ _ _

L A P I L U D O T = _ _ _ _ _ + _ _ _ _

S E V E N I P E S = _ _ _ _ _ + _ _ _ _

★★ ABC

Enter the letters A, B, and C into the diagram so that each row and column has exactly one A, one B, and one C. The letters outside the diagram indicate the first letter encountered, moving in the direction of the arrow. Keep in mind that after all the letters have been filled in, there will be two blank boxes in each row and column.

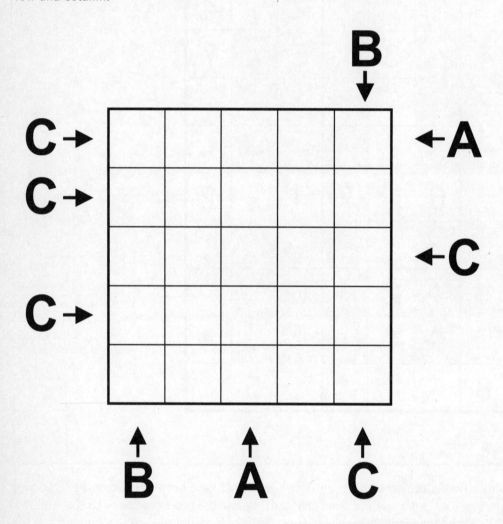

NATIONAL TREASURE

Using the letters in ETHIOPIA, we were able to form only one common uncapitalized five-letter word. Can you find it?

— — — — —

★★ Thievery by Daniel R. Stark

ACROSS

1 Cat's foot
4 Pong maker
9 Thumbs (through)
14 Wanted-poster letters
15 Pushed, as a raft
16 Banish
17 Strike obliquely
19 Put on airs
20 Kroft of *60 Minutes*
21 Type of computer
23 Simplicity
24 Gives off steam
26 Timber wolf
29 Beginning
31 __-de-sac
32 Like some knife edges
36 Lap dogs
38 Makes happy
39 Texas city
41 Buoy up
42 Food for whales
43 Have a cold
44 Glossy fabrics
47 Take it easy
49 Mockery
50 "The __ the merrier!"
54 Ploy
56 Nuclear reactors
57 Microscopic swimmer
59 Skier's need
62 Began a poker hand
63 Conversation starter
64 Engage in rivalry
65 Gawks at
66 Ran in neutral
67 Cousteau's summer

DOWN

1 Behind the times
2 Japanese hunting dog
3 Walks through water
4 Church alcove
5 Drag along
6 Foreman foe
7 Wrote back
8 High standards
9 __ we forget
10 Pay tribute to
11 Turbulence cause
12 Winter complaint
13 Tennis-match part
18 *The Three Faces of* __
22 Tire pressure meas.
24 __ noire
25 Rightmost column
27 Good, in Guatemala
28 Johnson's vaudeville partner
29 Neon and nitrogen
30 Whirls
32 Pickle serving
33 J.R.'s mama
34 Super bargain
35 Squeal (on)
37 Forest grazer
39 First Obi-Wan portrayer
40 Cause of distress
42 Sitting on a stool, perhaps
45 P.M.
46 Martial art
48 Postpone, as a bill
50 Wire measure
51 Martini extra
52 Tailoring job
53 Rival of Helena
55 Cool dudes
56 Jab at
57 Big flap
58 Tilly or Ryan
60 Completely
61 Spot in the Seine

★★ Wheels and Cogs

When the rugby player turns the handle on the cog, toward which ball will the pointer move?

BETWEENER

What four-letter word belongs between the word at left and the word at right, so that the first and second word, and the second and third word, each form a common two-word phrase?

SPARE _ _ _ _ BEING

★★ Find the Ships

Determine the position of the 10 ships listed to the right of the diagram. The ships may be oriented either horizontally or vertically. A square with wavy lines indicates water and will not contain a ship. The numbers at the edge of the diagram indicate how many squares in that row or column contain parts of ships. When all 10 ships are correctly placed in the diagram, no two of them will touch each other, not even diagonally.

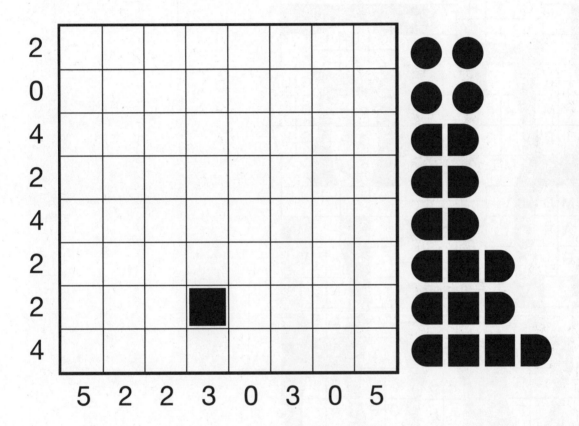

TWO-BY-FOUR

The eight letters in the word TELETHON can be rearranged to form a pair of common four-letter words in only one way. Can you find the two words?

___ ___ ___ ___   ___ ___ ___ ___

★★ Triad Split Decisions

In this clueless crossword puzzle, each answer consists of two words whose spellings are the same, except for the consecutive letters given. All answers are common words; no phrases or hyphenated or capitalized words are used. Some of the clues may have more than one solution, but there is only one word pair that will correctly link up with all the other word pairs.

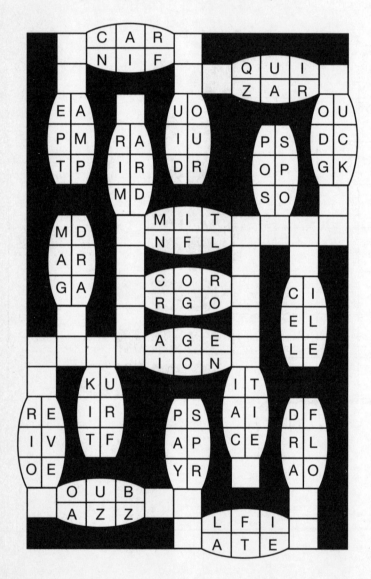

TRANSDELETION

Delete one letter from the word LEPRECHAUN and rearrange the rest, to get a word that means "big."

_____

★★ Get Out by Fred Piscop

ACROSS

1 "For __ sake!"
6 Handles clumsily
10 Rum cake
14 March 17 marchers
15 Lone Star State sch.
16 Battery fluid
17 Michelangelo masterpiece
18 Nasty look
19 Trawler's gear
20 Brunch fare
23 General on Chinese menus
24 "So's __ old man!"
25 Drop, as pounds
28 Tax-law expert
31 Blubbered
36 Volcano spew
37 Fast Amtrak train
39 Cable installer
40 Arcade attraction
43 Show the ropes to
44 Belgrade natives
45 Contend
46 Like most bar snacks
48 Aussie hopper
49 Crystal-ball consulter
50 Figs.
52 Bus. directors
54 Ditzes
61 "We're in trouble!"
63 Singer Braxton
64 Military data, for short
65 Sponge opening
66 Cupid alias
67 La __ (Milan opera house)
68 Seethe
69 Cubicle item
70 Brit's boob tube

DOWN

1 Domino spots
2 Norse navigator
3 Stadium section
4 Ritzy spread
5 Hoaxes
6 Door-handle sign
7 Suit to __
8 Like neglected lawns
9 Shoppers' binges
10 Backfire sound
11 Air heroes
12 Took the bait
13 Billboard messages
21 Italian bowling
22 Dogs' warnings
25 Cobblers' forms
26 Milo of *The Verdict*
27 Sailing hazard
29 Pigs' digs
30 *Luck and Pluck* author
32 Cartoonist Keane
33 Alla __ (music term)
34 Like Poe works
35 Salon appliance
37 Parthenon goddess
38 Farming word form
41 World Series mo.
42 *Enola Gay* load
47 Like some lines
49 Batter's position
51 Keep for later
53 Mill input
54 Needing liniment
55 Enjoy gum
56 Son of Seth
57 Wager
58 Emphatic type: Abbr.
59 Dudley Do-Right's love
60 Do in
61 FedEx rival
62 On a roll

★★ 123

Fill in the diagram so that each rectangular piece has one each of the numbers 1, 2, and 3, under these rules: 1) No two adjacent squares, horizontally or vertically, can have the same number. 2) Each completed row and column of the diagram will have an equal number of 1s, 2s, and 3s.

SUDOKU SUM

Without repeating any digits, complete the sum at right, by filling one digit in each of the five blanks.

```
    5  1  9
+   _  _  _
─────────────
 _  2  _
```

★★ Fences

Connect the dots with vertical or horizontal lines, so that a single loop is formed with no crossings or branches. Each number indicates how many lines surround it; squares with no number may be surrounded by any number of lines.

```
3 3               2
1       0 3 1     2
2     3     3
                0 2
3 3
        1     3   2
3     2 1 1       2
3             1 2
```

ADDITION SWITCH

Switch the positions of two of the digits in the incorrect sum at right, to get a correct sum.

```
  4 9 2
+ 5 1 8
-------
  7 1 3
```

★★ Join the Club by Daniel R. Stark

ACROSS

1 Bad actor
4 Sir, in India
9 Military student
14 Presidential nickname
15 Ouzo flavoring
16 Whirlpool competitor
17 Large glass alcove
19 Nash output
20 Just right
21 Complain about
23 Danson and Kennedy
24 Trunk contents
26 Complacent
29 Stiff straw hats
31 __ whim
32 Get cozy
36 Heaps kudos on
38 Vague discomfort
39 Get going
41 Skips past
42 Baseball feature
43 Countdown number
44 Writers on glass
47 Margin
49 Hold the floor
50 Bouquet holder
54 Hair dryer
56 Pulitzer poet Conrad
57 Expect
59 Gum flavor
62 Saguaros
63 Short-winded
64 Swimming-pool tester
65 Little kids
66 Ginger cookies
67 Be off base

DOWN

1 Regular routine
2 Dwelling
3 Asked for milk, like a young 35 Down
4 Wind catcher
5 Actress Jillian
6 Kept under wraps
7 Pinpoint
8 Word of warning
9 Collapse, with "in"
10 Sermon enders
11 New Hampshire school
12 USNA grad
13 Menlo Park monogram
18 Did exist
22 Cousteau's domain
24 Heirs, often
25 Stride
27 Not deserved
28 Shocked reactions
29 Oregon Trail town
30 Wooden strips
32 Chew the scenery
33 Put the finger on
34 Woman's shoe
35 Household leaper
37 Fly-ball path
39 Dele canceler
40 Get tuckered out
42 Improve, as skills
45 Wrecker's job
46 Wave heights
48 Upper-crust
50 Spirit
51 "Go fly __!"
52 Sir, in Seville
53 Put in a log
55 Singer Redding
56 Warmonger of myth
57 Circus routine
58 Customary manner
60 Geologic division
61 African viper

★★ Go With the Flow

Enter the maze at top right, pass through all the yellow circles exactly once, and then exit at bottom left. You must go with the flow, making no sharp turns, and you may use paths more than once.

SAY IT AGAIN

What five-letter word meaning "to shut," when pronounced differently, is also an adjective meaning "near"?

— — — — —

bRaIn BReAtHer
OUT-OF-THIS-WORLD WAYS TO COOK WITH O.J.

Orange juice may be the breakfast beverage of champions, but it has many more culinary uses than you may realize. Try it in one of the ingenious meal solutions and pick-me-ups below and you'll never look at the citrus fruit the same way again!

To stir up a fast and fabulous vinaigrette, whisk together 1/4 cup fresh orange juice, 1 teaspoon grated orange zest, 1 tablespoon fresh lemon juice, 1/2 teaspoon Dijon mustard, and 1/2 teaspoon salt. Gradually whisk in 1/2 cup fruity olive oil. Excellent on spinach salads.

For an herb-scented Bundt cake, add chopped fresh rosemary, fresh orange juice, and grated orange zest to the batter. Replacing half of the recipe's butter with olive oil also adds to the fruity flavor.

To freshen up spaghetti sauce, squeeze in the juice from one to two oranges.

To make a refreshing brine for fish, in a large bowl, combine 2 cups fresh orange juice, 2 tablespoons fennel seeds, 2 tablespoons sugar, 3 tablespoons kosher salt, and 1/2 teaspoon freshly ground black pepper. Add thick fish steaks or fillets and refrigerate for up to two hours. Remove from the brine and grill, broil, or pan-fry fish.

To give steamed rice an uplifting aroma, add 1/4 cup fresh orange juice to the cooking water.

For a surprisingly delicious chicken marinade, grate the zest and squeeze the juice from 1 lime and 1 lemon into a large zipper-lock bag. Stir in 1 can (6 ounces) thawed orange juice concentrate, 1/2 cup tomato sauce, 2 minced garlic cloves, 1 teaspoon dried Italian seasoning, and 1/2 teaspoon hot-pepper sauce. Drop in 2 pounds boneless chicken parts and marinate in the refrigerator for four to eight hours. Grill or broil the chicken and serve with a prepared salsa.

For a quick, creamy orange smoothie, combine orange-tangerine juice, vanilla ice cream, vanilla extract, and orange sherbet in blender. Process until smooth.

For a new twist on tapioca pudding, In a medium saucepan, combine 2 cups fresh orange juice, 1/3 cup sugar, 3 tablespoons quick-cooking tapioca, and a pinch of salt. Let stand for 5 minutes. Bring to a boil over medium heat, stirring constantly. Remove from the heat and cool for 20 minutes. The pudding will thicken as it cools. Stir until smooth and serve warm or chilled.

★★ Coin Boxes

Find the 20 monetary units of the world (past and present) that are arranged in various box shapes in the diagram. One answer is shown to get you started.

```
B A T K U C W O E R R I S C B
T H G A N P Q Y E I L A F O B
V B M C C E F D I R K K I R J
K L I D T N V M A H A X N T E
H A R D A F H D J A L F D P E
Y R P E R U F V A V N V M O S
A L E S P F H U T J A Q P E U
I F T A R E R J D S H I L D K
A E P U G D A F D G N I L R A
E U Y R U A L H D R J F D D N
O R B I V S I Q M A A H T A E
Y U R R J F A J V N C M A L D
H D O Q I F D I D A S H E O Q
H L L D A F E M H J L E K S T
L A R R N W Q O P F D K L A J
```

BAHT
BIRR
CENT
DALASI
DIME
DIRHAM
DOLLAR
DRAM
EURO
FORINT
KUNA
LIRA
~~PESETA~~
PESO
RAND
RIAL
SHEKEL
SHILLING
TALA
VATU

WHO'S WHAT WHERE?

The correct term for a resident of Oslo, Norway, is:

A) Oslite

B) Oslovian

C) Oslani

D) Osalian

★★ Hyper-Sudoku

Fill in the blank boxes so that every row, column, 3x3 box, *and* each of the four 3x3 gray regions contains all of the numbers 1 to 9.

		5	2			3		4	
4		3	1			9	6		
8							5		
	7			8	2	5	4		
	2		3						9
	9	4				2			
7		8							4

MIXAGRAMS

Each line contains a five-letter word and a four-letter word that have been mixed together (the order of the letters in each word has not been changed). Unmix the two words on each line and write them in the spaces provided. When you're done, find a two-part answer to the clue by reading down the letter columns in the answers.

CLUE: Redundant dog

C A N T A S I C H = _ _ _ _ _ + _ _ _ _

S H A W I S T H E = _ _ _ _ _ + _ _ _ _

O R A D I N Y O X = _ _ _ _ _ + _ _ _ _

W A L H E L O W N = _ _ _ _ _ + _ _ _ _

★★★ By Degrees by Doug Peterson

ACROSS

1 Shredded side dish
5 Actress Penélope
9 Brook dweller
14 Simpson sibling
15 Gardener's coil
16 Zing
17 European peaks
18 All tucked in
19 To a great degree
20 Cornflower
23 Miss __ (Clue suspect)
24 Novelist Harper
25 Frequently, in verse
26 Ft. Worth school
28 Bit of rain
32 Translator's obstacle
35 *Butterfield 8* author
37 Lateral lead-in
38 Painting used to promote gramophones
41 Popular ISP
42 Dapper
43 Dogpatch name
44 Lacking color
46 Feathery scarf
47 Martians, e.g.
48 Durocher of baseball
50 Bison habitat
54 How prescriptions are taken
59 Han River city
60 *The Grapes of Wrath* name
61 "Let's leave __ that"
62 Much, slangily
63 Up to the task
64 "Rule, Britannia" composer
65 First sign
66 Schools of thought
67 Roulette bet

DOWN

1 Hefty slices
2 Pastel shade
3 Animal lovers' org.
4 Spot with sinks
5 Swiss home
6 Sci-fi machine
7 Manipulator
8 Canadian finales
9 Brimless hat
10 Beat handily
11 Leave out
12 As far as
13 Not now
21 *Dharma & Greg* star
22 Fuzzy images
26 Greek letter
27 Roger in *North by Northwest*
29 Botch
30 First word of "The Raven"
31 Spot for docking
32 "If __ a Hammer"
33 "New Look" designer
34 Cuba, to Carlos
35 Grid great Graham
36 Incarnation
39 Clunky shoe
40 Arrowhead material
45 Woman's top
47 Whittles away
49 Brilliance
50 Sacred song
51 Back in vogue
52 Tabriz resident
53 Organic compound
54 Cold capital
55 Gas in a sign
56 Finishes a "j"
57 City near Santa Barbara
58 Filches

★★ One-Way Streets

The diagram represents a pattern of streets. P's are parking spaces, and the black squares are stores. Find the route that starts at a parking space, passes through all stores exactly once, and ends at the other parking space. Arrows indicate one-way traffic for that block only. No block or intersection may be entered more than once.

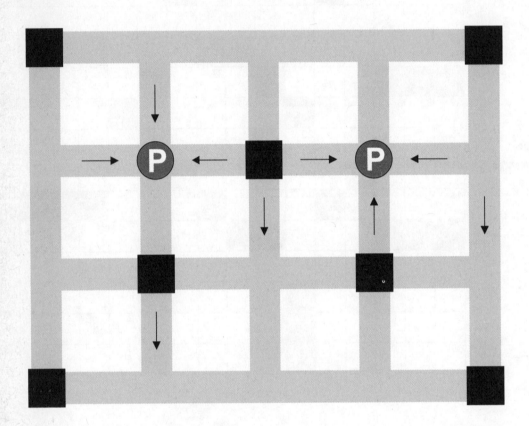

SOUND THINKING

What is the only common uncapitalized word whose only consonant sounds are R, S, and W, in that order?

_____

★★ Star Search

Find the stars that are hidden in some of the blank squares. The numbered squares indicate how many stars are hidden in the squares adjacent to them (including diagonally). There is never more than one star in any square.

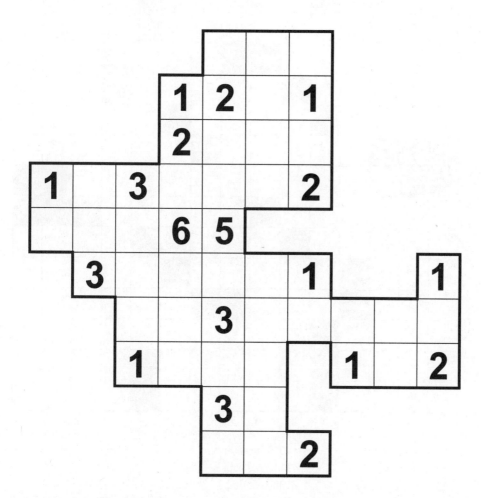

TELEPHONE TRIOS

Using the numbers and letters on a standard telephone, what three seven-letter words or phrases from the same category can be formed from these telephone numbers?

227-2663   _ _ _ _ _ _ _

744-7688   _ _ _ _ _ _ _

826-6673   _ _ _ _ _ _ _

★★★ Musical Notes by Adam Cohen

ACROSS

1 Colorful Apple
5 Quarterback Brett
10 They may be liberal
14 "__ know my ABC's ..."
15 "Are you in __?"
16 Sudden pull
17 "Ring of Fire" singer
19 Neuter
20 Bring out
21 Chinese dynasty
23 K-O connectors
24 Church cup
25 Bell town of fiction
27 "Am __ brother's keeper?"
28 Anecdote filler
29 "Immediately!" in the E.R.
30 More amiable
32 Bumppo of fiction
34 George in *Knute Rockne, All American*
35 "Quarter to Three" singer
37 Part of payments at the pump
39 "Ain't neither!" reply
40 Up and about
41 Fed. lending agency
42 Cheers for a torero
46 USPS delivery
47 Make __ (strike it rich)
49 Right, in Rouen
50 *Love Story* composer
51 Business card abbr.
52 Linking verb
53 "__ kleine Nachtmusik"
55 "Baby Hold On" singer
58 Associations: Abbr.
59 Citizen rival
60 Pointed arch

61 Noun suffix
62 Boundaries
63 "__ me your ears"

DOWN

1 Introduce arbitrarily
2 Half the theme of this puzzle
3 Not briefly
4 The Queen City
5 Four-time Indy 500 victor
6 Rainbow shape
7 Intl. radio service
8 Charge towards
9 Uma's ex

10 5 Down et al.
11 Close copies
12 Restrain
13 Lynyrd __ (rock band)
18 Reject
22 Repetitive negative
25 Unalaska neighbor
26 Hotel chain with a sunburst logo
29 River of Hades
31 Natatorium
33 Biblical landing site
34 *Godfather* composer
35 Violin parts
36 Real estate listing abbr.

37 Spanish Armada craft
38 Dancing legend
41 Made overly ornate
43 Place for cocktails
44 Brennan of *Private Benjamin*
45 Didn't leave
48 Attorney General before Thornburgh
49 __ Pérignon
52 Bus. leaders
54 Slalom course shape
56 Understand, to hipsters
57 '50s campaign-button name

★★★ Sets of Three

Group all the symbols into sets of three, with each set having either all the same shape or all the same color. The symbols in each set must all be connected to each other by a common horizontal or vertical side.

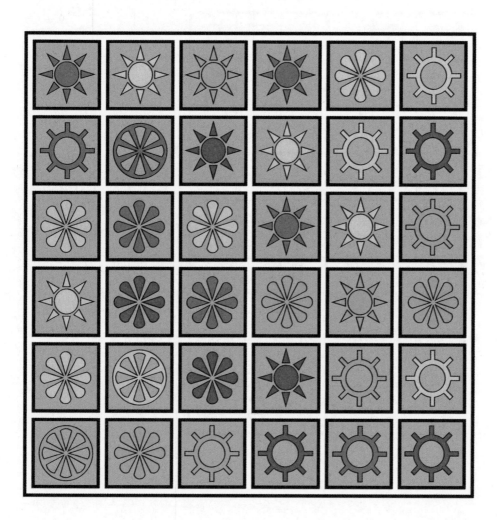

THREE AT A RHYME

Rearrange these letters to form three one-syllable words that rhyme.

B E G H H I I L T Y

_____   _____   _____

★★ Sudoku

Fill in the blank boxes so that every row, column, and 3x3 box contains all of the numbers 1 to 9.

1	7			6			5	3
8			4		5			1
		3	1		8	9		
		8				6		
		7	3		6	1		
3			8		9			2
4	8			1			6	7

COUNT UP

Inserting plus signs and minus signs, as many as necessary, in between the digits from 1 to 9 below, create a series of additions and subtractions whose final answer is 44. Any digits without a sign between them are to be grouped together as a single number.

1 2 3 4 5 6 7 8 9 = 44

★★★ Hard Stuff by Fred Piscop

ACROSS

1 Goalie's wear
5 Music-video cable station
9 Necklace fastener
14 Condo division
15 October birthstone
16 Puts a spell on
17 Hard-hit baseball
19 Florida Keys, e.g.
20 Take the tiller
21 Move to a MASH, maybe
23 Superlative suffix
24 Winter-hat parts
27 __ May Clampett
29 Hard puzzle
34 Bill picturing Cleveland
38 Jeansmaker Strauss
39 Bring in
40 Bench-clearer
43 Go sprawling
44 Iranian money
45 Not permanent, as ink
47 Hard form of lava
51 Fuss over, with "on"
52 Cold dessert
57 Politico Landon
60 Blowgun missile
62 Tractor maker
63 Porcupine's spine
65 Hard still product
68 Excessive
69 Leer at
70 Not "fer"
71 Molecule's makeup
72 Zip
73 Hive hummers

DOWN

1 Vital beat
2 Baker or Loos
3 Roadside eatery
4 Mill product
5 FYI part
6 News org.
7 Bullpen stat
8 TV nightly news hour
9 Gum base
10 Guitarist __ Paul
11 Wheel holder
12 Takes a gander at
13 "Hey, you!"
18 Olive __ (military uniform)
22 Cockpit fig.
25 British buggy
26 Of sound mind
28 1945 summit site
30 Do-nothing
31 Belgrade native
32 Diabolical
33 Auspicious, as time
34 Garr or Hatcher
35 Reagan Secretary of State
36 Algerian port
37 Lacking guidance
41 Love god
42 Unit-pricing word
46 Depot postings, informally
48 Lots and lots
49 Actress Hagen
50 Sunday delivery
53 Get-well spot, for short
54 Hosiery hue
55 Baseball great Banks
56 Many mall rats
57 Bluish green
58 Fontanne's partner
59 Generic pooch
61 Forum garb
64 Abner's radio partner
66 Moth-eaten
67 Teachers' org.

★★ Split Decisions

In this clueless crossword puzzle, each answer consists of two words whose spellings are the same, except for the consecutive letters given. All answers are common words; no phrases or hyphenated or capitalized words are used. Some of the clues may have more than one solution, but there is only one word pair that will correctly link up with all the other word pairs.

TRANSDELETION

Delete one letter from the word ARTICHOKES and rearrange the rest, to get a two-word term for something an athlete might wear.

_____

★★ Number-Out

Shade squares so that no number appears in any row or column more than once. Shaded squares may not touch each other horizontally or vertically, and all unshaded squares must form a single continuous area.

2	1	4	6	2	5
1	3	3	3	4	2
3	2	6	5	6	1
1	4	6	3	3	3
5	6	6	3	1	2
1	5	2	1	1	3

OPPOSITE ATTRACTION

Unscramble the letters in the phrase LEASE TURF to form two common words that are opposites of each other.

_____   _____

★★★ Spelling Bees by Doug Peterson

ACROSS

1 Skewed view
5 Pillowy
9 Like a rainbow
14 Together, musically
15 Six-sided state
16 Casals' instrument
17 Quaint stopover
20 Reebok rival
21 Debussy's sea
22 Caustic solutions
23 Chief Norse god
25 Scruff
27 *The Big Sleep* costars
33 Pickle holder
34 Italian wine center
35 Dogcatcher's quarry
36 "Don't dawdle!"
38 El Paso's home
41 Autograph
42 Concern for Keats
44 Actress Raines
46 Census datum
47 Livelihood
51 Minstrel's instrument
52 Taj Mahal site
53 Hamlet opener
56 Egg cells
58 Going public with
62 "Greatest show" twosome
65 B.B. King's genre
66 Copenhagen citizen
67 Lawyer employer
68 Baseballer Pee Wee
69 Not much
70 G-men

DOWN

1 Ali __
2 Picked from a lineup
3 Imported auto
4 Old salt
5 Most foamy
6 Gambling site, briefly
7 *Green Acres* locale
8 Last words, often
9 Comics cry
10 Thinks quietly
11 Sculpting medium
12 If that fails
13 Things kids connect
18 Gymnast Comaneci
19 Saudi, for one
24 NBA great Thurmond
26 Family men
27 More dishonorable
28 Make a speech
29 Put the kibosh on
30 Crop up
31 Tavern selection
32 Short-tailed cat
33 Doorway part
37 Nutty confections
39 Jessica of *Fantastic Four*
40 Lazybones
43 University URL ender
45 Skylit courtyards
48 Unit of matter
49 15 Across neighbor
50 Import fee
53 Shortened wd.
54 Racer Yarborough
55 In alignment
57 Med. school study
59 "Would __ to you?"
60 Uncool one
61 Workout locations
63 Function
64 Something inherited

★★ ABC

Enter the letters A, B, and C into the diagram so that each row and column has exactly one A, one B, and one C. The letters outside the diagram indicate the first letter encountered, moving in the direction of the arrow. Keep in mind that after all the letters have been filled in, there will be two blank boxes in each row and column.

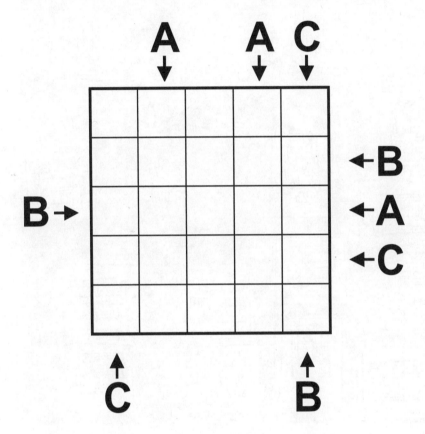

CLUELESS CROSSWORD

Complete the crossword with common uncapitalized seven-letter words, based entirely on the letters already filled in for you.

★★ Set In Stone

To unlock the jewel, which of the numbered stone tablets fits into each of the slots?

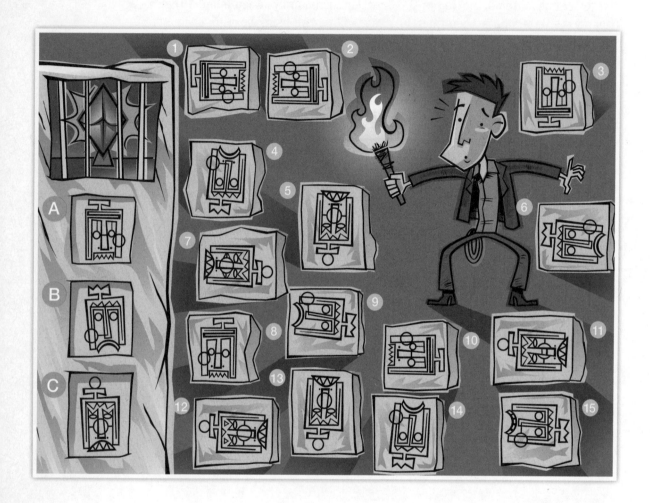

BETWEENER

What four-letter word belongs between the word at left and the word at right, so that the first and second word, and the second and third word, each form a common two-word phrase?

REST __ __ __ __ CHAIR

★★★ Line Drawing

Draw two straight lines, each from one edge of the square to another edge, so that the words in each region have something in common.

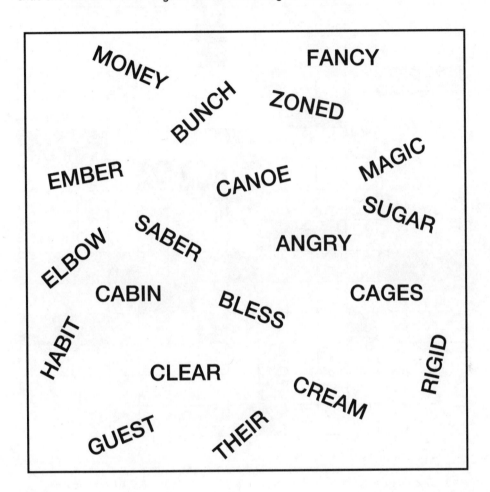

THREE OF A KIND

Find the three hidden words in the sentence that, read in order, go together in some way.

The mystery novel's hero may be strong,
but the outlaw is hesitant.

★★★ Digital Display by Adam Cohen

ACROSS

1 *Same Time, Next Year* actor
9 After the fact
15 Water-ski alternative
16 "Anybody there?"
17 Barnum star
18 Still around
19 HST beat him in '48
20 Janis' comics husband
22 Actress Charlotte
23 Indiana city
26 Onetime library catalog need
28 Unclose, poetically
29 ___ *for Space* (Bradbury book)
31 Zeno's classroom
32 Pullman, for one
35 Gretchen on *Benson*
39 Moderate
43 *Born Free* feline
44 Fall down
45 Mild oath
49 Opposite of paleo-
50 Microbrewery product
51 Burger topper, perhaps
55 Tom Sawyer affirmative
56 Letters from the post office?
57 Musical postscript
58 ___ rule
60 *Lost Horizon* star
62 '50s TV host
67 Less than confident
68 Contractor's offering
69 Blush or flush
70 Admission in court?

DOWN

1 Fitting
2 Vientiane native
3 Law's long feature
4 Dressed to the nines
5 His racket is in the Smithsonian
6 Hail
7 Slow-witted
8 Composer Berg
9 Lace place
10 Hugs and kisses, symbolically
11 Something to sweeten
12 *Butterfield 8* author
13 Kin of echolocation
14 Carried along
21 Hwys.
23 "I have no idea!"
24 Arbor Day month
25 Enjoys a novel
26 Aoki of golf
27 Largest African city
29 NBC premiere of 1975
30 Rocks at a bar
33 Where Moscow is
34 1960s NY senator
36 Variable stars
37 Highlanders
38 Legally germane
40 Mao's successor
41 Laugh syllable
42 "Telephone Line" group
46 Pack, in a way
47 Ameche's *Cocoon* costar
48 *Teletubbies* fan
51 Come to mind
52 Opposite of everybody
53 Was in neutral
54 Massage targets
55 "I did it!"
58 Architectural pier
59 Variety-show segment
61 Steaming
63 Occupational ending
64 Where white coats are worn
65 Info from the cockpit
66 Cannon conclusion

★★ Find the Ships

Determine the position of the 10 ships listed to the right of the diagram. The ships may be oriented either horizontally or vertically. A square with wavy lines indicates water and will not contain a ship. The numbers at the edge of the diagram indicate how many squares in that row or column contain parts of ships. When all 10 ships are correctly placed in the diagram, no two of them will touch each other, not even diagonally.

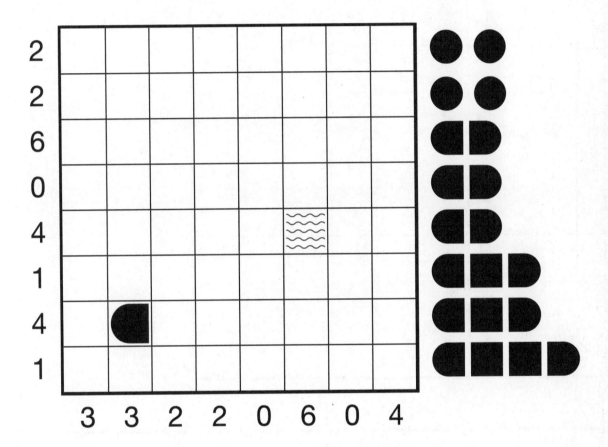

TWO-BY-FOUR

The eight letters in the word PURVEYOR can be rearranged to form a pair of common four-letter words in only one way. Can you find the two words?

— — — —   — — — —

★★★ Hyper-Sudoku

Fill in the blank boxes so that every row, column, 3x3 box, *and* each of the four
3x3 gray regions contains all of the numbers 1 to 9.

		5						2
	4	5		7			3	9
1	9			2	8			
			1		5		9	7
5					9			
						4		
	5		4					
							8	
4	1	8						

MIXAGRAMS

Each line contains a five-letter word and a four-letter word that have been mixed together (the
order of the letters in each word has not been changed). Unmix the two words on each line and
write them in the spaces provided. When you're done, find a two-part answer to the clue by
reading down the letter columns in the answers.

CLUE: Pan letters

```
R O U G H O T O M  =  _ _ _ _ _  +  _ _ _ _
S T O A L A G A D  =  _ _ _ _ _  +  _ _ _ _
W R I S T A R I E  =  _ _ _ _ _  +  _ _ _ _
C H O V O W E L T  =  _ _ _ _ _  +  _ _ _ _
```

★★★ All Those In Favor ... by Doug Peterson

ACROSS

1 Verne's circumnavigator
5 Equinox month
10 Neighbor of Turkey
14 Furniture giant
15 Central Florida city
16 List of options
17 Klinger on *M*A*S*H*
18 Heavy volumes
19 Chess finale
20 Makeup case items
23 Anthem contraction
24 Without a date
25 Mass-transit alternative
28 Obstruct
31 Spin doctor
35 Colored
37 "__ clear day ..."
38 Speak highly of
39 Sitcom created by Sidney Sheldon
42 Pint-sized
43 Tease playfully
44 Sondheim title character
45 Lucy's landlady
46 Cavalry weapon
48 Marina del __, CA
49 Horse follower
51 Lisa Simpson's instrument
53 Words from Hamlet
60 Teutonic three
61 Country estate
62 Function
63 Runnin' Rebels' sch.
64 '50s Ford
65 Somewhat circular
66 Clinton opponent
67 Yorkshire city
68 Lucy Lawless TV role

DOWN

1 Military-band instrument
2 Approve
3 *Chicago* star
4 Reclusive actress
5 Recreational vehicle
6 "Don't have __, man!"
7 Interstate access
8 Monty Python member
9 Does not possess
10 ESL student, often
11 Concrete
12 Certain farm population
13 Canadian prov.
21 VCR button
22 *It Happened One Night* director
25 Easter Island owner
26 Sit in on
27 Pullman feature
29 Lennon's love
30 *The Metamorphosis* author
32 Trivial
33 Digression of a sort
34 Down-and-out
36 Spade or Marlowe
38 Stands for busts
40 Fifth word of the Koran
41 Three-sided sail
46 Take big steps
47 Stadium cry
50 Make merry
52 Ricoh rival
53 Ponte Vecchio site
54 Stadium cry
55 Alternatively
56 Winter toy
57 Wander around
58 __ Bator
59 Composer Bartók
60 Washout

★★★ Fences

Connect the dots with vertical or horizontal lines, so that a single loop is formed with no crossings or branches. Each number indicates how many lines surround it; squares with no number may be surrounded by any number of lines.

```
3       1 3       2
3 2           3 3
    3 1       2
1                   3
1                   2
    1       0 2
2 3               1 2
0       3 3       2
```

ADDITION SWITCH

Switch the positions of two of the digits in the incorrect sum at right, to get a correct sum.

```
  1 2 3
+ 8 5 6
-------
  7 0 9
```

★★★ Tri-Color Maze

Enter the maze at bottom right, pass through all the color squares exactly once, then exit, all without retracing your path. You must pass through the color squares in this sequence: red, blue, yellow, red, blue, etc.

SAY IT AGAIN

What five-letter word for a type of vehicle, when pronounced differently, is also the past tense of a verb?

— — — — —

★★ Number-Out

Shade squares so that no number appears in any row or column more than once. Shaded squares may not touch each other horizontally or vertically, and all unshaded squares must form a single continuous area.

1	2	4	2	5	4
3	2	3	6	1	4
4	1	3	4	2	4
1	5	3	4	6	3
6	4	2	4	3	6
5	6	6	1	4	2

OPPOSITE ATTRACTION

Unscramble the letters in the phrase POLO SCENE to form two common words that are opposites of each other.

_____   _____

★★★ Something Wick-ed by Patrick Jordan

ACROSS

1 Bus-schedule listing
5 "Ask away!"
10 Caesar's boast beginner
14 Surfer's surface
15 Flying monster of myth
16 Persian Gulf adjoiner
17 Logging camp tools
18 Austrian psychiatrist Alfred
19 Gentle touches
20 Item with a candle
23 "On the other hand ..."
24 Jots
28 Flowerless plants
32 Little
35 *Titanic* backdrop
36 Chromosome constituent
37 Dallas NBAer
38 Item with a candle
42 In the manner of
43 Many Christmas trees
44 Personnel manager, at times
45 Notable sort
48 Person from Pyongyang
49 CEO's aide
50 Wintertime utterance
51 Item with a candle
59 Generic dog
62 __ Ulysses Grant
63 Inkling
64 "Fine with me!"
65 Clued in
66 Odds' partners
67 Lapidary's inventory
68 Kitchen-floor installer
69 Hyphen cousin

DOWN

1 Mariner's mop
2 Something to hail
3 No longer bothered by
4 Nudnik
5 Sunglasses, slangily
6 Lit into
7 Paris airport
8 11-nation cartel
9 Supermodel Banks
10 MTV segments
11 The __ of Good Feeling
12 Seize
13 Mentality measures
21 "Laughing" beast
22 Tool set
25 Musical tone quality
26 Rhododendron relative
27 Great Britain's longest river
28 Quagmire
29 Mexican wildcat
30 Halvah ingredient
31 Minded the kids
32 Arctic explorer
33 Lodging locations
34 Badminton barrier
36 Crisscross pattern
39 Sci-fi spacecraft
40 Paw woe for Androcles' lion
41 It's about 78% nitrogen
46 Delights in
47 Plumed neckpiece
48 *Seinfeld* character
50 Strident sound
52 Online discussion
53 Fuzzy fruit
54 Like the Sabin vaccine
55 In a dead heat
56 *Show Boat* author Ferber
57 Warren Beatty film of '81
58 Humorous poet
59 Visibility hamperer
60 Mamie's man
61 Structure with a spillway

★★★ 123

Fill in the diagram so that each rectangular piece has one each of the numbers 1, 2, and 3, under these rules: 1) No two adjacent squares, horizontally or vertically, can have the same number. 2) Each completed row and column of the diagram will have an equal number of 1s, 2s, and 3s.

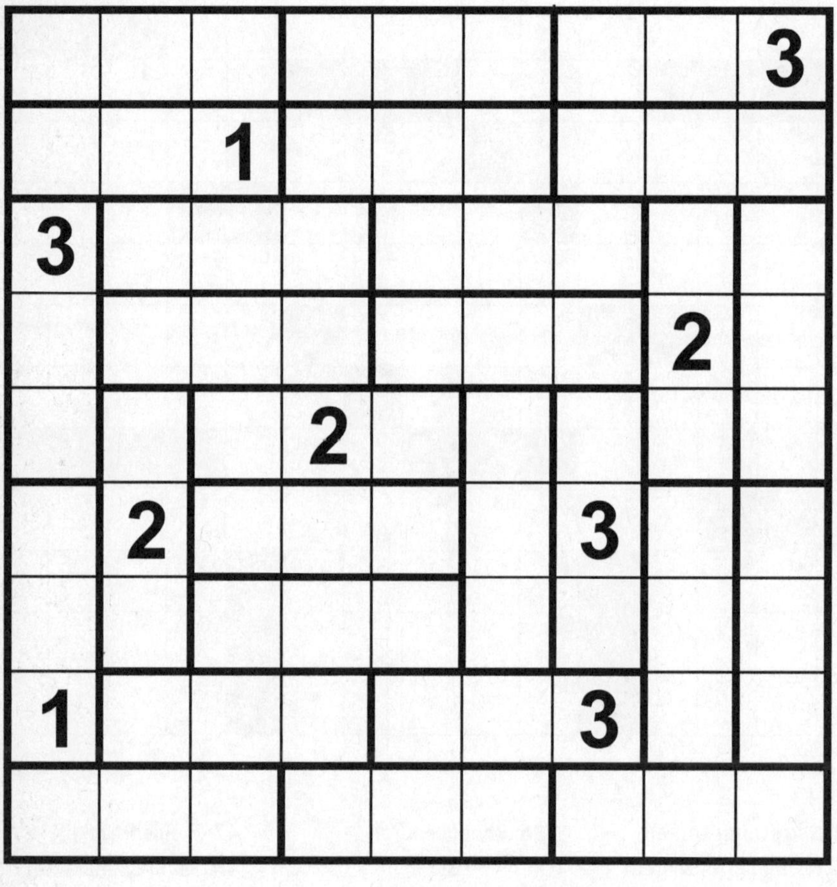

								3
		1						
3								
							2	
		2						
	2				3			
1					3			

SUDOKU SUM

Without repeating any digits, complete the sum at right, by filling one digit in each of the five blanks.

$$\begin{array}{r} \_\ 2\ \_ \\ +\ 7\ \_\ 9 \\ \hline \_\ \_\ 5 \end{array}$$

★★★ Find the Ships

Determine the position of the 10 ships listed to the right of the diagram. The ships may be oriented either horizontally or vertically. A square with wavy lines indicates water and will not contain a ship. The numbers at the edge of the diagram indicate how many squares in that row or column contain parts of ships. When all 10 ships are correctly placed in the diagram, no two of them will touch each other, not even diagonally.

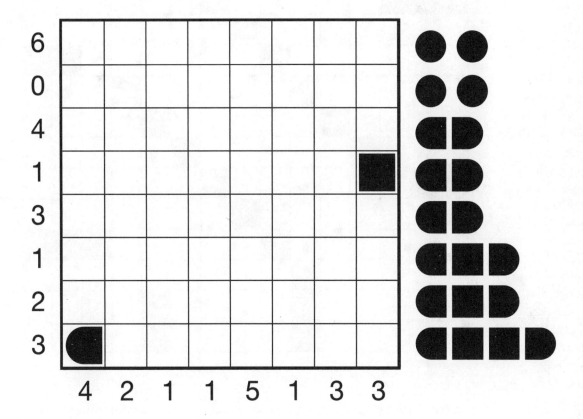

TWO-BY-FOUR

The eight letters in the word OUTVOTED can be rearranged to form a pair of common four-letter words in only one way. Can you find the two words?

— — — —   — — — —

★★★ I Love L.A. by Adam Cohen

ACROSS

1 Bivouac
5 Mag formerly titled *Modern Maturity*
9 __ *Shrugged* (Rand novel)
14 Most populous continent
15 Cognac letters
16 "Mule Train" singer
17 Tibetan dog
19 Bend in a river
20 Winter festivals
21 Dairy-case offering
22 Pillbox hat designer
25 Burnt
26 Freight unit
27 Singer Julius
28 Home Depot competitor
29 Prima __
30 __-di-dah
33 Variety of 21 Across
34 Law-school class
35 __-cake (kids' game)
36 Home of Dover AFB
37 Tours "Thank you"
38 Water craft
39 Secure
41 Summed (up)
42 Property recipient
44 Blixen's pen name
45 Easter parade headgear
46 Vacation goal, briefly
47 Home of a Biblical witch
48 Tomato
52 Greek marketplace
53 Tofu bean
54 "Hi, sailor!"
55 Gourmet mushroom
56 Pre-1992 map abbr.
57 World's longest river

DOWN

1 "Silent" president
2 Fireplace residue
3 Farrow of *Peyton Place*
4 Broadcast medium
5 Frequent Funicello costar
6 Colorado resort
7 Supremes lead singer
8 Health insurance grp.
9 Farewell song at a luau
10 Revenue collectors
11 Academic track
12 Win by __
13 Put in stitches
18 Mercury and Saturn
21 Rock of comedy
22 Like loose-leaf paper
23 Battery terminal
24 Abdul-Jabbar, formerly
25 Desert sights
27 Variety of pine
29 What dynes measure
31 __ *Grows in Brooklyn*
32 *The Creation* composer
34 Former CIA director
35 Barrie boy
37 Twenty Questions category
38 *On Golden Pond* star
40 Poe woman
41 Musical liability
42 At 90-degree angles, nautically
43 Start and end of "O Sole Mio"
44 Jones and Crockett
46 Some marsupials
48 Pelican State sch.
49 __ Beta Kappa
50 Chat-room chuckle
51 Hurricane center

★★★ Ship Spirals

The names of these historic ships are arranged in spirals in the diagram, either starting or finishing in the center, either clockwise or counterclockwise. Some of the spirals may overlap. One answer is shown to get you started.

```
Z T Z Y U A N M E R W
C E N D N G E C K R N
X U R E E I S A M I L
I O V A H G P D Y R E
E N D E F P R U I D V
C E U M Q C H R S C O
N A R A M N A I D L E
I P E S I I T S H S I
I I I L L D B W E F F
A D V D X A X C U T K
R E E R U R A R K T U
U T N P T I M A S Y C
Y R A O A L Y S T O T
U Q M R E W Q L M C Y
E E N A M O W O H K N
N O R Y F L A M B R I
I E M F L G Z E I A T
D N A I N M N Z N N A
S J Q A A H E J E R O
E G U I T X T A Y V N
U Y S D A I H B S I Y
U A I N A C T Q Y E S
L U L A R P A R E N R
V S I T K L K H W J E
L L I R F F S M H G R
H C H V B H A M D E U
U R C Q V R E P I N B
H Z T C K I H S A W B
A B G V J O O C J S J
```

ADVENTURE
AQUITANIA
BRITANNIA
CARPATHIA
CHRISTINA
CHURCHILL
CUTTY SARK
DISCOVERY
EDINBURGH
ENDEAVOUR
ENDURANCE
GNEISENAU
HAMPSHIRE
ITALY MARU
JERVIS BAY
LUSITANIA
~~MAYFLOWER~~
MERRIMACK
NEW JERSEY
NORMANDIE
QUEEN MARY
RAMILLIES
SHEFFIELD
STOCKHOLM

IN OTHER WORDS

There is only one common uncapitalized word that contains the consecutive letters IGP. What is it?

_____

★★★ Stagecoach Maze

Enter the maze at bottom, pass through all the stars exactly once, and then end at the setting sun, all without retracing your path.

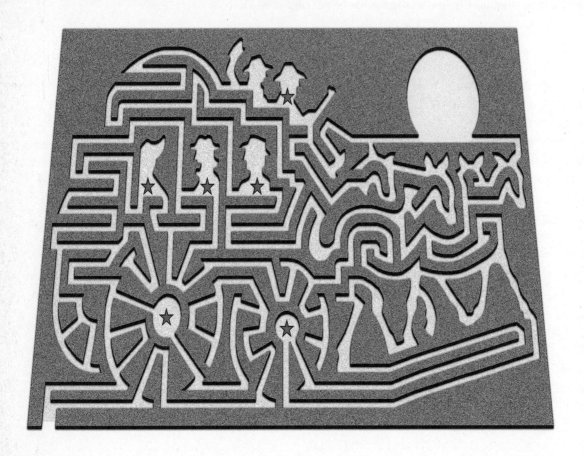

THREE AT A RHYME

Rearrange these letters to form three one-syllable words that rhyme.

A A A C D E E H I S S T T W

_____   _____   _____

★★★ Star Search

Find the stars that are hidden in some of the blank squares. The numbered squares indicate how many stars are hidden in the squares adjacent to them (including diagonally). There is never more than one star in any square.

	1	1	1	1				
						3	2	
1				4				
		1	4			2		3
1				3		2		
	2		3				2	
				1		3		
		1		1				
					1			

TELEPHONE TRIOS

1	ABC 2	DEF 3
GHI 4	JKL 5	MNO 6
PRS 7	TUV 8	WXY 9
*	0	#

Using the numbers and letters on a standard telephone, what three seven-letter words or phrases from the same category can be formed from these telephone numbers?

235-5478   _ _ _ _ _ _ _

378-6637   _ _ _ _ _ _ _

742-6478   _ _ _ _ _ _ _

★★★ Say What? by Doug Peterson

ACROSS

1 Cornfield noises
5 Zhivago's beloved
9 Minty drink
14 Minimally
15 Norwegian royal name
16 Computer of the '40s
17 Green gem
18 Verdi masterpiece
19 Roger the reviewer
20 Complete washout
23 '60s jacket style
24 Linger in the tub
25 18 Across solo
29 Compass reading
31 Straightens up
33 Churl
36 Imperturbable one
39 Brief fracas
40 Annual televised address
43 Comic-strip frame
44 Has a hunch
45 Flock member
46 Acid neutralizers
48 Java holder
50 Bard's adverb
51 Pet lovers' grp.
54 Caribbean island
58 "12 items or less" places
61 Windmill part
64 "What time __?"
65 Contends
66 Large-eyed primate
67 Zilch
68 Novel ending
69 Baseball-card giant
70 One of the *Brady Bunch* boys
71 For fear that

DOWN

1 Louisiana cuisine
2 Taper off
3 Loafer specification
4 Takes the tiller
5 Bakery purchase
6 Assumed name
7 Satellite medium
8 Himalayan hazard
9 Catcall
10 Without a loss
11 Golf position
12 Sense of pitch
13 Batting avg., e.g.

21 British philosopher/ mathematician
22 Guitar relative
26 Fix a loose lace
27 Following behind
28 Without dissent
30 WWII arena
32 Unsurprisingly
33 House broadcaster
34 Dickens title starter
35 Thanks, in Thuringia
37 Kids
38 Follower's suffix
41 Got misty

42 Source of shade
47 DSL offerer
49 Rough road surface
52 Labor activist Chavez
53 Out of the way
55 Bring together
56 Red veggies
57 Plus
59 Gen-__ (baby boomer's 37 Down)
60 Antlered animal
61 Diner order
62 Heavenly lion
63 Band booster

★★★ Sudoku

Fill in the blank boxes so that every row, column, and 3x3 box contains all of the numbers 1 to 9.

6		8		5				
						8		1
	5	2	8	3				
			2			7	6	
				4				
	4	5			9			
			8	3	5	9		
1		9						
				2		6		3

MIXAGRAMS

Each line contains a five-letter word and a four-letter word that have been mixed together (the order of the letters in each word has not been changed). Unmix the two words on each line and write them in the spaces provided. When you're done, find a two-part answer to the clue by reading down the letter columns in the answers.

CLUE: Wonder-ful period

S N O C E D E N T = _ _ _ _ _ + _ _ _ _

P A L A J I N A R = _ _ _ _ _ + _ _ _ _

B U D R O Y N E S = _ _ _ _ _ + _ _ _ _

U L N A F S T E D = _ _ _ _ _ + _ _ _ _

★★★ One-Way Streets

The diagram represents a pattern of streets. A and B are parking spaces, and the black squares are stores. Find the route that starts at A, passes through all stores exactly once, and ends at B. Arrows indicate one-way traffic for that block only. No block or intersection may be entered more than once.

SOUND THINKING

There are three common uncapitalized six-letter words whose only consonant sounds are N and Z, in that order. Two of them are IONIZE and ANNOYS. What's the other?

_____

★★★ ABC

Enter the letters A, B, and C into the diagram so that each row and column has exactly one A, one B, and one C. The letters outside the diagram indicate the first letter encountered, moving in the direction of the arrow. Keep in mind that after all the letters have been filled in, there will be two blank boxes in each row and column.

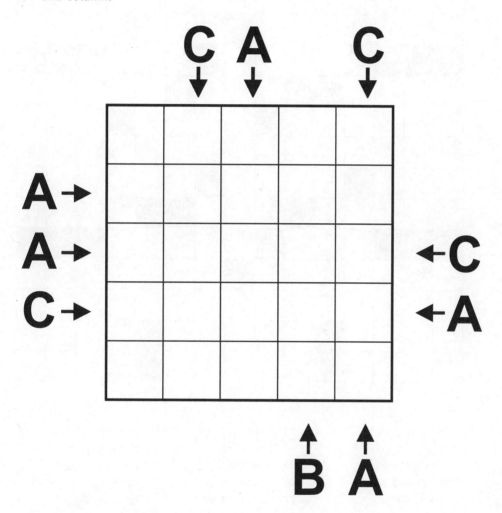

NATIONAL TREASURE

Using the letters in LITHUANIA, we were able to form five common uncapitalized five-letter words. Can you find them all?

— — — — —   — — — — —   — — — — —

— — — — —   — — — — —

★★★ Kid-Lit King by Doug Peterson

ACROSS

1 Aerial maneuver
5 Truckers, often
10 Frame of mind
14 Run smoothly
15 Charge towards
16 Beef-rating org.
17 Book by 23 Down
20 Withdrawn
21 Settles up in advance
22 Signed, as a lease
24 Hitter's stat
25 Ala. neighbor
28 Lacking liquid
30 Sorority letters
34 Geological periods
37 Final Four game
39 Cold-blooded crawler
40 Book by 23 Down
43 Phone-line abbr.
44 __ cheese dressing
45 Boxer's souvenir
46 Keep an __ (watch)
48 Payroll ID
50 Sandberg of Cooperstown
51 "Cool!"
53 Does a number
56 Holiday Inn actor
60 Competition
64 Story by 23 Down
66 Toledo's lake
67 Green blades
68 Finished, as a cake
69 Hangs loosely
70 Brief squabble
71 Advanced degs.

DOWN

1 Org. for women drivers
2 Family pronoun
3 Sweet sandwich
4 Voting sector
5 Sound from a floorboard
6 Sounded reveille
7 H.S. subject
8 Coarse tool
9 One of the Beatles
10 Tot's messy creation
11 Dept. of Labor branch
12 Jazz singer Anita
13 Stops up
18 Palindromic diarist
19 Milquetoast
23 Notable author/illustrator
25 Little laugh
26 Strong adhesive
27 Opposite of sur
29 Nay opposite
31 Brownish yellow
32 Pallid
33 Germ cell
35 Heavy sole fastener
36 NBC debut of '75
38 Muir or Miniver
41 Bucks and boars
42 No-frills takeoff site
47 Speaks at length
49 Most gracious
52 Least valuable part
54 Untrue
55 Veldt grazer
56 Assents at sea
57 Transfusion fluids
58 Math course
59 French 101 verb
61 Mark permanently
62 Winter toy
63 Bill and __ Excellent Adventure
65 Monopoly token

★★ Glass Act

Which of the reflections does the princess see in the mirror?

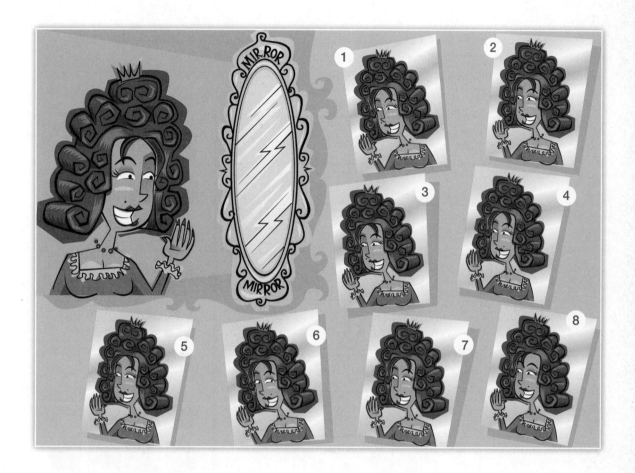

BETWEENER

What five-letter word belongs between the word at left and the word at right, so that the first and second word, and the second and third word, each form a common two-word phrase?

ROLE _ _ _ _ _ TRAIN

★★★ Find the Ships

Determine the position of the 10 ships listed to the right of the diagram. The ships may be oriented either horizontally or vertically. A square with wavy lines indicates water and will not contain a ship. The numbers at the edge of the diagram indicate how many squares in that row or column contain parts of ships. When all 10 ships are correctly placed in the diagram, no two of them will touch each other, not even diagonally.

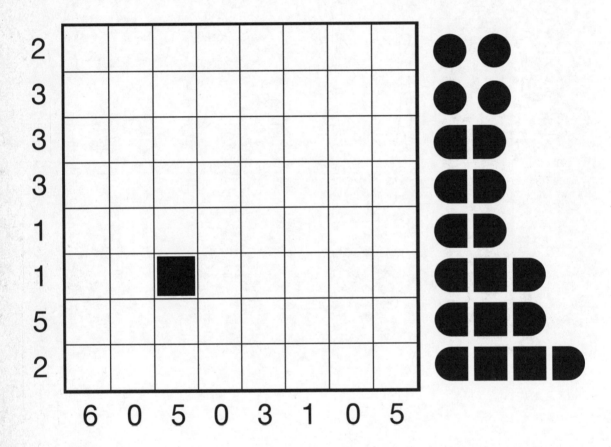

TWO-BY-FOUR

The eight letters in the word NARRATOR can be rearranged to form a pair of common four-letter words in only one way. Can you find the two words?

__ __ __ __   __ __ __ __

★★★ 123

Fill in the diagram so that each rectangular piece has one each of the numbers 1, 2, and 3, under these rules: 1) No two adjacent squares, horizontally or vertically, can have the same number. 2) Each completed row and column of the diagram will have an equal number of 1s, 2s, and 3s.

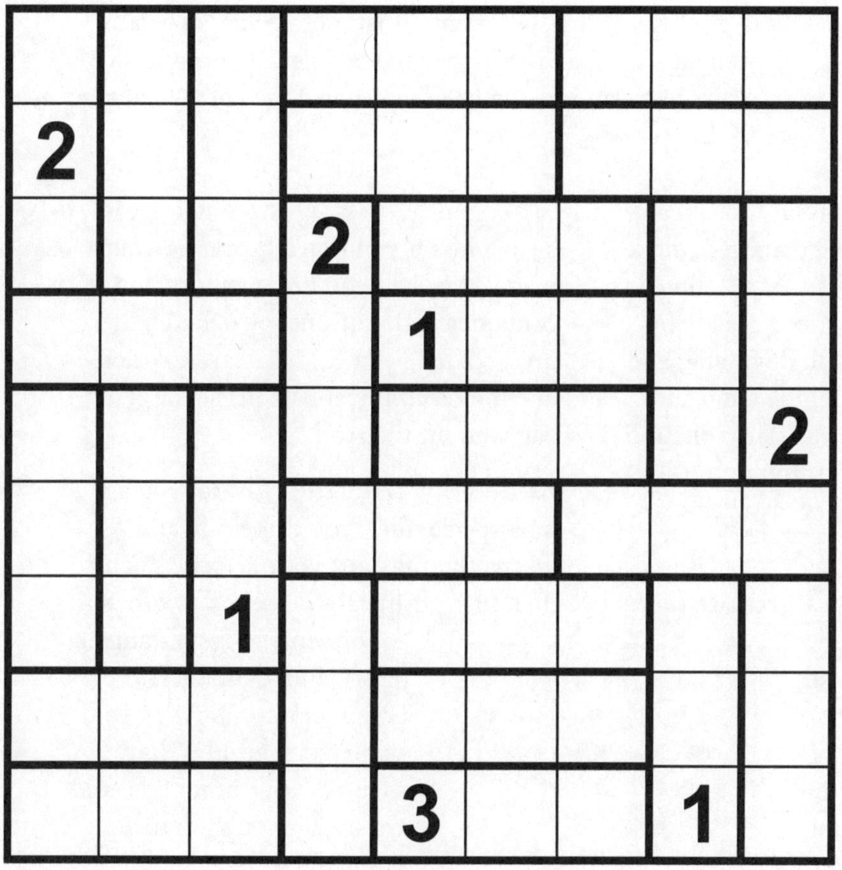

SUDOKU SUM

Without repeating any digits, complete the sum at right, by filling one digit in each of the five blanks.

```
    5  2  _
+   _  _  9
───────────
    _  _  7
```

bRaiN BREaTHEr
INGENIOUS USES FOR FILM CONTAINERS

We throw them into junk drawers never to be seen again—or toss them out with the trash. But we bet you didn't know how handy those plastic, cylindrical containers that protect your camera's film can be after you've developed the pictures. Here are some ways that film canisters can be useful around the house long after you've said "cheese."

Handy stamp dispenser To keep a roll of stamps from being damaged, make a stamp dispenser from an empty film container. Hold the container steady by taping it to a counter with duct tape, and use a utility knife to carefully cut a slit into the side of the canister. Drop the roll of stamps in, feed it out through the slit, snap the cap on, and it's ready to use.

On-the-road pill dispensers Use empty film containers as travel-size pill bottles for your purse or overnight bag. If you take more than one medication, use a separate container for each. Write the medication and dosage on a peel-and-stick label and attach to each container. For at-a-glance identification, color the labels with different-colored highlighter pens.

Store fishing flies You can save a lot of money and grief by storing fishing flies and hooks in film containers. They don't take up much room in a fishing vest, and if you do drop one in a stream, the airtight lid will keep it floating long enough for you to fish it out.

Emergency sewing kit You'll never be at a loss if you pop a button or your hem unravels if you fill an empty film container with buttons, pins, and a prethreaded needle. Make several; tuck one into each travel bag, purse, or gym bag, and hit the road.

Bring your own diet aids If you are on a special diet, you can easily and discreetly transport your favorite salad dressings, artificial sweetener, or other condiments to restaurants in plastic film containers. Clean, empty canisters hold single-size servings, have snap-on, leak-proof lids, and are small enough to tuck into a purse.

"With the rise of digital cameras, it's getting harder and harder to find film containers to put to good use. Ask for them at one-hour photo shops, or at a professional film developing lab."

Emergency nail polish remover Create a small, spill-proof carry case for nail polish remover by tucking a small piece of sponge into a plastic film container. Saturate the sponge with polish remover and snap on the lid. For an emergency repair, simply insert a finger and rub the nail against the fluid-soaked sponge to remove the polish.

★★★★ Around the Bend by Merle Baker

ACROSS

1 *Baseball Tonight* channel
5 Airplane parts
10 Religious offshoot
14 King of nursery rhyme
15 The Balance
16 First name in scat
17 Grub
18 __ a kind
19 Trucker, at times
20 Roadside warning
23 Sculler's need
24 God of war
25 Strapping
27 Scullers
30 Celebration
32 Brings in
33 Diplomatic skill
34 Canadian oil company
37 Key letter
38 Draft animal attachment
41 Debtor's letters
42 Remove from office
44 Carries laboriously
45 Attacked
47 Musical motifs
49 Apple tools
50 Interstellar cloud
52 Transmitted
53 Words on a menu
54 Apply oneself earnestly
60 Predicament
62 Thin as __
63 Falco of *The Sopranos*
64 Bookie's concern
65 Small role
66 Filches
67 Kindest regards
68 Glides downhill
69 Mine finds

DOWN

1 O.T. book
2 London neighborhood
3 Oxen's burden
4 Some talking heads
5 Mosaic handiwork
6 *Peanuts* kid
7 Genesis son
8 Egg on
9 Cinches
10 Jiffy
11 Usurp the place of
12 Unsoiled
13 Don't run off
21 Strident
22 Monopoly foursome: Abbr.
26 Took a meal
27 Seized vehicle
28 Molokai neighbor
29 Tennis accessories
30 Viper feature
31 Cools down
33 Authentic
35 Fly like an eagle
36 Expels
39 Fact books
40 Excelled
43 Cal. heading
46 Radio City Music Hall style
48 Lodge member
49 Viola cousins
50 Influential person
51 Slur over
52 Hit the slopes
55 Russia's __ Mountains
56 Presented oneself
57 Telltale sign
58 Help with the dishes
59 Costner role
61 It ends in Oct.

★★★ Fences

Connect the dots with vertical or horizontal lines, so that a single loop is formed with no crossings or branches. Each number indicates how many lines surround it; squares with no number may be surrounded by any number of lines.

```
1 0       2 3
              2       2
      3 1       1 1
                  3 3
  1 2
  3 1       3 3
  3     2
      2 1       2 2
```

ADDITION SWITCH

Switch the positions of two of the digits in the incorrect sum at right, to get a correct sum.

$$
\begin{array}{r}
458 \\
+103 \\
\hline
671
\end{array}
$$

★★★ Number-Out

Shade squares so that no number appears in any row or column more than once. Shaded squares may not touch each other horizontally or vertically, and all unshaded squares must form a single continuous area.

5	3	2	1	1	4
5	2	6	1	4	1
6	2	5	2	3	4
1	4	3	3	3	5
3	3	1	1	2	6
2	1	3	4	5	2

OPPOSITE ATTRACTION

Unscramble the letters in the phrase CRAFT KNOB to form two common words that are opposites of each other.

_____   _____

★★★★ Manual Operation by Merle Baker

ACROSS

1 Noteworthy achievement
5 "Sealed With __"
10 Things to believe in
14 Cornerstone word
15 Pie-chart lines
16 D.C. baseballer, e.g.
17 In knots
18 List heading
20 Cost add-on
22 Assumes the role of
23 Words from Caesar
24 WWW address starter
27 "Calendar Girl" singer
31 Uneasy feeling
35 Inter __
37 Lamb alias
38 Coziness
41 Erupter of 1169
42 Ballpark figs.
43 Exams for would-be attys.
44 Exclamation of startling abruptness
46 Thérèse Raquin novelist
48 Embassy VIP
50 What you see
55 It might make you cry
59 Soup or salad ingredient
60 Needle case
61 Composer Satie
62 Rubbish
63 Bio word
64 Desires
65 Fished for morays
66 Work without __

DOWN

1 Jazz pianist Hines, familiarly
2 Early computer
3 Concerning
4 Michael and Sweeney
5 Proficient performer
6 Blazing Saddles actress
7 "__ Rock and Roll Music"
8 Counting from
9 Visited tourist spots
10 Gate-crashers
11 Trudge
12 Ancient Persian
13 Hit sign
19 Gorge
21 Chicago Hope actress
25 Where prices are shown
26 Faint from excitement
28 __ mater
29 Singer Eartha
30 Satisfied sounds
31 Not many
32 Neighbor of Belg.
33 Actress Rowlands
34 Sure things
36 Should that be true
39 Novice
40 Battle site of 1836
45 Mickey and Jerry
47 Described
49 Free, to Martí
51 Tiny creature
52 Board
53 Toughen
54 Be frugal
55 Make weary
56 Scandinavian god
57 Topper dog
58 Stare in wonder
59 Paramount

★★★ No Three in a Row

Enter the maze at top right, pass through all the squares exactly once, and then exit at bottom left, all without retracing your path. You may not pass through three squares of the same color consecutively.

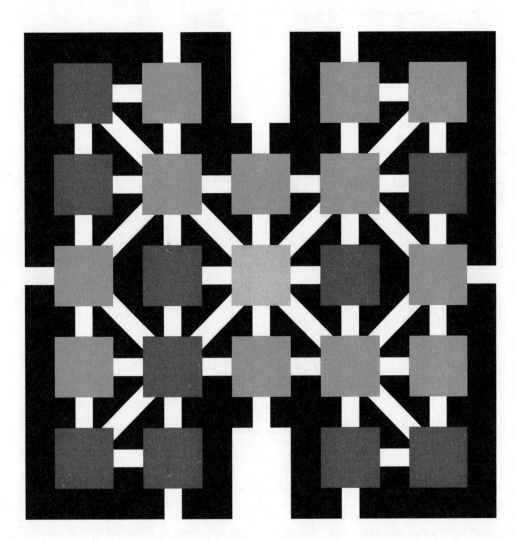

BETWEENER

What five-letter word belongs between the word at left and the word at right, so that the first and second word, and the second and third word, each form a common two-word phrase?

HOLD _ _ _ _ _ MAIN

★★★ Hyper-Sudoku

Fill in the blank boxes so that every row, column, 3x3 box, *and* each of the four 3x3 gray regions contains all of the numbers 1 to 9.

			2				7	
	3		8					
8				1		4	9	2
3	4			6	5			
		5		2				
					4			
	9							
5	2	6				8		9
4							6	

MIXAGRAMS

Each line contains a five-letter word and a four-letter word that have been mixed together (the order of the letters in each word has not been changed). Unmix the two words on each line and write them in the spaces provided. When you're done, find a two-part answer to the clue by reading down the letter columns in the answers.

CLUE: Where tiles are laid

A S W E G E A T S = _ _ _ _ _ + _ _ _ _

L A T O V T E A M = _ _ _ _ _ + _ _ _ _

T A M I R D U S T = _ _ _ _ _ + _ _ _ _

R E A D I N E U T = _ _ _ _ _ + _ _ _ _

★★★ "D" As in Geography

All these 10-letter "D" places around the globe can be found in D shapes in the diagram below. All the answers have the same shape and are oriented right-side-up. One answer is shown to get you started.

```
H G O T D R F D A R L D E T T I L I E R
U G A J E P U O N T H E L V B O N T Y D
A E A S I F M N E O D R A O D A L T P A
D R V G H N L A D N U I D N U N O A S L
S T P I T I K G I D M H S Q D I C E B E
L I N R K O G H D I F R O D Y L A Y L S
R B A I P H A A N G K I S H A R N D C S
O N K D I A V L B D A H R U B S B I A D
D L A G L R P A E D B S D E R B Y D U B
E I G O T H I R T A R T I N E R H S G L
E T H A R T L A M W A Y A N D T A T S E
D A B R F I S X C A D I B U M H R E R V
O S H O B D B H E A N R L D J E T L I N
N U I D A U A P D J E K E D A L O D E S
R B R L K S Y L O Z S C R J E L O N G H
E A A E S L I U D E F I T B E R I H I I
G K N F L R O N T E N K E A J E N S N R
G I K R B A N G R J I O L N R T G Y G E
O D U K I D S T D E K G D K A D F B E D
C A R D G N O R F D U D Q U C A N R E Y
```

DALBEATTIE
DAMARALAND
DARJEELING
DARLINGTON
DAUGAVPILS
DENT DU MIDI
DERBYSHIRE
DEVONSHIRE
DIABLERETS
DIRK HARTOG
~~DIYARBAKIR~~
DOGGER BANK
DONAGHADEE
DODECANESE
DRUMLITHIE
DUKINFIELD
DUNCANS BAY
DUNNET HEAD
DÜSSELDORF

INITIAL REACTION

Identify the well-known proverb from the first letters in each of its words.

T. H. A. B. T. O. _____

★★★★ Keep Quiet by Richard Silvestri

ACROSS

1 It makes every stop
6 Get fresh with
10 Track section
14 Thunderstruck
15 Court order
16 Loosen
17 Dutch genre painter
18 Cannon contents
19 Snooty sort
20 *West Side Story* song
22 Urban road hazard
24 Erstwhile sporty car
25 Islamic Almighty
26 Beanery
30 Lincoln in-laws
34 Scary street of cinema
35 GNP or RBI
36 Sweet bay
37 Pub orders
39 Eat away at
41 Hard to find
42 Rambled
44 Hamelin pests
46 Hot off the presses
47 Seat belt
48 Tackle-box contents
50 Old photo tint
52 Circle section
53 North Carolinian
56 Move like a snake
60 "Here comes trouble!"
61 Oscar nominee for *The Aviator*
63 Unsophisticated
64 Java neighbor
65 Mgmt. VIPs
66 Over
67 Help a hood
68 Engrave with acid
69 Omen interpreters

DOWN

1 Be inclined
2 Not fooled by
3 Columnist Herb
4 Anchor position
5 Horse racing units
6 Hit like Ruth
7 Hand holder
8 Mere
9 Bar perch
10 Traffic-report time
11 Part of AD
12 Elvis, for one
13 Leaf division
21 Yelled derisively
23 "Cheerio!"
25 Oregon city
26 Gets the news
27 Distribute
28 Spread sloppily
29 Former Mideast monogram
31 Liquid-Plumr alternative
32 Joshua in *The Ten Commandments*
33 Big bunches
36 __ *Weapon* (Gibson/Glover film)
38 Big success
40 German article
43 Olympic weapon
45 Hallowed places
48 Debone
49 Number on the pump
51 Inner contentment
53 Big brass
54 Great white hunter?
55 Portrayal
56 Pageant entrant's wear
57 Hole up
58 At any time
59 Beatty film
62 *Gunsmoke* character

★★ Triad Split Decisions

In this clueless crossword puzzle, each answer consists of two words whose spellings are the same, except for the consecutive letters given. All answers are common words; no phrases or hyphenated or capitalized words are used. Some of the clues may have more than one solution, but there is only one word pair that will correctly link up with all the other word pairs.

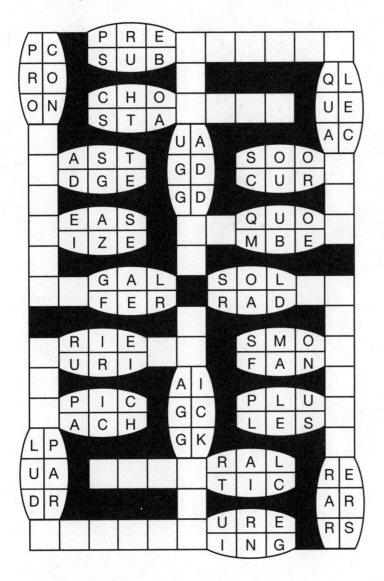

TRANSDELETION

Delete one letter from the word FOOTRACES and rearrange the rest, to get a weather term.

_____

★★★ One-Way Streets

The diagram represents a pattern of streets. A and B are parking spaces, and the black squares are stores. Find the route that starts at A, passes through all stores exactly once, and ends at B. Arrows indicate one-way traffic for that block only. No block or intersection may be entered more than once.

SOUND THINKING

The only consonant sounds in what two common seven-letter adjectives are M, N, and S, in that order?

_____   _____

★★★★ Sense of Yuma by Patrick Jordan

ACROSS

1 Run scared
6 Janitorial tools
10 Levels off the lawn
14 Without help
15 Magazine in the fashion section
16 Deviltry
17 More peeved
18 Spiffy
19 Flat-topped elevation
20 Arizona city's Latin motto?
22 Cauldron concoction
23 __ Mahal
24 Battering-ram target
26 Apt. stat
29 Barn attics
32 Rough files
36 Unfathomable stretches
38 Tigger's playmate
39 Title for Juan's wife
40 Enamored of an Arizona city?
43 In every case
44 Time period
45 Corresponding
46 Do a roaster's job
47 Whimsically amusing
49 Hi-__ graphics
50 Gouda alternative
52 "__ Woman" (1972 tune)
54 How Dino greets Fred
57 Arizona city boxer?
63 Move viscously
64 All over again
65 Fantasy Island transport
66 Rock gently
67 __ of the above
68 Toss out
69 What headphones cover
70 Dance, drama, etc.
71 Dollywood diversions

DOWN

1 Bygone
2 Fleshy-leafed plant
3 Cheers character
4 Ham-handed
5 Bowl filler
6 Café card
7 Designer Cassini
8 Kilt patterns
9 Brief argument
10 Tissue layers
11 No longer concerned about
12 Like Confucius
13 Side dish with crab cakes
21 Norwegian waterways
25 Crunchy ice cream flavor
26 Healing treatment, briefly
27 Do-re-mi
28 Falls in flakes
30 Egg __ yung
31 Xerography powder
33 Sub detector
34 Word before number or rate
35 Wind instruments
37 Rink visitors' needs of yore
39 Media critic Gene
41 Took a look at
42 NFLer, e.g.
47 F's analogue
48 1980s pop singer
51 Frigidaire competitor
53 1,156, to Vergil
54 Get outscored
55 South Dakota adjoiner
56 Former Kremlin despot
58 Metropolis journalist
59 Moms in meadows
60 Put into words
61 Without a recurrence
62 Cod catchers

★★★ Solitaire Poker

Group the 50 cards into ten poker hands of five cards each, so that each hand contains two pairs or better. The cards in each hand must be connected to each other by a common horizontal or vertical side. Hint: Three of the cards in the top row are used to form a flush.

SAY IT AGAIN

What six-letter word for a unit of time, when pronounced differently, is also an adjective meaning "tiny"?

_ _ _ _ _ _

★★★ Star Search

Find the stars that are hidden in some of the blank squares. The numbered squares indicate how many stars are hidden in the squares adjacent to them (including diagonally). There is never more than one star in any square.

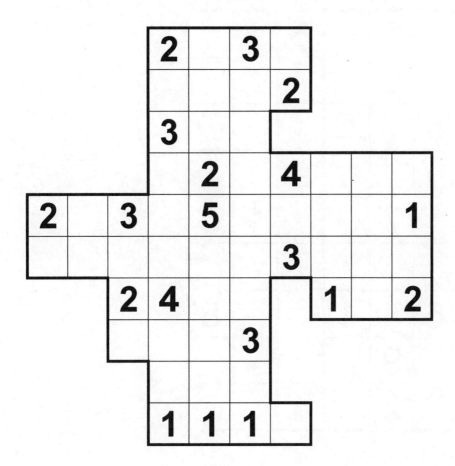

TELEPHONE TRIOS

	ABC	DEF
1	**2**	**3**
GHI **4**	JKL **5**	MNO **6**
PRS **7**	TUV **8**	WXY **9**
✳	**0**	**#**

Using the numbers and letters on a standard telephone, what three seven-letter words or phrases from the same category can be formed from these telephone numbers?

286-2236   _ _ _ _ _ _ _

538-8823   _ _ _ _ _ _ _

786-7546   _ _ _ _ _ _ _

★★★ Sudoku

Fill in the blank boxes so that every row, column, and 3x3 box contains all of the numbers 1 to 9.

		1		3		5		
				6				
6			8		5			7
		2				9		
3	8			7			1	6
		6				7		
7			6		1			8
				9				
		9		2		4		

COUNT UP

Inserting plus signs and minus signs, as many as necessary, in between the digits from 1 to 9 below, create a series of additions and subtractions whose final answer is 74. Any digits without a sign between them are to be grouped together as a single number.

$$1 \quad 2 \quad 3 \quad 4 \quad 5 \quad 6 \quad 7 \quad 8 \quad 9 \quad = \quad 74$$

★★★★ Praiseworthy Comment by Doug Peterson

ACROSS

1 Dovetail
5 Woodland ways
10 Charitable offering
14 Golden State coll.
15 Milkmaid's perch
16 Blue-green
17 Start of a quote by Otto van Isch
19 Take it easy
20 Bookstore section
21 Made a small adjustment
23 Utmost
24 Ranch visitors
25 Lipstick mishap
28 Part 2 of quote
32 Tourist transports
33 Hasty escape
34 Get smart
35 *Wheel of Fortune* buy
36 Part 3 of quote
38 Shaq's pos.
39 *Barney Miller* star
41 Remote targets
42 Loan number
43 Part 4 of quote
45 Author Verne
46 Less dicey
47 Taker of vows
48 Morning hour
51 Bottled drink
55 Prom-night sight
56 End of quote
58 Stead
59 Susan Lucci role
60 Ark. neighbor
61 Frowned-upon contraction
62 "Blowin' in the Wind" composer
63 Southernmost Florida

DOWN

1 Sierra Club cofounder
2 Repeat
3 Close with force
4 Humidor items
5 Coll. major
6 Suit to __
7 Young one
8 Soaking spot
9 Delays
10 Oversized volumes
11 Security problem
12 Creation of Daedalus
13 *Citizen Kane* prop
18 __'acte
22 Unsettling
24 Persephone's mother
25 Resell illegally
26 Obsession
27 Black-key material
28 Comic-book sound
29 Colorful sticker
30 City in Montana
31 Belgian battle site
33 Noticeably glum
36 French lawmakers
37 Eggs: Lat.
40 Distribute
42 Go berserk
44 Computer buyer's concern
45 Dame __ Dench
47 Strikeout king Ryan
48 She, in Siena
49 Grandfather clock numeral
50 FBI operatives
51 Animal lovers' grp.
52 Diminutive dog
53 Part of SRO
54 School orgs.
57 Wire measurement

★★★ ABC

Enter the letters A, B, and C into the diagram so that each row and column has exactly one A, one B, and one C. The letters outside the diagram indicate the first letter encountered, moving in the direction of the arrow. Keep in mind that after all the letters have been filled in, there will be two blank boxes in each row and column.

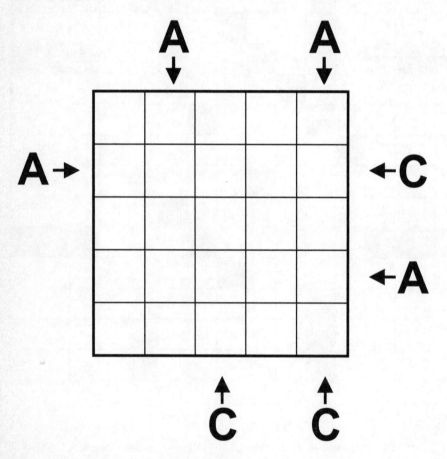

CLUELESS CROSSWORD

Complete the crossword with common uncapitalized seven-letter words, based entirely on the letters already filled in for you.

★★★ Find the Ships

Determine the position of the 10 ships listed to the right of the diagram. The ships may be oriented either horizontally or vertically. A square with wavy lines indicates water and will not contain a ship. The numbers at the edge of the diagram indicate how many squares in that row or column contain parts of ships. When all 10 ships are correctly placed in the diagram, no two of them will touch each other, not even diagonally.

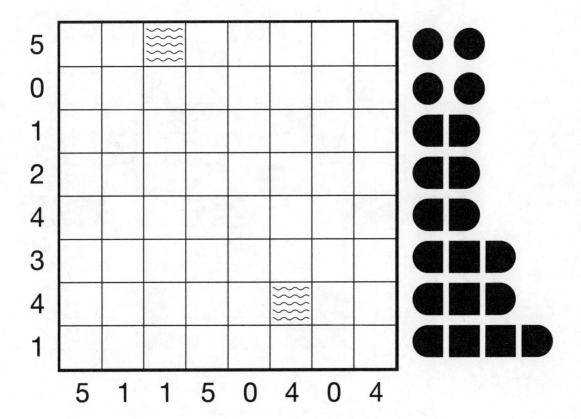

TWO-BY-FOUR

The eight letters in the word MULTIPLY can be rearranged to form a pair of common four-letter words in only one way. Can you find the two words?

___ ___ ___ ___   ___ ___ ___ ___

★★★★ Sport Play by Shirley Soloway

ACROSS

1 NATO mem.
5 Covered
9 XXXV x X
13 Romanian prename
14 Engaged
16 Angler's item
17 Umpires?
20 Designer Miller
21 Makes possible
22 Boxer Laila
23 Crater's edge
24 NHL draftees?
29 Swiss food conglomerate
34 Annoy
35 Going with
37 Substandard
38 Hebrew letter
40 Teachers' org.
41 Two loins of beef
42 MLB playoff round
43 More stylish
45 Qualifiers
46 Franciscan's mecca
48 Hipster bowler?
50 Actress Thompson
52 Pan Am rival
53 The latest places to go
57 German city
60 Wimbledon match?
63 Comics dog
64 Some high clouds
65 Parka piece
66 Trawling needs
67 Litchfield's loc.
68 Helper: Abbr.

DOWN

1 Clothes protector
2 High spirits
3 "__ Marlene"
4 Medicinal medium
5 Sacred goblet
6 Former Calabrian currency
7 Neighbor of Okla.
8 Yield
9 Social group
10 Dumbbell exercise
11 Ontario Indian
12 Comparative word
15 Cruise-ship activity
18 Spit's partner
19 Willing
24 Trump ex
25 Honeycomb units
26 Business leaders
27 Gambling game
28 Tuscany city
30 Baden-Baden feature
31 Doughnutlike
32 Bath sponge
33 Physicist Mach
36 Catch in the act
39 Greek letter
41 "Music, Music, Music" singer
43 Haberdashery accessory
44 Chicago conveyance
47 Job opening
49 Maker of pianos and motorcycles
51 Savory jelly
53 Computer image
54 Stem joint
55 Business wear
56 C. in C.
57 Swiss city
58 Son of Seth
59 Sgts., e.g.
61 Debate side
62 St. Pete summer setting

★★ Cut That Out

Which of the pieces has been snipped from the greeting card?

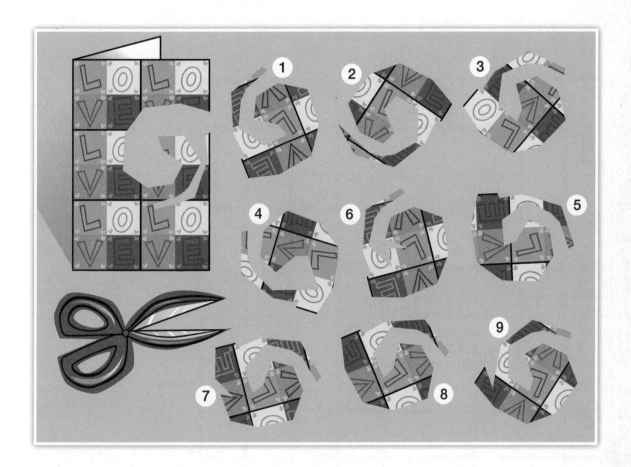

THREE AT A RHYME

Rearrange these letters to form three one-syllable words that rhyme.

C C E E E H I I K M P Q U

_____ _____ _____

★★★ 123

Fill in the diagram so that each rectangular piece has one each of the numbers 1, 2, and 3, under these rules: 1) No two adjacent squares, horizontally or vertically, can have the same number. 2) Each completed row and column of the diagram will have an equal number of 1s, 2s, and 3s.

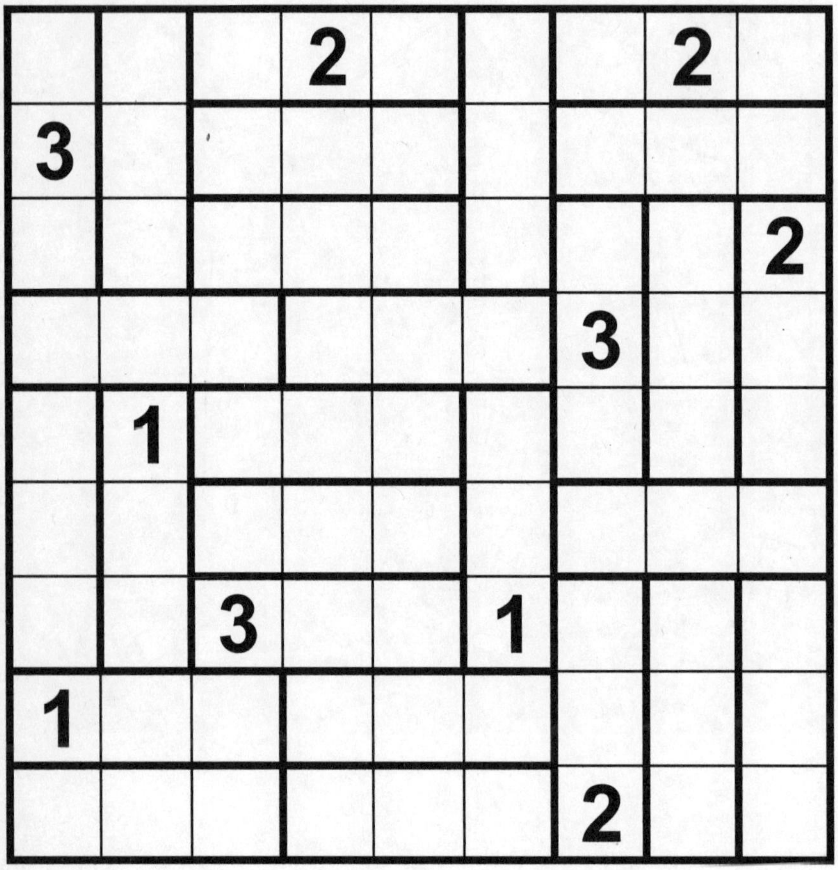

			2				2	
3								
								2
						3		
	1							
		3			1			
1								
						2		

SUDOKU SUM

Without repeating any digits, complete the sum at right, by filling one digit in each of the five blanks.

$$
\begin{array}{r}
7\ 0\ \_ \\
+\ \_\ \_\ 5 \\
\hline
\_\ \_\ 4 \\
\end{array}
$$

★★★ Fences

Connect the dots with vertical or horizontal lines, so that a single loop is formed with no crossings or branches. Each number indicates how many lines surround it; squares with no number may be surrounded by any number of lines.

```
.   .   .   .   .   .   .

    0       0           1

.   .   .   .   .   .   .

    3               2

.   .   .   .   .   .   .

  2   1               3

.   .   .   .   .   .   .

        2           1

.   .   .   .   .   .   .

  3           2

.   .   .   .   .   .   .

  1               2   3

.   .   .   .   .   .   .

    3               0

.   .   .   .   .   .   .

  1       1       3

.   .   .   .   .   .   .
```

ADDITION SWITCH

Switch the positions of two of the digits in the incorrect sum at right, to get a correct sum.

```
  5 3 7
+ 2 1 6
-------
  9 5 1
```

★★★★ Playing Politics by Shirley Soloway

ACROSS

1 "Trolley Song" sound
6 Critical remark
10 One-half fl. oz.
14 Nighttime quaff
15 Phone letters
16 Sing soulfully
17 Nullifies
18 Sweeney of *Anything Goes*
19 A fan of
20 Nonpartisan celebration?
23 Mule of song
24 Oxford adjuncts
25 *Nova* network
28 Editor, often
32 Tiny amount
34 Fruit center
35 Any Sha Na Na song
40 Reagan's jelly beans?
43 Unaggressive
44 City of Peru
45 Bygone person of Peru
46 Speaks freely
49 Cal. column
50 Yom Kippur instrument
54 "Da __ Ron Ron"
56 Statehouse collection?
63 Quite a while
64 Ground grain
65 Bracelet attachment
66 Segment
67 Not very bright
68 Red dyestuff
69 Pitchers' concerns
70 Prehistoric menace
71 Caravan stops

DOWN

1 206
2 __ *Lake* (Doctorow novel)
3 Scathing, as criticism
4 Geometric points
5 Travelmate of Melchior
6 Natural
7 Sounded like
8 Glassmaker Lalique
9 Rochester's creator
10 Plot device
11 Monopoly railroad
12 18- or 19-string instrument
13 Sneaky maneuvers
21 Campaign-poster word
22 *Reversible Errors* author
25 Painter Mondrian
26 Not very sleek
27 Choreography unit
29 Plain-woven fabric
30 *Empire Strikes Back* director Kershner
31 Looks to be
33 Old pro
36 Ring of flowers
37 Small measure of progress
38 Wanderlust, perhaps
39 "Hairy man" of the Bible
41 WWII vessel
42 King Abdullah, e.g.
47 On time
48 Over-the-head cloak
50 Land ender
51 "Horrible" cartoon character
52 La Scala offering
53 Symbols of strength
55 *Waking Ned Devine* character
57 Big name in small planes
58 Strong wind
59 The A in A-Rod
60 Prepares leather
61 *Comus* composer
62 12/25

★★★ Hyper-Sudoku

Fill in the blank boxes so that every row, column, 3x3 box, *and* each of the four 3x3 gray regions contains all of the numbers 1 to 9.

9					8	2		4
			3	2				
			5	9				
	8			7			3	6
1					3			2
	1	3	4	5	9			
							7	
	2				4			

MIXAGRAMS

Each line contains a five-letter word and a four-letter word that have been mixed together (the order of the letters in each word has not been changed). Unmix the two words on each line and write them in the spaces provided. When you're done, find a two-part answer to the clue by reading down the letter columns in the answers.

CLUE: Pipe material

C I C L I N U G E = _ _ _ _ _ + _ _ _ _

O R G O B R I E N = _ _ _ _ _ + _ _ _ _

B A F R I K E D E = _ _ _ _ _ + _ _ _ _

I S N U E P T E T = _ _ _ _ _ + _ _ _ _

★★ Split Decisions

In this clueless crossword puzzle, each answer consists of two words whose spellings are the same, except for the consecutive letters given. All answers are common words; no phrases or hyphenated or capitalized words are used. Some of the clues may have more than one solution, but there is only one word pair that will correctly link up with all the other word pairs.

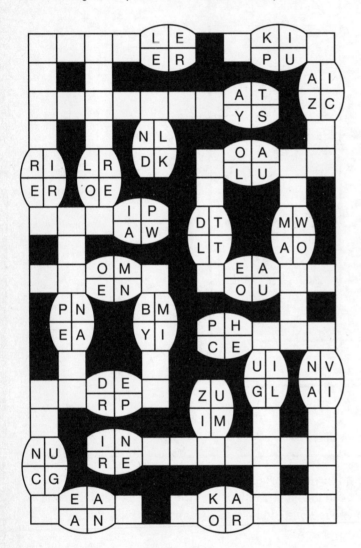

TRANSDELETION

Delete one letter from the word OCEANFRONT and rearrange the rest, to get a period of time.

_____

★★★★ By the Numbers by Richard Silvestri

ACROSS

1 Blockbuster movie of 1975
5 Kid
9 Tollbooth area
14 Condo division
15 Voice above tenor
16 Schooner filler
17 Fuddy-duddy
18 Down in the dumps
19 Deal maker
20 Difficulty
23 MLB stat
24 Insect with eyespots
28 Deerstalker, for one
31 Cleopatra's attendant
34 Of the lips
36 Stray from the script
38 Child, e.g.
40 First name in scat
41 Math approximation technique
44 Sicilian resort
45 Ship out
46 To the left or right
47 Notary's need
49 *Mayor* author
51 Three times, in prescriptions
52 Trawler trailers
54 Western Indian
56 With hesitation
62 Something to rattle
66 Brewer's kiln
67 Bread spread
68 City on the Mohawk
69 Mayberry moppet
70 Muscle stiffness
71 Dizzy's music
72 Compote flavor
73 Leisurely manner

DOWN

1 Dojo activity
2 In a while
3 Off the mark
4 Supply
5 It's spotted in South America
6 Corner shapes
7 Knock the socks off
8 *What Women Want* actress
9 Gamma-globulin source
10 Fall back
11 Epoch
12 Meditation system
13 Skill
21 African antelope
22 Musical syllables
25 Toes the mark
26 Edam alternative
27 Chlorine compound
28 Paris sights
29 Aphrodite's love
30 Nosedive
32 Bit of farmland
33 Part of the leg
35 Surgical tool
37 Rasht resident
39 Opposite of exo-
42 Aerin Lauder's grandmother
43 *Chicago Hope* Emmy winner
48 Lure into wrongdoing
50 Coast Guard vessel
53 Nose around
55 Elicit
57 Paper patcher
58 China setting?
59 "Modern Gallantry" essayist
60 Camera eye
61 A tie that binds
62 Fill-in
63 Filled up on
64 Chest protector
65 System starter

★★★ Turn Maze

Entering at the bottom and exiting at the top, find the shortest path through the maze, following these turn rules: You must turn right on red squares, turn left on blue squares, and go straight through yellow squares. Your path may retrace itself and cross at intersections, but you may not reverse your direction at any point.

BETWEENER

What five-letter word belongs between the word at left and the word at right, so that the first and second word, and the second and third word, each form a common two-word phrase?

ROLLING _ _ _ _ _ AGE

★★★ Number-Out

Shade squares so that no number appears in any row or column more than once. Shaded squares may not touch each other horizontally or vertically, and all unshaded squares must form a single continuous area.

4	4	5	3	6	2
5	2	2	1	5	3
2	4	4	4	1	6
4	3	2	5	2	1
6	5	6	2	3	2
3	5	1	6	2	4

OPPOSITE ATTRACTION

Unscramble the letters in the phrase KNIT HITCH to form two common words that are opposites of each other.

_____   _____

★★★ One-Way Streets

The diagram represents a pattern of streets. A and B are parking spaces, and the black squares are stores. Find the route that starts at A, passes through all stores exactly once, and ends at B. Arrows indicate one-way traffic for that block only. No block or intersection may be entered more than once.

SOUND THINKING

The only consonant sounds in what 10-letter word (not a plural) are L, T, H, and S, in that order?

_____

★★★★ Pardon My French by Merle Baker

ACROSS

1 *Pygmalion* playwright
5 Dolphins' home
10 Fed. agent
14 Singing syllables
15 Synthetic fabric
16 Corn Belt state
17 Soon, in poems
18 Catches red-handed
19 Jacket fastener
20 Tennis star
23 Tiny Tim instrument
24 Light at a corner
25 Plans
27 Detergent target
30 Ripped
31 May honoree
34 Work of David
36 Bamboo eater
39 Heavy metal
41 1980s TV group
43 Recipe directive
44 Sounds of music
46 Cape Cod catch
48 Wine designation
49 Cobblers' tools
51 Male voice
53 Spreads rumors
56 Child's treat
60 Do something
61 Payment methods
64 Thing
66 Cowboy contest
67 LAX stats
68 Infamous emperor
69 Bigeye and bluefin
70 Short letter
71 Eye annoyance
72 Gaze fixedly
73 Little piggies

DOWN

1 Criticizes
2 Asian capital
3 Together (with)
4 In decline
5 Louvre work
6 Investment options
7 "I cannot tell __"
8 Gangsters' girlfriends
9 Entomology specimen
10 US soldiers
11 Some statuary
12 No longer out
13 Where to pick up kittens
21 Complain
22 Patronize, with "at"
26 Periods
28 Padded surfaces
29 Vote in
31 Cambridge sch.
32 Pizarro's quest
33 Religious residence
35 Stable mother
37 Cube to roll
38 Multi-episode story line
40 Part of CNBC
42 Cobra predator
45 Unlikely
47 Way out
50 Bowling and badminton
52 Mickey Mouse, e.g.
53 Acquisitions
54 Eightsome
55 Dog's muzzle
57 Artoo __
58 Ticked off
59 Mountain curves
62 Author Ferber
63 Diary duration
65 *Simpsons* bar owner

★★★ Sudoku

Fill in the blank boxes so that every row, column, and 3x3 box contains all of the numbers 1 to 9.

		6			5			9
5				4			3	
	7			1				
4						9		
			9	7	6			
		3						8
				6			4	
	4			5				1
8			3			5		

MIXAGRAMS

Each line contains a five-letter word and a four-letter word that have been mixed together (the order of the letters in each word has not been changed). Unmix the two words on each line and write them in the spaces provided. When you're done, find a two-part answer to the clue by reading down the letter columns in the answers.

CLUE: Whale feature

B A T H R U M E B = _ _ _ _ _ + _ _ _ _

B A R U G L I E D = _ _ _ _ _ + _ _ _ _

C U R M B A G E R = _ _ _ _ _ + _ _ _ _

K A P N O P L E B = _ _ _ _ _ + _ _ _ _

★★★ Star Search

Find the stars that are hidden in some of the blank squares. The numbered squares indicate how many stars are hidden in the squares adjacent to them (including diagonally). There is never more than one star in any square.

			1	1	1	1	
		2					
2		3			2		2
		3					
	1	4				6	3
				3			
	1					1	
	2	2	2	2			

TELEPHONE TRIOS

	ABC	DEF
1	**2**	**3**
GHI	JKL	MNO
4	**5**	**6**
PRS	TUV	WXY
7	**8**	**9**
*****	**0**	**#**

Using the numbers and letters on a standard telephone, what three seven-letter words or phrases from the same category can be formed from these telephone numbers?

246-3464   _ _ _ _ _ _ _

242-7837   _ _ _ _ _ _ _

359-5323   _ _ _ _ _ _ _

★★★★ Wild and Woolly by Fred Piscop

ACROSS

1 Trunk, in art class
6 Under control
11 __ Na Na
14 __ Irish Rose
15 Unaided
16 By what means
17 Scram, like an ovine?
19 NASA spacewalk
20 Small sofa
21 Mix up
22 Toon shriek
23 Antarctic explorer
25 Paint with dots
27 Toe the line
30 Cue-stick end
32 School cheer
33 Murphy had one
34 Leave unsaid
36 Is afraid of
39 Played to a tie
41 They're taboo
43 Minimally
44 "Us" and "them"
46 Subject word
47 Slangy suffix
48 Makes a choice
50 Sgt., e.g.
51 Poker card
52 Middlesex middles
55 Pueblo Indian
57 Chart topper
58 Numerical word form
60 Sorority hopeful
64 Web pop-ups
65 Ovine city?
67 Teachers' org.
68 How we stand
69 Former Senator Lott
70 Take a stab at
71 French Open champ at 16
72 Couldn't stomach

DOWN

1 Gets "it"
2 Double reed
3 Knee-slapper
4 "Halt!" caller
5 It means "bone"
6 __ kwon do
7 "__ fair ..."
8 Zoo barriers
9 Ill will
10 Question after a mission
11 Ovine workers?
12 Wretched abode
13 Up and about
18 Kennedy Center honoree of '97
24 Simpleton of rhyme
26 Appeal
27 Reo builder
28 Adriatic seaport
29 Ovine "No kidding?"
31 Attach, as a corsage
35 Modicum
37 Rub the wrong way
38 Don't move
40 Blubbered
42 Does detective work
45 Disco lights
49 Safe from harm
51 __ del Fuego
52 Gregorian, for one
53 Down source
54 Mill product
56 Colossus poet
59 In olden times
61 Legislative body
62 Heredity unit
63 Business sign abbr.
66 NBA tiebreakers

★★★ Minuteman Maze

Enter the maze under the Minuteman's right foot, pass through all the stars exactly once, and then exit the maze, all without retracing your path. Hint: Make a left turn immediately after entering the maze, then turn right at the bottom left corner.

SAY IT AGAIN

What six-letter word meaning "to deny," when pronounced differently, is also a word for something that people throw out?

— — — — — —

★★★ Musical Trail

Beginning with SILK STOCKINGS, then moving up, down, left, or right, one letter at a time, trace a path of these 41 musicals in the diagram.

```
M E K A T E Y C O M P J A I L H O T P A
S S I M A D D L O O T S N N I Y U O I L
N E K I L A D C E S H O L I D A S E L J
A J Y T A C R A N L E M B Z Z T A R L O
O K L A H A M J O O C A A R A J H O E E
Y S E L O M E N G T N U G N U L T C Y Y
O G O B E S I Y U D D O R U M L A K L L
B D L A R S M S A N L L Y O A D D Y B I
N E D S L E T N I E S E T N N U O T T N
S I O E H T O H T I G G E I S B W E H O
K L O W T A I G E R I B L U E M N W A Y
S T O C S R L P X A M O R E M A A D T E
W S G K Y T I R S E E S G I R L O O T E
I C N I H A R E S V I T Y N N H R B T R
E K E T C U N E V O F A G O U E L P S N
D M E A E E Q S A L R W A N F M M C H I
C A W S B E S E I L U O Y T T Y O T I A
K A S T T H C R O T Y D A N H E B O C M
D N E L D N A Y O R I C N I A Y O G A D
M A B B E A U T G E D I N G P F R I E N
```

ALL THAT JAZZ	JAILHOUSE ROCK
ANNIE GET YOUR GUN	KISS ME KATE
	LES MISERABLES
AVENUE Q	MACK AND MABEL
BARNUM	
BEAUTY AND THE BEAST	MAIN STREET TO BROADWAY
BILLY ELLIOT	MAME
BUDDY	OKLAHOMA
CALAMITY JANE	ON THE TOWN
CAMELOT	PAINT YOUR WAGON
CARMEN JONES	PAL JOEY
CHICAGO	
DADDY COOL	ROSE MARIE
DIRTY DANCING	SCROOGE
EVITA	~~SILK STOCKINGS~~
FOLLIES	STARLIGHT EXPRESS
FUNNY GIRLS	STOMP
G I BLUES	SWEET CHARITY
GOLDEN BOY	THE BOY FRIEND
GUYS AND DOLLS	TOMMY
HELP	WICKED
HOLIDAY INN	
INTO THE WOODS	

WHO'S WHAT WHERE?

The correct term for a resident of Prince Edward Island, Canada, is:

A) Peirian   B) Edwardian

C) Islander   D) Eddite

★★★ ABC

Enter the letters A, B, and C into the diagram so that each row and column has exactly one A, one B, and one C. The letters outside the diagram indicate the first letter encountered, moving in the direction of the arrow. Keep in mind that after all the letters have been filled in, there will be two blank boxes in each row and column.

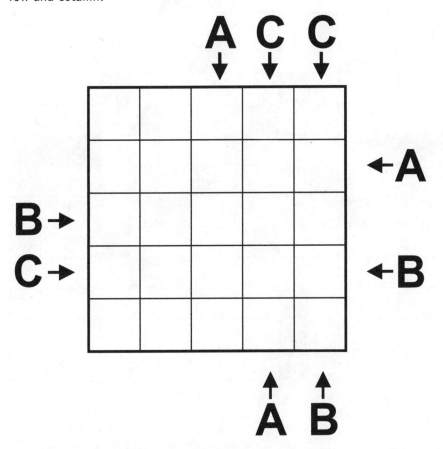

CLUELESS CROSSWORD

Complete the crossword with common uncapitalized seven-letter words, based entirely on the letters already filled in for you.

★★★★★ Themeless Toughie by Anna Stiga

ACROSS

1 Big name in sorcery
10 Ethnic starter
15 Sort of swimsuit
16 Asian peninsula
17 One of the World Heritage Sites
18 Takes care of trays
19 Chief
20 Perform as expected
22 Center starter
23 Mideast carrier
24 *Swan Lake* character
25 Certain Jamaican
27 Bothers
29 Occupational ending
30 Expresses contempt
32 Point
33 Large-scale
34 Poky
36 Paint holder
38 "__ for Boss" ('92 campaign slogan)
41 Catch
43 Cereal topper
47 *Wheel of Fortune* purchase
48 Helga's husband
50 One in a box
51 Pol's promise
53 Capital of Qatar
55 UA partner
56 Western farewell
58 Opposite of *matin*
59 Predictor's pack
60 Post-adolescence
62 Wake Island, e.g.
63 Ballgame souvenirs
64 Present __
65 Commercial device

DOWN

1 They're not serious

2 Patella
3 Poker ploy
4 Place for essays
5 Beat all
6 OK
7 Mountaintop feature, perhaps
8 Sore
9 Brave quality
10 Fixes deeply
11 Brownish gray
12 Ancient French region
13 Father of Odysseus

14 Seafood serving
21 Hotel amenity
23 Count equivalent
26 Julia, in *Ocean's Eleven*
28 Foster Brooks persona
31 Haydn piece
33 Choice list
35 Quipster
37 Lower, in Lima
38 Sound of a knock
39 Seeing someone
40 Fairway club

42 It won't fly
44 Clothes holder
45 Invitation phrase
46 Chair feature
48 Work hard
49 Untrustworthy ones
52 Chills
54 *The Planets* composer
57 Kitty's friend
58 Buttonhole
61 Not just any

6 INEXPENSIVE, EASY WAYS TO TRANSFORM A ROOM

Tired of your boring brown sofa, and your blah window treatments? The following "aha!" tips can easily bring you out of your decor doldrums. Considering how much time you spend in your family room, you may as well love how it looks!

Think of your sofa as your favorite shirt. In other words, cover it in a color you love to wear instead of in a neutral—what most people choose—that disappears in the room. If you choose your favorite color, one that looks best on you, the sofa will take center stage. And you'll never get tired of sitting on it.

Use bold fabric patterns in small doses. A little on a footstool or accent pillows will go a long way. It won't overwhelm, but it will stand out. This is a good way to use an expensive fabric you love without having to break the bank buying several yards to cover an entire couch.

For large chairs, choose a small print. If you're covering a large chair, such as a wingback, choose a small-print fabric. These chairs are dramatic enough. A small print helps balance that drama and create a more sophisticated look.

Got kids? Choose a forgiving sofa fabric. Patterns help hide spills and crumbs. You probably already know that by now. But did you also know that a fabric with a texture—a cotton velvet or some other textile with a pile—will do wonders for masking the mess? Try it. You'll worry less and enjoy more.

Dress up boring window shades. Those vanilla-colored roller shades are about as blah as it gets. But they're inexpensive, and they do the job. For a few dollars more, you can transform the shades—and an entire room in the process—by gluing a bold wallpaper print to the insides of the shades. This works best with shades 27 inches wide or less—the width of a standard wallpaper roll. Measure the length of the fully extended shade, and cut the wallpaper to fit, leaving an extra two inches. Roll out the shade and cover it with wallpaper adhesive using a sponge roller. Lay the wallpaper on the glue, letting the two extra inches wrap under the bottom of the shade. Use a rolling pin to smooth out air bubbles. Trim away any excess wallpaper. Because the wallpaper makes the shade a little harder to roll up and down, this trick works best on windows where you don't mind leaving the shade partially down.

Make a decorative bulletin board. Is your ho-hum brown corkboard not doing your decor any favors? Wrap it in a pretty, decorative fabric and either glue or staple the edges to the back. Since you will be putting pins through the fabric, you probably want to pick something durable, like canvas.

★★★★ Find the Ships

Determine the position of the 10 ships listed to the right of the diagram. The ships may be oriented either horizontally or vertically. A square with wavy lines indicates water and will not contain a ship. The numbers at the edge of the diagram indicate how many squares in that row or column contain parts of ships. When all 10 ships are correctly placed in the diagram, no two of them will touch each other, not even diagonally.

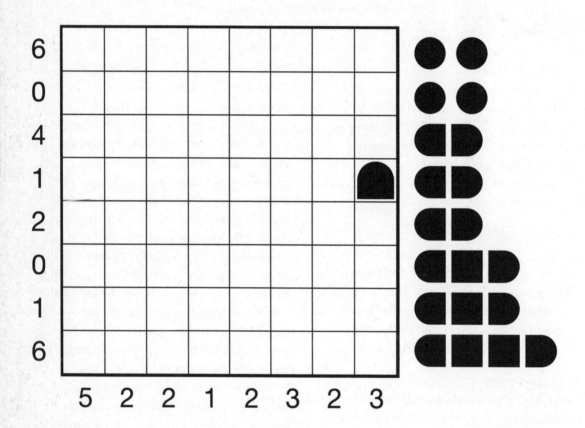

TWO-BY-FOUR

The eight letters in the word IDENTIFY can be rearranged to form a pair of common four-letter words in only one way. Can you find the two words?

— — — —   — — — —

★★★★ Hyper-Sudoku

Fill in the blank boxes so that every row, column, 3x3 box, *and* each of the four 3x3 gray regions contains all of the numbers 1 to 9.

					7			
3				4				
					2	7		
			8			3		
				5				
	2							
	7		6				5	9
	3	4			8			
		6		2	8	4		

BETWEENER

What five-letter word belongs between the word at left and the word at right, so that the first and second word, and the second and third word, each form a common two-word phrase?

CUTTING __ __ __ __ __ GAME

★★★★★ Themeless Toughie by Daniel R. Stark

ACROSS

1 U.S. ballistic missile
8 Shut, as a gate
15 More aloof
16 Function
17 OK
18 Universal
19 Level expanse
20 __ wheels
22 Papyrus relative
23 Where some stock is held
24 More competent
26 Reduce intake
27 Summer on the Seine
28 Offender
30 Before
31 Software editions
33 Turned sharply
35 Bonsai and ikebana
36 Like some controls
37 Kitchen device
40 Needing no quarters
44 Tours turndown
45 Sneezer's needs
47 Doctrine
48 Major Hoople
50 Not touching
51 Be checkmated
52 "Luck of the Draw" singer
54 East ender
55 Oxonian's parent
56 Family tree
58 Blowing away
60 Keyed in
61 Library's need
62 Overbearing rulers
63 Used a loofah

DOWN

1 Hide seeker
2 Stuffed
3 Form a jury
4 Name meaning "bountiful"
5 School near Windsor Castle
6 Ariz. neighbor
7 Quails
8 Frequent feller
9 Chest beater
10 Dice throws
11 Postmen have one
12 More robust
13 Knickknack holder
14 Struck out
21 Where the Po rises
24 Freud's homeland
25 Brook
28 Insert mark
29 Wild ducks
32 Munch on
34 Gnome
36 Habitual gloom
37 Like old oak trees
38 Long-leaf lettuce
39 Puts oil on
40 Bygone autocrat
41 Going wild
42 Inherent quality
43 Surfaced
46 Risks a fine
49 Ready tea
51 Fraught
53 Polynesian staple
55 Game with goals
57 Figure out
59 Clothing defect

★★ What's Next?

Which one of the numbered squares should replace the question mark, to follow the logical pattern in each of these three sequences?

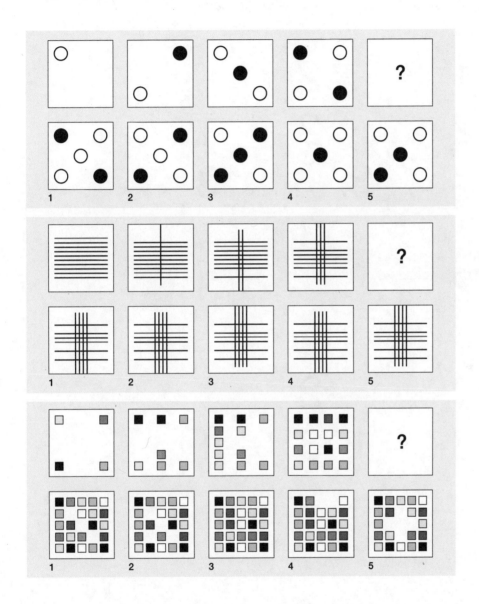

THREE AT A RHYME

Rearrange these letters to form three one-syllable words that rhyme.

E E G I I I M N N N S S T

_____   _____   _____

★★★★ Fences

Connect the dots with vertical or horizontal lines, so that a single loop is formed with no crossings or branches. Each number indicates how many lines surround it; squares with no number may be surrounded by any number of lines.

```
1   1 3   2
1   2   2   1
        3     3
2       3
    2         3
  1   3
  1   0   2   1
    3   1 3   1
```

ADDITION SWITCH

Switch the positions of two of the digits in the incorrect sum at right, to get a correct sum.

```
  362
+ 459
-----
  701
```

★★★★★ Themeless Toughie by Merle Baker

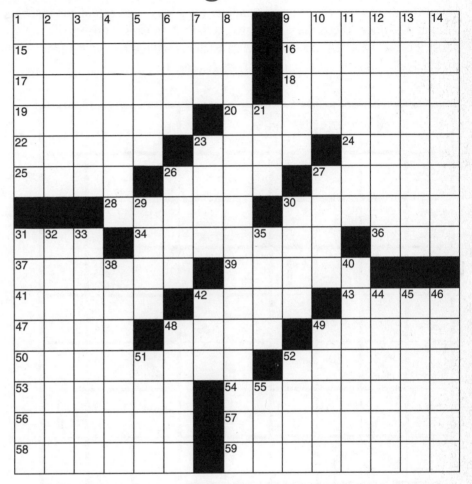

ACROSS

1 Rested
9 Much of Argentina
15 Spenser sonnet cycle
16 Bake
17 Burt Reynolds film of '88
18 Are compelled
19 Somber sounds
20 Evolves
22 Onetime New York natives
23 Put away
24 Saponification product
25 Mild oath
26 Wayne or Knox
27 *Compás* direction
28 Earth mover
30 Trusted teacher
31 Meas. of discomfort
34 Flustered
36 Yearbook buyers: Abbr.
37 Prepares to bow
39 *CSI* venue
41 In the company of
42 Livestock fare
43 Park Ave. abodes
47 Memory measure
48 Toss down
49 __ Loops
50 Stand out
52 Candy-heart phrase
53 Crescentlike
54 Cagliari is its capital
56 Crème de la crème
57 Added up
58 Suspend a sitting
59 Sirens, e.g.

DOWN

1 *Dracula* character
2 Egyptian "father of the gods"
3 Succeeded
4 Frank
5 Makes final
6 Sundries, for short
7 Z preceder
8 Weighs
9 "Balderdash!"
10 Put __ on (limit)
11 Goes
12 Saves on postage
13 Relay device
14 Circular target
21 Sweetie
23 Na, in some compound names
26 Cal. pages
27 Red-spotted scooter
29 Sharp sound
30 Coordinate
31 Careless one, perhaps
32 Gandhi's quest
33 Like a square
35 Baker's meas.
38 Tuition category
40 Oater slur
42 Alluvial deposit
44 Ballet position
45 More exclusive
46 Places
48 Gather
49 Patient no more
51 Itineraries: Abbr.
52 Ichabod foe
55 Soul, to Sartre

★★★★ 123

Fill in the diagram so that each rectangular piece has one each of the numbers
1, 2, and 3, under these rules: 1) No two adjacent squares, horizontally or
vertically, can have the same number. 2) Each completed row and column of the
diagram will have an equal number of 1s, 2s, and 3s.

SUDOKU SUM

Without repeating any digits, complete the sum at right,
by filling one digit in each of the five blanks.

```
  4 _ 8
+ _ 1 _
_ _ 7
```

★★★ Number-Out

Shade squares so that no number appears in any row or column more than once. Shaded squares may not touch each other horizontally or vertically, and all unshaded squares must form a single continuous area.

1	5	4	2	3	2
1	3	6	1	4	5
5	5	1	6	2	2
6	2	6	5	6	4
1	1	3	1	6	2
2	6	4	3	1	6

OPPOSITE ATTRACTION

Unscramble the letters in the phrase GROWTH RING to form two common words that are opposites of each other.

_____   _____

★★★★★ Themeless Toughie by Daniel R. Stark

ACROSS

1 Like some audio books
9 Field workers
15 A real Renaissance man
16 Sort of paint
17 Bomb big-time
18 Stem (from)
19 Where to hear Farsi
20 Unseld of the NBA
21 Nicked
22 Conger catcher
24 Poker player's giveaway
26 Groovy, today
27 Dr. of rap
28 Marked down
31 Whitish
32 On deck
33 Diminish, with "out"
34 Spelunker hangout
36 Pulled down
38 Sari wearers
39 Have collected
41 Some ceramics
42 Part of the Corn Belt
43 German 101 verb
46 Egg __ yung
47 Tight gripper
48 Stately home
50 Conductor's concern
52 Floor
55 Actress Falco
56 Cruise carriers
57 Reluctant to talk
59 Box up
60 Heightened
61 Regarded as
62 Newborns

DOWN

1 In the pact
2 Bwana's helper
3 Isle __ National Park
4 Nonsensical
5 Martial-arts level
6 Matured
7 Trim
8 Canis Major component
9 Get snoopy
10 TV newsman Roger
11 Put on guard
12 Change citizenship
13 Made public
14 Luge driver
23 Duds with belts
25 Chief's advisers
29 Postal Creed word
30 Year-end temps
31 Madonna ex
32 Bird: Lat.
33 Geometric solid
34 Former First Daughter
35 Make public
37 Literary miscellany
38 Frilly
40 Left over
42 Touched lightly
43 Prepare for service
44 Evening gala
45 General drifts
47 Lines from Lowell
49 Hartford competitor
51 Wagon pullers
53 Dwindle
54 Repeat
58 Auric's creator

★★★ Shakespearean Jigsaw

Find these characters from Shakespeare's plays that are arranged in jigsaw puzzle shapes in the diagram. One piece is shown to get you started.

```
D E S C O M A L J K G O N E R O H C O C
A L D E G A I V U I N G B T I L E L R E
R A E L I A J O L I U L O R L U K E D N
T D M O N A E L I O S E L I N C O B E O
E Y R O O R S O R M C A I N G B R Y L T
M M E H B K S T E A A R S I R T O B I S
I A H T I C I H G C E S A R L P C T A H
D C B E N O C E A B T C S M A E O O U C
O C U P G L A L N E I A E I U R B W E B
R K R A O Y O L H T T L B S N I C L E S
U S I D O H S B I N A I A T C E L O T G
W L E F A T T O A N A B S R C L E O P O
O L L E D O H T H N A I T E O F R R A B
M I R A N M G K C I U Q S S L A O O T B
R Y T H E E I L N O R E B O I L M S R O
N R U C H I O Y H A M R O P V S E A A D
E T O L B E S B E N L I R A I T O L I N
H E S D R I A E P E E C T P O A F F B A
T P S O M H K C I D T H I H A L O I V N
E I L U J T E H T D R A A E L I A O U Q
```

ARIEL
ARTEMIDORUS
BANQUO
BENEDICK
BOLINGBROKE
BOTTOM
CALIBAN
CELIA
CLEOPATRA
COBWEB
CORDELIA
~~DESDEMONA~~
FALSTAFF
GONERIL
HAMLET
HENRY THE EIGHTH
HERO
IAGO
JESSICA
JULIET
JULIUS CAESAR
KING LEAR
LADY MACBETH
LAUNCELOT GOBBO
MACBETH

MALVOLIO
MIRANDA
MISTRESS QUICKLY
OBERON
OLIVIA
OPHELIA
OTHELLO
PEASEBLOSSOM
PERICLES
PETRUCHIO
PORTIA
PUCK
REGAN
RICHARD THE THIRD
ROBIN GOODFELLOW
ROMEO
ROSALIND
SEBASTIAN
SHYLOCK
SIR TOBY BELCH
TITANIA
TOUCHSTONE
TRINCULO
VIOLA

IN OTHER WORDS

There is only one common uncapitalized word that contains the consecutive letters MCE. What is it?

_____

★★★★ Straight Ahead

Enter the grid at the second white square from the top at left, pass through all of the blue squares, and then exit at the white square at left directly above the one you entered. You must travel horizontally or vertically in a straight line, and turn only to avoid passing through a black square. It is okay to retrace your path.

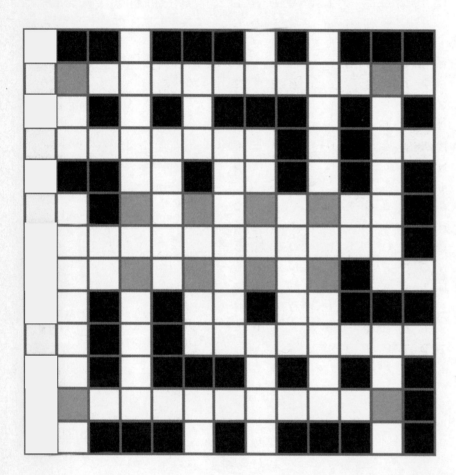

SAY IT AGAIN

What six-letter word meaning "to quit," when pronounced differently, is also a word meaning "to continue to serve"?

__ __ __ __ __ __

★★★★★ Themeless Toughie by S.N.

ACROSS

- **1** Gap
- **7** Checked
- **15** Good with one's hands
- **16** Tall, thin one
- **17** Angolan money
- **18** Cole Porter film score
- **19** Rankles
- **20** John Glenn in *The Right Stuff*
- **21** Respectful address
- **22** Saddle sticker
- **24** *Boys of Summer* subject
- **25** One way to say yes
- **26** Martinique's group
- **30** Easter preceder
- **31** *Children of the Albatross* author
- **32** One out
- **33** Shell filler
- **34** Source of warmth
- **35** Marceau character
- **38** Screen lines
- **40** *M*A*S*H* extras
- **43** Sweater letter
- **44** Toaster, at times
- **45** Stuff in seams
- **46** New York Public Library benefactor
- **48** Profile
- **49** Retreat
- **50** *To Venus and Back* artist
- **54** Rusher's dismissal
- **56** Emulate Cousteau
- **57** Medicinal plant
- **58** Island that bans autos
- **59** Literature Nobelist of '71
- **60** Top secret
- **61** Britten opera hero

DOWN

- **1** Acquires copiously
- **2** *Braveheart* villain
- **3** GI meal
- **4** A dog's age
- **5** Not to be sneezed at
- **6** Lofty
- **7** Fit
- **8** Thatching material
- **9** Precipitate
- **10** Fighting words
- **11** High point
- **12** Outburst
- **13** Hughes protégé
- **14** Trifle, perhaps
- **23** Pops up again
- **27** Middle
- **28** Coolness
- **29** Transferee's activity
- **35** Clueless one's comment
- **36** "Don't worry!"
- **37** Name meaning "of noble descent"
- **38** Subject of some FCC regulations
- **39** Gumshoe
- **40** Bit
- **41** Ready when you arrive
- **42** Iroquois League members
- **47** Pen complaints
- **51** F. Scott Fitzgerald's birthplace
- **52** Kiwi-like
- **53** Executive dept. head
- **55** Blythe's daughter in *Meet the Parents*

★★★★ ABCD

Enter the letters A, B, C, and D into the diagram so that each row and column has exactly one A, one B, one C, and one D. The letters outside the diagram indicate the first letter encountered, moving in the direction of the arrow. Keep in mind that after all the letters have been filled in, there will be two blank boxes in each row and column.

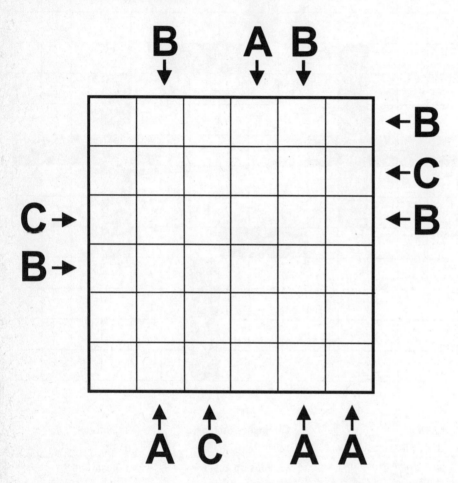

NATIONAL TREASURE

Using the letters in VIETNAM, we were able to form two common uncapitalized six-letter words. Can you find them both?

— — — — — —   — — — — — —

★★★★ Sudoku

Fill in the blank boxes so that every row, column, and 3x3 box contains all of the numbers 1 to 9.

				6		9		
		5	1					
	4					2		5
	9			2				
6			3		1			7
				7			3	
5		7					6	
					2	8		
		4		8				

MIXAGRAMS

Each line contains a five-letter word and a four-letter word that have been mixed together (the order of the letters in each word has not been changed). Unmix the two words on each line and write them in the spaces provided. When you're done, find a two-part answer to the clue by reading down the letter columns in the answers.

CLUE: Canadian import

A S P O N O T E F = _ _ _ _ _ + _ _ _ _

R A N I S O N E E = _ _ _ _ _ + _ _ _ _

L U C K R I L E N = _ _ _ _ _ + _ _ _ _

A F T O L A P M E = _ _ _ _ _ + _ _ _ _

★★★★★ Themeless Toughie by Daniel R. Stark

ACROSS

1 Exotic vacation
7 Literally, "in sailor's style"
15 Looked into
16 More than worried
17 Slide specimen
18 Archer partner
19 Southern capital
21 Edge of a sort
22 Poison Ivy portrayer
23 Don Juans
24 Take the check
26 Actor Ayres
27 Mesa Verde attraction
29 Dutch master
30 Santa __ winds
31 Yonder
33 Comic Philips
35 Baffles
37 Port on the Clyde
41 Subject for Keats
42 Lacking detail
43 Hockey great
44 Shar-Pei shakers
47 Baby, maybe
49 Oklahoma town
50 Port near Kyoto
52 Defensive rings
55 Relay segment
56 Air-pump meas.
57 Accounting record
60 Passé
62 Home of Deere and Company
63 Something for nothing
64 More level
65 Searched (out)
66 Unites again

DOWN

1 Paint spreaders
2 Weaponry
3 Squander
4 First shepherd
5 Steel rod
6 Its highest point is Borah Peak
7 Health-club staffer
8 Graf's mate
9 Kind of apple
10 Map detail
11 Bit of cold
12 Member of the rhododendron family
13 Phone button
14 Skilled ones
20 Psychics may see them
25 P P P
28 Jodie Foster film of '94
31 Empty space
32 __ shui
34 Totally impractical
36 Perfume ingredient
37 Fundraisers, often
38 Objective of some sports
39 Meant to be
40 Bathrobes
42 Acted moody
44 Complain
45 Sew up
46 Order handler
48 Hamper
51 Put on a pedestal
53 Cook's need
54 Cook's need
58 Touch up
59 Vast number
61 Debussy subject

★★★★ One-Way Streets

The diagram represents a pattern of streets. Ps are parking spaces, and the black squares are stores. Find the route that starts at a parking space, passes through all stores exactly once, and ends at the other parking space. Arrows indicate one-way traffic for that block only. No block or intersection may be entered more than once.

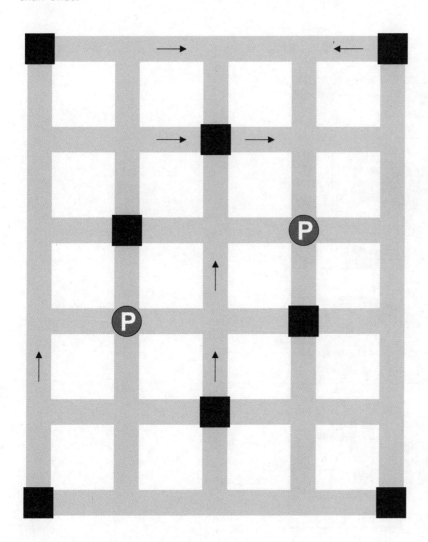

SOUND THINKING

The consonant sounds in the word UXORIAL (pronounced "uck-SORE-ee-ul," meaning "of a wife") are K, S, R, and L, in that order. What more common word, a culinary term, consists of exactly the same consonant sounds in the same order?

_____

★★ Split Decisions

In this clueless crossword puzzle, each answer consists of two words whose spellings are the same, except for the consecutive letters given. All answers are common words; no phrases or hyphenated or capitalized words are used. Some of the clues may have more than one solution, but there is only one word pair that will correctly link up with all the other word pairs.

TRANSDELETION

Delete one letter from the word EMBATTLES and rearrange the rest, to get a two-word term for something found in a car.

_____

★★★★★ Themeless Toughie by Daniel R. Stark

ACROSS

1 Derisive sounds
8 Like some exercise
15 Issue forth
16 Grade-school project
17 Extension
18 Romance, for 14 Down
19 1987 Peace Prize winner
20 Relax, with "out"
22 Bart's mother
23 Object to
24 Craze
26 Roulette bet
27 Islanders' surface
28 Great numbers
30 Name in Beatles history
31 Tumbled down
33 Flower part
35 At __ (conflicting)
36 Hit the water
37 Mole's work
40 Oater heroes
44 *Femenino* suffix
45 Some pro golfers
47 Edge
48 Telejournalist Cosby
50 Overindulges
51 News follower
52 Vibrant
54 Poodle pro
55 Triumphal outburst
56 Branch off
58 Major unrest
60 Ceaseless
61 Inherent quality
62 Organized ways
63 Came out

DOWN

1 Like terra cotta
2 "Ventura Highway" band
3 Four teeth
4 Work clay
5 Passed bills
6 Depot info
7 Fabric edges
8 Ballet duet
9 Austrian article
10 Travel far and wide
11 Bach instrument
12 Saloon
13 Think of
14 *Terminator 2* director
21 Camelot lady
24 Interfered
25 What some keys have
28 Takes on cargo
29 Moves a bit
32 Bilk
34 End of Jack's boast
36 Closet item
37 Diatribes
38 Public service
39 You find them in your travels
40 Place
41 On the lam
42 Get behind
43 Freeloaded
46 Long stories
49 Head off
51 After a while
53 Bird of prey
55 Model
57 Herd of whales
59 Belief

★★★★ Looped Path

Draw a continuous, unbroken loop that passes through each of the red, blue, and white squares exactly once. Move from square to square in a straight line or by turning left or right, but never diagonally. You must alternate passing through red and blue squares, with any number of white squares in between.

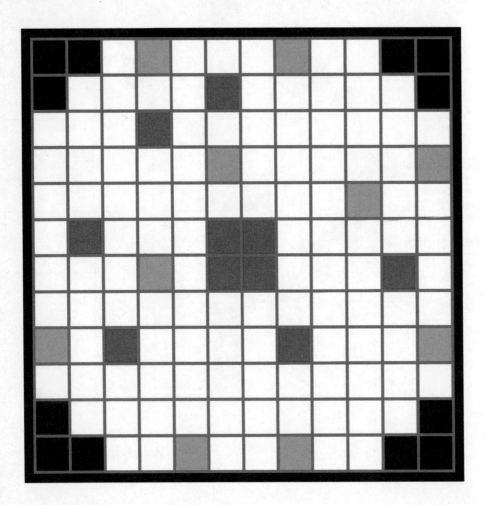

SAY IT AGAIN

What seven-letter word meaning "to create," when pronounced differently, is also a word for a section of a supermarket?

— — — — — — —

★★★★ Star Search

Find the stars that are hidden in some of the blank squares. The numbered squares indicate how many stars are hidden in the squares adjacent to them (including diagonally). There is never more than one star in any square.

				2		**1**	
		1					
2		**2**		**4**		**2**		**1**
						2	
			2		**3**			**2**
			3					
					5	**3**		**3**
		3		**3**			**2**	
					3			
		2		**2**		**2**		

TELEPHONE TRIOS

	ABC	DEF
1	**2**	**3**

GHI	JKL	MNO
4	**5**	**6**

PRS	TUV	WXY
7	**8**	**9**

*	**0**	**#**

Using the numbers and letters on a standard telephone, what three seven-letter words or phrases from the same category can be formed from these telephone numbers?

287-8246   _ _ _ _ _ _ _

748-8837   _ _ _ _ _ _ _

825-2623   _ _ _ _ _ _ _

★★★★★ Themeless Toughie by Doug Peterson

ACROSS

1 Tabloid topic
8 Woodstock group
15 Heat measure
16 Trimmed
17 They're revolting
18 Acted as oracle
19 Wings
20 Certain solvents
21 Took a gander
22 Moxie
23 *M* actor
25 English earldom
29 Pillar of Islam
33 "That's not good"
34 Selling point
35 Noggin nugget
36 Fast-food order
38 Sparkle
39 Blanch, perhaps
41 Paddington Bear's origin
42 Artist Bonheur
43 Meaning
44 Pick up on
46 Shooter's support
48 Tackle
53 Made eyes
56 Pavlova role
57 Filled food
58 Ohio college town
59 Formally designates
60 Most simple
61 Superlatively short
62 Former Mexican president Zedillo

DOWN

1 Come to blows
2 Minesweeper of fiction
3 Exclusively
4 Observant one
5 Dragons' school
6 Vented
7 Take away
8 Where a lariat is looped
9 Parting word
10 Green bunch
11 Br'er Rabbit, for one
12 Rice, e.g.
13 Poetic adverb
14 Contributes
22 Press on
24 Reciter of Homer
26 Number for one
27 Prohibition et al.
28 '90s TV action heroine
29 Fountain collaborator
30 Chick follower
31 Anouilh of drama
32 Pioneer photojournalist
37 It goes through a lot of seaweed
40 Half-octave
45 Start gently
47 Hides
49 Ella Fitzgerald record label
50 They, to Monet
51 Select names
52 Near the hour
53 __ house
54 Pins' place
55 Composer Novello
56 Out of sight

★★★★ Number-Out

Shade squares so that no number appears in any row or column more than once. Shaded squares may not touch each other horizontally or vertically, and all unshaded squares must form a single continuous area.

5	1	5	6	2	3
2	3	6	2	1	2
3	4	5	2	2	1
6	5	6	4	6	3
1	6	3	6	4	5
6	4	2	5	2	4

OPPOSITE ATTRACTION

Unscramble the letters in the phrase HOWLED PLEAS to form two common words that are opposites of each other.

_____   _____

★★★★ Line Drawing

Draw four straight lines, each from one edge of the square to another edge, so that four circles have no lines touching them, five circles have one line passing through them, and one circle has two lines passing through it. Hint: None of the four lines you draw will intersect with another.

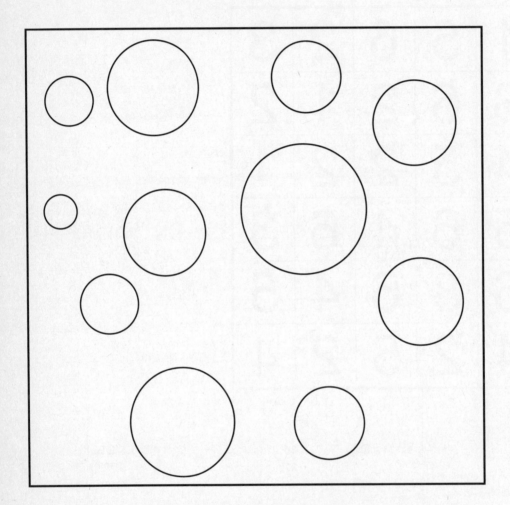

TWO-BY-FOUR

The eight letters in the word HYDROGEN can be rearranged to form a pair of common four-letter words in only one way. Can you find the two words?

— — — — . — — — —

★★★★★ Themeless Toughie by Anna Stiga

ACROSS

1 Music to a griller's ears
9 PC accessory
15 Monocled mascot
16 Maryland state bird
17 The sexes, supposedly
18 Scully's partner
19 Winner of seven Tonys
20 Source of warmth
22 Repudiate
23 Something to save
24 Ate
25 Despicable one
29 Scold
33 Encouraging words
36 Dijon's home
38 Prince William, circa 1999
39 Displays
41 As Nestor would
42 Blade of a windmill
43 NLer since '62
45 Ceremonial attire
48 Soother
52 It may help start your day
55 Toots
56 Most together
57 Bull feature
59 Access
60 Source for "It's Now or Never"
61 Flipped, to investors
62 Sears subsidiary

DOWN

1 Fix well
2 Want in the worst way
3 Choose to participate
4 Meshlike
5 '40s First Family member
6 Compass reading
7 Saw some sites
8 One of the Apostles
9 Most people
10 Blow
11 Like big waves
12 Pas de deux part, perhaps
13 Former Earl of Home
14 Trifling
21 Roxie in *Chicago*
23 Seconder's response
24 They're in for a while
26 Jon's dog
27 Unaffected
28 A raft of
29 Where Martin Short first played Ed Grimley
30 Ibsen character
31 Oodles
32 Philly Pops founder
34 Between ports
35 Just right
37 Charge
40 Johnson & Johnson brand
44 Brunch drink
46 Bill Ford's grandfather
47 Like some exclusive communities
48 Drags
49 Foreign film geanre
50 *The State and Revolution* author
51 Cry of astonishment
52 Not a true friend
53 Stamp sheet
54 Symbols of industry
55 Stood firm
58 Business partner, perhaps

★★ Triad Split Decisions

In this clueless crossword puzzle, each answer consists of two words whose spellings are the same, except for the consecutive letters given. All answers are common words; no phrases or hyphenated or capitalized words are used. Some of the clues may have more than one solution, but there is only one word pair that will correctly link up with all the other word pairs.

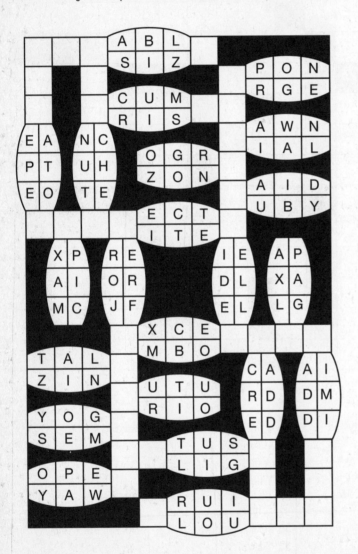

TRANSDELETION

Delete one letter from the word OMNIPRESENT and rearrange the rest, to get a dinner course usually served hot.

_____

★★ Space Holders

Which of the numbered satellites will fit into each dock of the space station?

THREE AT A RHYME

Rearrange these letters to form three one-syllable words that rhyme.

B E E E H I L O R S S S U U

_____   _____   _____

★★★★★ Themeless Toughie by Merle Baker

ACROSS

1 Keen & Co., e.g.
8 Rose
15 Important guest
16 Like Nadia Comaneci
17 They may be taken seriously
19 *Love Story* composer
20 Coup victim of '67
21 Vanderbilt acquisitions: Abbr.
22 Env. contents
24 Vincent successor
25 Giovanni Dandolo was one
26 Societal breakdown
28 *Arabian Nights* menace
29 Caged tiger, perhaps
30 Lowers
32 Superlatively peppy
34 Bullfighting maneuver
35 Brace
36 Spenser subjects
39 Scorsese subject
42 Finicky one, maybe
43 Period
45 Like leaves
46 Saudi provincial leader
47 Stiff collars
49 One-channel
50 English __
51 Writing names
53 Drug-stds. publication
54 Flighty fellow
57 Entangle
58 Balloon car
59 Crows' homes
60 Flirtatious glance

DOWN

1 Something to get out
2 Steve Martin film of '87
3 Monopolistic
4 NT book
5 Start of a Cockney toast
6 Mythical twin
7 Quidditch players
8 Some brothers
9 Name of two Chinese dynasties
10 Playground retort
11 E. Lansing school
12 Didn't let sleeping dogs lie
13 Surfaces
14 Ambrosia, for one
18 Saint-__ (French port)
23 Mudslinging pol
25 Pool-table spot, perhaps
27 Big name in Mideast history
29 Groom oneself
31 Eleanor Roosevelt, __ Roosevelt
33 One of the majors
36 Be healthy
37 *It's Too Late Now* autobiographer
38 Some Vonnegut novels
39 Action on the set
40 Not slack
41 Home addition
44 Fall guy
47 *École* attendee
48 *Who's Afraid of Virginia Woolf?* actor
51 Having the means
52 Vittorio De __
55 Sonny Rollins style
56 Breakfast partner

PAGE 17
Instructive

R	A	L	P	H		S	C	A	M		S	A	V	E
A	L	A	M	O		P	O	L	E		O	X	E	N
F	I	R	S	T	C	L	A	S	S		R	E	A	D
T	E	D		T	A	I	L		S	H	E	L	L	S
			N	E	S	T		P	I	E	S			
T	O	R	E	A	T			R	E	F	U	N	D	S
A	V	O	W		E	W	E	S		B	A	I	T	
R	E	D	S		F	L	E	E	T		J	I	M	I
P	R	E	P		O	V	E	N		E	V	E	R	
S	T	O	R	A	G	E			A	C	C	E	S	S
			O	I	L	S		S	L	A	T			
E	N	I	G	M	A		T	E	E	N		B	O	G
L	E	A	R		M	A	I	N	C	O	U	R	S	E
S	A	G	A		P	A	N	S		P	S	A	L	M
A	T	O	M		S	A	T	E		Y	O	Y	O	S

PAGE 18
Five Squares

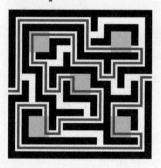

COUNT UP
1+23+45+67-89 = 47

PAGE 19
Puzzle Pieces

INITIAL REACTION
Talk Is Cheap

PAGE 20
Sudoku

8	9	5	6	4	3	2	1	7
7	2	6	9	5	1	3	8	4
1	4	3	7	8	2	9	6	5
5	6	8	4	2	7	1	9	3
3	1	2	5	9	8	7	4	6
4	7	9	1	3	6	8	5	2
9	5	7	3	1	4	6	2	8
2	3	4	8	6	9	5	7	1
6	8	1	2	7	5	4	3	9

MIXAGRAMS

B R O I L   P A C E
I N L E T   W H O A
L E G I T   R U D E
L I V E R   D A Y S

PAGE 21
Falling

C	H	A	O	S		R	O	A	D		T	O	T	S
O	O	M	P	H		A	N	T	E		U	H	O	H
E	N	T	E	R		N	E	O	N		M	A	D	E
D	E	S	C	E	N	D	A	N	T		B	R	A	D
			W	A	R			A	L	L	E	Y	S	
S	H	O	D	D	Y		M	E	L	E	E			
O	M	N	I		S	O	O	T		A	W	A	K	E
S	O	L	V	E		G	O	T		P	E	R	I	L
A	S	Y	E	T		R	E	E	L		E	E	L	S
			B	A	A	E	D		U	P	D	A	T	E
S	T	O	O	L	S		A	K	A					
T	E	R	M		S	L	I	D	E	R	U	L	E	S
A	H	A	B		E	Y	R	E		O	S	A	K	A
M	E	T	E		T	R	A	P		L	E	V	E	L
P	E	E	R		S	E	N	T		E	R	A	S	E

PAGE 22
Fences

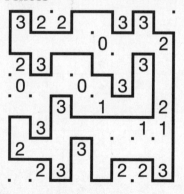

ADDITION SWITCH
5 8 3 + 2 9 1 = 8 7 4

PAGE 23
Line Drawing

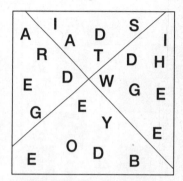

STAID, GRADE, WEIGHED, OBEYED

THREE OF A KIND
MOST HAWAII MAPS INCLUDE A SHELF, REEF, OR A VALLEY

PAGE 24
The Caped Crusader

WHO'S WHAT WHERE?
Neapolitan

PAGE 25
Join the Group

T	A	R	A		F	L	E	E		B	U	T	T	E
E	L	A	L		E	A	R	P		O	N	A	I	R
M	I	N	I		D	I	R	E		W	I	L	L	A
P	A	C	K	H	O	R	S	E		T	O	L	L	S
		S	H	E	A	R		S	P	I	N			
			S	A	S	H		R	E	J	E	C	T	
N	O	T	C	H		P	O	L	O		A	R	L	O
A	B	E	L		S	A	L	A	D		C	L	A	Y
P	E	R	U		O	M	E	N		S	K	E	W	S
S	Y	M	B	O	L		S	E	A	T				
			S	H	E	A		L	O	A	D	S		
W	R	O	T	E		G	A	N	G	P	L	A	N	K
R	I	P	E	N		O	R	E	O		L	I	O	N
A	L	T	A	R		N	E	A	R		A	L	O	E
P	E	S	K	Y		Y	A	L	E		H	Y	P	E

PAGE 26

Number-Out

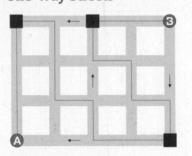

OPPOSITE ATTRACTION
SOFT, HARD

PAGE 27

Stringalong

THREE AT A RHYME
CLAY, HEY, WEIGH

PAGE 28

Don't 56 Down

M	I	A	M	I		F	L	A	G		A	S	T	I
O	S	C	A	R		L	I	L	Y		U	P	O	N
P	E	R	P	E	T	U	A	L	M	O	T	I	O	N
S	E	E	M		O	K	R	A		A	U	N	T	S
	A	T	T	Y		B	D	R	M					
S	P	O	K	E	S		F	O	E		N	E	I	L
T	E	P	E	E		F	E	A	S	T		A	D	E
E	T	E	R	N	A	L	T	R	I	A	N	G	L	E
P	A	R		S	T	A	I	D		B	A	L	E	R
S	L	A	B		M	U	D			B	L	U	E	S	Y
		L	I	S	T		B	E	E	T				
M	E	D	A	L		I	S	L	E		I	T	E	M
E	V	E	R	L	A	S	T	I	N	G	L	O	V	E
R	I	S	E		A	T	O	P		P	U	G	E	T
E	L	K	S		A	S	P	S		A	S	O	N	E

PAGE 29

One-Way Streets

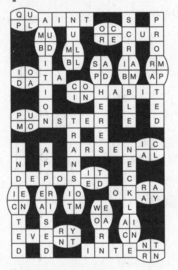

SOUND THINKING
WISE GUY

PAGE 30

Split Decisions

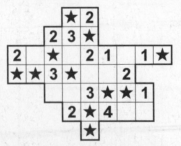

TRANSDELETION
TOPSOIL

PAGE 31

Star Search

TELEPHONE TRIOS
DEFIANT, GALLANT, VALIANT

PAGE 32

Leap Day

B L K E C E E Y E P M H
V A O G L L R B G E Q T
Y E W L O E N U I E E A
R P L P C A P A B L E E
J P D A L P K H L S Q L
L A U A L U L L A A A F P
T A P V L E P A D N L S
F S I A A N E L P A T S
E A F C C T T L Y E C Z
Z O P P E Y S E P A L J
P E A R L P R T P A E L
X D J N M S S X H T I W

Unlisted words are ELEPHANT and TADPOLE

IN OTHER WORDS
SAUCY

PAGE 33

Watch Your Step

E	B	B	S		S	C	R	A	P		S	H	O	P
R	E	A	L		O	H	A	R	E		L	I	N	E
A	L	S	O		F	E	V	E	R		I	D	E	A
S	L	I	P	S	T	R	E	A	M		D	E	S	K
	S	L	E	E	T			S	I	Z	E			
			T	O	G	A		T	O	R	E	U	P	
P	A	N	T		P	I	T	A		N	U	R	S	E
S	N	O	R	E		F	L	U		E	L	M	E	R
S	T	R	I	P		T	A	N	G		E	A	S	T
T	E	M	P	E	R		S	T	O	P				
			M	E	E	K			L	O	C	A	L	
C	A	P	E		F	A	L	L	F	L	O	W	E	R
A	L	I	T		E	R	A	S	E		S	A	V	E
L	O	N	E		R	A	D	A	R		T	R	E	E
L	E	E	R		S	T	E	T	S		S	E	L	L

PAGE 34

Hyper-Sudoku

4	8	7	5	2	3	9	6	1
3	6	2	8	1	9	5	7	4
9	1	5	4	7	6	2	3	8
5	9	3	7	6	4	1	8	2
8	2	6	3	5	1	7	4	9
1	7	4	2	9	8	6	5	3
6	5	8	1	4	2	3	9	7
2	3	9	6	8	7	4	1	5
7	4	1	9	3	5	8	2	6

MIXAGRAMS
K N I F E   E A S Y
O N I O N   S C A R
A B O U T   Z E A L
S H I R K   A S E A

PAGE 35
Window Dressing
A: #6, B: #8, C: #1

BETWEENER
BOY

PAGE 36
123

3	2	1	3	1	2
1	3	2	1	2	3
2	1	3	2	3	1
1	2	1	3	2	3
3	1	3	2	1	2
2	3	2	1	3	1

SUDOKU SUM
4 1 2 + 3 9 5 = 8 0 7

PAGE 37
"A in Geography

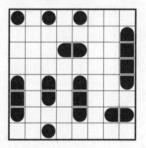

O	P	A	L	S		S	L	U	M		C	O	O	L
A	L	L	O	T		P	O	S	E		A	U	R	A
T	E	A	S	E		E	Y	E	S		S	T	I	R
S	A	N	T	A	C	L	A	R	A		A	G	O	G
			L	U	L	L	S		T	B	O	N	E	
E	S	T	A	T	E			P	O	L				
R	E	A	C	H		S	I	D	E	W	A	L	K	S
M	A	R	C		O	S	C	A	R		N	E	I	L
A	T	T	R	A	C	T	E	D		S	C	A	L	E
			A	N	T			M	E	A	D	O	W	
B	A	G	G	Y		C	A	J	U	N				
U	T	A	H		M	A	D	A	G	A	S	C	A	R
L	A	V	A		O	D	D	S		T	A	U	P	E
G	L	E	N		V	E	T	O		E	M	B	E	D
E	L	L	A		E	T	O	N		S	E	E	D	S

PAGE 38
ABC

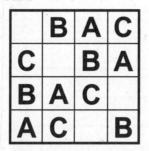

	B	A	C
C		B	A
B	A	C	
A	C		B

CLUELESS CROSSWORD

L	U	C	K	I	E	R
I		O		N		E
K	I	N	G	D	O	M
A		C		U		A
B	R	O	I	L	E	R
L		R		G		K
E	N	D	L	E	S	S

PAGE 39
Find the Ships

TWO-BY-FOUR
LAMA, BORN; ROAN, LAMB (or BALM); LOAM, BARN (or BRAN)

PAGE 40
National League

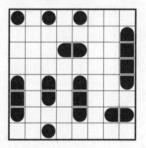

Missing word is BELARUS

INITIAL REACTION
Look Before You Leap

PAGE 41
Face Invaders

A	J	A	R		P	A	L	M		R	I	S	K	S
L	O	R	E		O	L	E	O		U	N	T	I	E
P	L	E	A		N	O	N	O		S	L	A	T	E
S	T	A	R	S	I	N	O	N	E	S	E	Y	E	S
				T	E	E			L	I	T			
C	A	M	P	U	S		A	S	I	A		G	A	B
A	T	E	I	N		A	B	I	T		T	U	B	A
R	O	C	K	S	I	N	O	N	E	S	H	E	A	D
O	N	C	E		O	N	U	S		T	A	S	T	E
L	E	A		S	W	A	T		C	E	N	T	E	R
			S	P	A			B	O	A				
F	O	O	T	I	N	O	N	E	S	M	O	U	T	H
R	O	B	I	N		W	I	L	T		A	C	R	E
O	Z	O	N	E		E	C	O	L		F	L	A	W
M	E	E	T	S		D	E	W	Y		S	A	Y	S

PAGE 42
Star Maze

THREE AT A RHYME
BUN, ONE, TON

PAGE 43
Fences

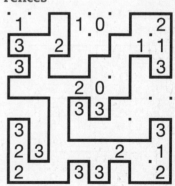

ADDITION SWITCH
2 3 4 + 5 6 7 = 8 0 1

PAGE 44

Multiple Meanings

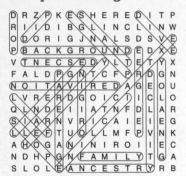

"Key" word is DESCENT

WHO'S WHAT WHERE?
Surinamer

PAGE 45

TV Talk

P	A	L	M		O	A	S	I	S		S	O	M	E
E	L	I	A		C	R	E	A	K		A	B	E	L
C	O	M	P	U	T	E	R	N	E	T	W	O	R	K
S	E	E		S	E	T			W	A	T	E	R	S
		M	E	T	H	O	D		P	O	S	Y		
	B	E	E	F		A	R	O	S	E				
S	E	A	L	U	P		D	C	I		S	A	G	E
G	A	S	O	L	I	N	E	S	T	A	T	I	O	N
T	M	E	N		T	A	R		E	R	O	D	E	D
		P	A	T	I	O		E	V	E	S			
	L	A	C	E		O	N	L	A	T	E			
T	O	W	A	R	D		D	U	O		U	F	O	
G	R	A	D	U	A	T	E	P	R	O	G	R	A	M
I	N	R	E		T	I	A	R	A		A	S	T	I
F	E	E	T		A	L	T	O	S		P	A	S	T

PAGE 46

Sudoku

7	6	4	9	5	2	8	1	3
1	3	2	7	8	6	9	4	5
9	8	5	4	1	3	6	7	2
8	5	3	2	4	7	1	6	9
2	1	6	8	3	9	7	5	4
4	9	7	1	6	5	2	3	8
5	2	9	3	7	1	4	8	6
6	4	1	5	2	8	3	9	7
3	7	8	6	9	4	5	2	1

MIXAGRAMS

B	E	L	L	Y		J	I	V	E
K	A	Z	O	O		O	M	I	T
A	R	E	N	A		H	A	W	K
R	O	U	G	E		N	E	X	T

PAGE 47

123

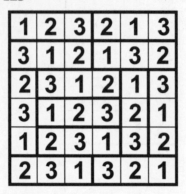

SUDOKU SUM
$1 6 9 + 2 3 8 = 4 0 7$

PAGE 48

At the Deli

PAGE 49

One-Way Streets

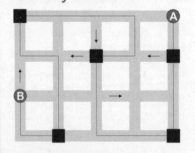

SOUND THINKING
OVERWROUGHT

PAGE 50

No Three in a Row

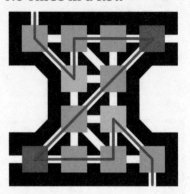

SAY IT AGAIN
SOW

PAGE 51

Star Search

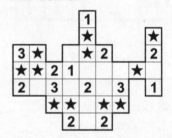

TELEPHONE TRIOS
LEBANON, UKRAINE, URUGUAY

PAGE 52

Lighten Up

B	O	N	U	S		G	A	S	P		V	A	T	S
O	B	E	S	E		O	R	E	O		E	R	I	E
L	O	W	E	R		L	E	A	N		R	I	D	E
D	E	S		B	A	L	A	N	C	E	B	E	A	M
	F	A	I	R	Y			H	A	S	S	L	E	
C	E	L	L	A	R		S	P	O	T				
A	R	A	B		O	T	T	O		S	H	A	F	T
S	A	S	E		W	O	O	L	S		A	F	R	O
A	S	H	E	S		B	O	O	T		S	T	I	R
		I	C	E	D		A	T	T	E	S	T		
A	C	C	U	S	E		C	L	E	A	R			
M	A	R	T	I	N	S	H	E	E	N		G	P	S
I	N	I	T		T	O	E	D		A	L	L	A	H
S	O	M	E		E	L	L	E		N	O	O	N	E
S	E	E	R		R	E	P	S		T	O	W	E	D

PAGE 53

I At Last

Unlisted word is BIKINI

IN OTHER WORDS
RASPBERRY

PAGE 55

Line Drawing

The first names in each region all start with the same letter, and are either all male or all female.

THREE OF A KIND
THE BUFFA<u>LO</u> STEAK'S <u>TI</u>NY WIDTH <u>OUGHT</u> TO BE LARGER.

PAGE 56

ABC

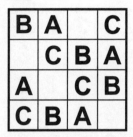

NATIONAL TREASURE
IMBUE, MAIZE, MAMBO

PAGE 57

Scare Words

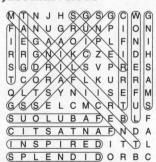

PAGE 58

Time Out
#4

BETWEENER
TIE

PAGE 59

Just Marvelous

Unlisted word is SPLENDID

INITIAL REACTION
To Err Is Human

PAGE 60

Find the Ships

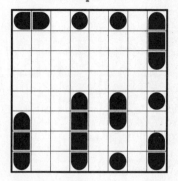

TWO-BY-FOUR
BARB, TICK

PAGE 61

Sudoku

9	2	5	1	6	8	3	4	7
3	8	6	4	7	5	2	9	1
4	1	7	9	2	3	5	6	8
2	9	8	7	5	1	6	3	4
5	7	4	6	3	2	8	1	9
1	6	3	8	4	9	7	5	2
8	3	2	5	9	4	1	7	6
7	5	9	2	1	6	4	8	3
6	4	1	3	8	7	9	2	5

MIXAGRAMS

```
P A S S E    B O D Y
S A W E D    E X I T
B O A S T    G I V E
L U N G E    S T E P
```

PAGE 62

Loved Ones

A crossword grid with the following answers filled in: OSCAR, ERAS, STAR, SNORE, MASC, HULA, HONEYBUNCH, ERIN, ABET, ISTOO, TAG, HAS, TOTALS, ICHABOD, LACE, DOE, SNUBS, MIDIS, ERASE, MEL, ADORE, AKRON, PEARL, VAN, TACT, WEEKEND, STREET, SSN, RAH, NOBLE, EARL, EURO, SWEETIEPIE, ATOP, EELS, CLEFS, DEBT, DRAT, ESSES.

PAGE 63

Fences

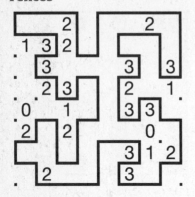

ADDITION SWITCH
3 4 5 + 2 7 8 = 6 2 3

PAGE 64

Triad Split Decisions

TRANSDELETION
STEEPLE

PAGE 65

123

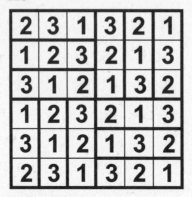

SUDOKU SUM
3 4 9 + 5 2 1 = 8 7 0

PAGE 66

Let's Be Candid

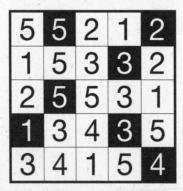

PAGE 67

Number-Out

OPPOSITE ATTRACTION
START, END

PAGE 68

Dicey

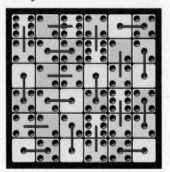

SAY IT AGAIN
DOVE

PAGE 69

Exotic Vacation

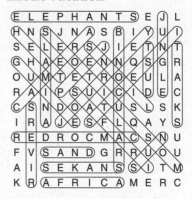

Missing word is RHINOS

WHO'S WHAT WHERE?
Albanian

PAGE 70

A Day At the Races

D	A	L	I		M	A	I	D		A	L	E	R	T
A	M	E	N		A	C	R	E		P	A	C	E	S
W	I	N	A	S	C	H	O	L	A	R	S	H	I	P
N	E	A	T	H		E	N	I	D		S	O	N	S
			R	E	V	S		C	I	A	O			
A	R	C	A	D	E		A	I	M	S		C	P	R
P	E	E	N		T	O	T	O		T	A	H	O	E
P	L	A	C	E	O	F	B	U	S	I	N	E	S	S
L	A	S	E	R		F	A	S	T		N	E	S	T
E	Y	E		G	A	I	T		A	D	O	R	E	S
			B	O	S	C		S	N	I	T			
E	S	S	O		T	I	M	E		O	A	T	E	R
S	H	O	W	T	O	A	D	V	A	N	T	A	G	E
P	O	L	L	S		T	I	E	R		E	C	O	N
N	O	O	S	E		E	I	R	E		S	O	S	O

One-Way Streets

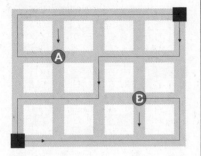

SOUND THINKING
TORPEDO

Hyper-Sudoku

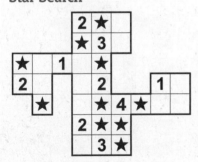

2	8	9	6	3	4	7	5	1
1	4	3	7	5	2	9	6	8
7	6	5	1	9	8	3	4	2
3	2	8	9	4	7	5	1	6
6	7	4	5	8	1	2	3	9
5	9	1	2	6	3	4	8	7
9	3	6	8	2	5	1	7	4
8	5	7	4	1	9	6	2	3
4	1	2	3	7	6	8	9	5

COUNT UP
12+34+56-7-8+9 = 96

Star Search

TELEPHONE TRIOS
ANXIOUS, JITTERY, KEYED UP

What's the Holdup?

A	T	W	A	R		A	M	P	S			S	E	T
L	O	O	S	E		L	O	S	E		B	O	R	E
S	L	O	T	S		E	L	A	L		A	S	I	A
O	L	D	I	E		C	E	L	L	B	L	O	C	K
		E	R	A	S			M	E	E	K			
P	A	N		L	A	M	A		R	E	S	A	T	
E	T	C		P	E	T	S		T	A	P	E	S	
G	O	L	F	S		A	L	E		S	T	R	A	W
S	N	O	O	P		T	A	M	E		I	R	A	
	E	G	R	E	T		S	I	R	S		C	S	T
	F	A	I	L			R	E	N	O				
S	P	A	R	K	P	L	U	G		A	E	T	N	A
H	A	R	E		P	A	N	E		M	A	J	O	R
A	C	M	E		E	M	I	R		A	T	A	R	I
H	E	Y		D	A	T	E		N	O	M	A	D	

ABC

B	C	A	
	A	B	C
C	B		A
A		C	B

CLUELESS CROSSWORD

W	E	T	L	A	N	D
I		R		C		R
T	R	A	P	E	Z	E
N		V		T		A
E	M	E	R	A	L	D
S		L		T		E
S	U	S	P	E	N	D

Jolly Roger Maze

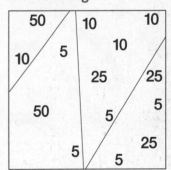

BETWEENER
HOT

Sudoku

9	7	2	6	3	1	8	4	5
8	3	6	4	7	5	9	2	1
4	1	5	2	9	8	7	3	6
5	6	8	9	4	7	2	1	3
1	2	7	5	6	3	4	8	9
3	9	4	8	1	2	6	5	7
7	5	9	1	2	4	3	6	8
6	4	1	3	8	9	5	7	2
2	8	3	7	5	6	1	9	4

MIXAGRAMS

R E H A B   E A S Y
B O O T Y   T R I O
D E B U T   R A Z E
P E A C E   D R E W

Hi, Guys

C	A	R	E		A	B	L	E		D	I	A	L
O	R	A	L		R	E	A	P		F	O	N	D	A
A	I	M	S		O	G	R	E		A	L	L	O	T
L	A	P	E	L	M	I	K	E		B	L	A	R	E
		I	A	N		P	L	A	Y	E	R			
S	N	I	F	F	S		C	H	E	E	R			
M	O	V	I	E		L	O	O	T		B	O	O	M
O	N	E	S		B	A	R	E	S		I	R	M	A
G	O	S	H		E	V	E	S		F	L	E	E	S
			I	D	E	A	S		S	A	L	O	N	S
B	M	I	N	U	S		S	E	T					
L	A	R	G	E		P	H	O	N	E	J	A	C	K
O	P	A	R	T		R	U	N	T		A	L	O	E
A	L	T	O	S		O	M	A	R		B	O	N	E
T	E	E	D		S	P	R	Y		S	T	E	P	

Line Drawing

THREE OF A KIND
YOU SHOULD READ THE AD
ABOUT TIP-TOP POTATOES.

PAGE 80

Find the Ships

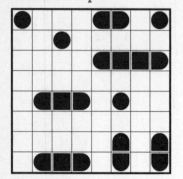

TWO-BY-FOUR
CAGY, HINT (or THIN); ACHY,
TING; HANG, CITY

PAGE 81

Fences

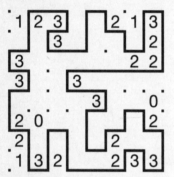

ADDITION SWITCH
7 0 9 + 1 3 6 = 8 4 5

PAGE 82

Food Money

C	R	E	P	E		A	L	A	S		H	I	N	T
A	O	L	E	R		T	A	L	C		E	D	I	E
P	A	S	T	A	D	O	U	G	H		A	O	N	E
E	R	E			S	E	N	D		O	O	D	L	E	S
			G	E	N	E		T	O	I	L			
O	S	C	A	R	S		C	O	L	L	E	C	T	
H	E	A	R	S		S	A	W	S			T	A	O	S
N	A	I	L		A	R	E			T	I	L	T	
O	M	N	I		S	L	E	D		P	U	R	E	E
	S	E	C	R	E	T	S		A	L	C	O	T	T
			B	E	V	Y		T	R	U	E			
S	W	E	R	V	E		M	A	I	M		B	A	G
H	I	V	E		R	E	D	C	A	B	B	A	G	E
A	R	E	A		A	L	S	O		E	R	R	O	R
M	E	N	D		L	I	E	S		R	A	N	G	E

PAGE 83

Out With the Old
#4

THREE AT A RHYME
APT, RAPT, TAPPED

PAGE 84

123

3	2	1	2	1	3	2	3	1
1	3	2	3	2	1	3	1	2
2	1	3	1	3	2	1	2	3
1	3	2	3	2	1	3	1	2
2	1	3	2	1	3	2	3	1
1	3	2	1	3	2	1	2	3
3	2	1	2	1	3	2	3	1
2	1	3	1	3	2	1	2	3
3	2	1	3	2	1	3	1	2

SUDOKU SUM
1 2 5 + 6 0 9 = 7 3 4

PAGE 85

Number-Out

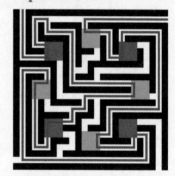

OPPOSITE ATTRACTION
GAIN, LOSE

PAGE 86

Reptile House

PAGE 87

Sequence Maze

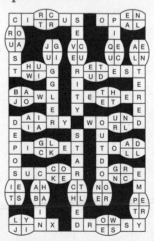

SAY IT AGAIN
LEAD

PAGE 88

Split Decisions

TRANSDELETION
ANTEATER

PAGE 89

Hyper-Sudoku

3	4	9	6	8	5	7	1	2
7	8	1	4	9	2	6	5	3
5	2	6	7	1	3	8	9	4
2	9	5	3	6	1	4	7	8
4	3	8	5	7	9	2	6	1
6	1	7	8	2	4	5	3	9
1	6	3	2	4	7	9	8	5
8	5	4	9	3	6	1	2	7
9	7	2	1	5	8	3	4	6

MIXAGRAMS

```
VIGOR   MALT
ADORN   SITE
COLOR   MACE
LIFER   PLUS
```

PAGE 90

Time For Bed

PAGE 91

On the Trail

IN OTHER WORDS
SOYBEAN

PAGE 93

One-Way Streets

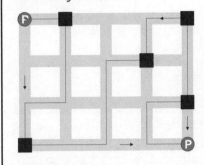

SOUND THINKING
SEAWEED

PAGE 94

Turkey Leftovers

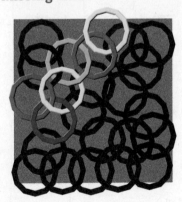

PAGE 95

Missing Links

THREE AT A RHYME
OFF, COUGH, SCOFF

PAGE 96

Star Search

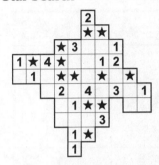

TELEPHONE TRIOS
GRAFTON, GRISHAM, ROWLING

PAGE 97

Triad Split Decisions

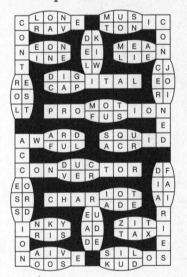

TRANSDELETION
RAGTIME

PAGE 98

Listen to the Blackbird

PAGE 99

ABC

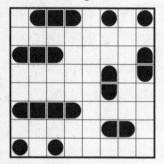

NATIONAL TREASURE
ABLOOM

PAGE 100

Find the Ships

TWO-BY-FOUR
DULY, WRAP (or WARP)

PAGE 101

Physical Figures

J	E	S	U		C	H	E	R		H	A	T	C	H
A	B	C	S		L	O	G	E		O	M	A	H	A
C	O	R	D		I	M	A	M		S	I	X	A	M
O	N	E	A	R	M	E	D	B	A	N	D	I	T	S
B	Y	E		A	B	S		R	B	I	S			
		N	A	G	S		C	A	Y		T	S	K	S
S	A	D	A	T		E	R	N	S	T		T	I	A
T	W	O	H	A	N	D	E	D	S	W	O	R	D	S
O	R	O		G	O	E	S	T		I	R	I	S	H
P	Y	R	E		B	L	T		S	N	A	P		
		K	N	E	W		O	L	E		M	A	S	
T	H	R	E	E	L	E	G	G	E	D	R	A	C	E
A	E	I	O	U		I	O	L	A		A	L	T	A
R	E	C	U	R		S	U	E	Z		K	L	U	M
P	L	A	T	O		S	P	R	Y		E	S	P	Y

PAGE 102

What's Next

Square 5 (10 straight lines per word), Square 3, Square 1

BETWEENER
FALL

PAGE 103

Sudoku

3	5	7	6	8	1	2	4	9
6	1	2	7	4	9	8	3	5
8	9	4	5	2	3	6	7	1
7	8	3	1	5	6	9	2	4
5	4	9	8	3	2	1	6	7
2	6	1	4	9	7	3	5	8
9	7	8	2	6	5	4	1	3
4	2	5	3	1	8	7	9	6
1	3	6	9	7	4	5	8	2

MIXAGRAMS

A	M	A	S	S		S	O	O	T
F	U	G	U	E		R	E	V	S
O	L	D	E	N		G	O	E	S
A	L	G	A	E		L	U	R	K

PAGE 104

Fences

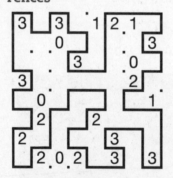

ADDITION SWITCH
384 + 267 = 651

PAGE 105

Just Imagine

N	O	R	A		R	U	E	S		C	P	A	S	
E	M	I	R		A	N	N	E		H	I	P	P	O
R	A	C	E		M	I	C	A		A	C	R	I	D
D	R	E	A	M	B	O	A	T		S	T	O	N	E
			I	O	N	S			T	U	N	E	S	
K	E	A	T	S		S	E	L	L	E	R			
E	I	G	H	T	H		S	A	O		E	D	A	M
P	R	A	I	S	E	D		P	O	T	H	O	L	E
T	E	R	N		R	O	B		M	E	A	N	E	R
	K	A	R	E	E	M		S	T	A	G	E		
P	E	S	T	S		L	A	S	T					
A	V	O	W	S		F	A	N	C	Y	F	R	E	E
G	E	N	I	E		E	T	N	A		R	I	P	E
E	N	A	C	T		T	E	E	M		E	V	I	L
	T	R	E	S		A	D	D	S		T	E	C	S

PAGE 106

Number-Out

2	2	6	5	4	3
3	2	3	4	5	5
5	2	1	2	5	4
6	3	4	1	1	2
4	6	2	1	6	6
4	1	5	1	2	6

OPPOSITE ATTRACTION
DAY, NIGHT

PAGE 107

Hyper-Sudoku

2	9	3	1	8	6	4	5	7
5	8	4	9	2	7	1	6	3
7	1	6	3	4	5	9	2	8
1	5	2	7	6	3	8	4	9
3	6	8	4	9	1	2	7	5
4	7	9	8	5	2	6	3	1
8	4	5	6	3	9	7	1	2
9	3	1	2	7	4	5	8	6
6	2	7	5	1	8	3	9	4

COUNT UP
123+45-67-8-9 = 84

PAGE 108
Grainy

PAGE 109
G Whiz

INITIAL REACTION
Out Of Sight, Out Of Mind

PAGE 110
Color Paths

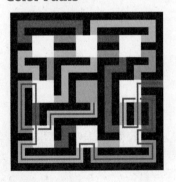

SAY IT AGAIN
WIND

PAGE 111
Double-O Four

PAGE 112
One-Way Streets

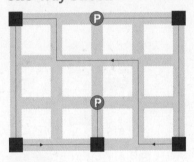

SOUND THINKING
PAISLEY

PAGE 113
123

2	1	3	1	2	3	1	3	2
3	2	1	2	3	1	2	1	3
1	3	2	3	1	2	3	2	1
3	2	1	2	3	1	2	1	3
1	3	2	3	1	2	1	3	2
3	2	1	2	3	1	3	2	1
2	1	3	1	2	3	1	3	2
1	3	2	3	1	2	3	2	1
2	1	3	1	2	3	2	1	3

SUDOKU SUM
8 3 7 + 1 0 5 = 9 4 2

PAGE 114
Line Drawing

The words in each region are spelled with the same vowels.

THREE OF A KIND
THE MAPLE AVENUE CAFÉ SERVES HOMEMADE VEAL ON EASTER.

PAGE 115
Say Cheese

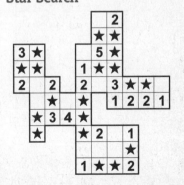

PAGE 116
Star Search

TELEPHONE TRIOS
CALGARY, HALIFAX, TORONTO

PAGE 117

Cat and Mouse Maze

THREE AT A RHYME
GUARD, HARD, BARRED

PAGE 118

Snack-Time Pairs

G	U	A	R	D		B	O	P		C	A	R	O	B
I	N	N	E	R		A	P	E		O	P	I	N	E
T	I	N	G	E		L	E	T		M	O	V	I	E
	T	E	A	A	N	D	C	R	U	M	P	E	T	S
	I	D	O			I	P	O						
P	A	W	N		F	O	X		I	N	C	I	T	E
A	B	A		T	E	P	E	E		M	A	R	A	T
C	O	F	F	E	E	A	N	D	D	A	N	I	S	H
E	V	E	R	S		L	O	G	I	N		S	T	E
R	E	R	A	T	E		N	E	T		C	H	E	R
			C	O	O			T	A	R				
M	I	L	K	A	N	D	C	O	O	K	I	E	S	
O	B	I	E	S		D	O	W		I	S	L	A	M
P	E	N	N	E		E	V	E		T	I	L	D	E
S	T	E	T	S		R	E	D		A	S	S	E	T

PAGE 119

Hyper-Sudoku

5	1	3	7	6	9	2	8	4
6	8	4	2	3	1	5	9	7
2	9	7	5	8	4	3	6	1
4	6	1	3	9	2	8	7	5
8	5	9	6	1	7	4	3	2
7	3	2	8	4	5	9	1	6
3	7	5	1	2	8	6	4	9
1	4	6	9	5	3	7	2	8
9	2	8	4	7	6	1	5	3

MIXAGRAMS
S T O O D   G A R B
A W A K E   P I K E
P I L O T   L A U D
S N I P E   E V E S

PAGE 120

ABC

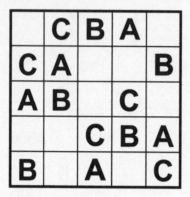

NATIONAL TREASURE
PATIO

PAGE 121

Thievery

P	A	W		A	T	A	R	I		L	E	A	F	S
A	K	A		P	O	L	E	D		E	X	I	L	E
S	I	D	E	S	W	I	P	E		S	T	R	U	T
S	T	E	V	E			L	A	P	T	O	P		
E	A	S	E		B	O	I	L	S		L	O	B	O
			G	E	N	E	S	I	S		C	U	L	
S	E	R	R	A	T	E	D		P	E	K	E	S	
P	L	E	A	S	E	S		A	B	I	L	E	N	E
E	L	A	T	E		P	L	A	N	K	T	O	N	
A	I	L		S	A	T	E	E	N	S				
R	E	S	T		F	A	R	C	E		M	O	R	E
	T	A	C	T	I	C			P	I	L	E	S	
A	M	E	B	A		C	H	A	I	R	L	I	F	T
D	E	A	L	T		H	E	L	L	O		V	I	E
O	G	L	E	S		I	D	L	E	D		E	T	E

PAGE 122

Wheels and Cogs
Ball B

BETWEENER
TIME

PAGE 123

Find the Ships

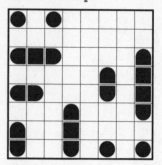

TWO-BY-FOUR
TENT, HOLE

PAGE 124

Triad Split Decisions

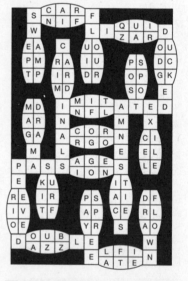

TRANSDELETION
HERCULEAN

PAGE 125

Get Out

P	E	T	E	S		P	A	W	S		B	A	B	A
I	R	I	S	H		U	T	E	P		A	C	I	D
P	I	E	T	A		L	E	E	R		N	E	T	S
S	C	R	A	M	B	L	E	D	E	G	G	S		
			T	S	O			Y	E	R				
L	O	S	E		C	P	A		S	O	B	B	E	D
A	S	H		A	C	E	L	A		W	I	R	E	R
S	H	O	O	T	I	N	G	G	A	L	L	E	R	Y
T	E	A	C	H		S	E	R	B	S		V	I	E
S	A	L	T	E	D		R	O	O		S	E	E	R
		N	O	S		M	G	T						
	S	C	A	T	T	E	R	B	R	A	I	N	S	
U	H	O	H		T	O	N	I		I	N	T	E	L
P	O	R	E		E	R	O	S		S	C	A	L	A
S	T	E	W		D	E	S	K		T	E	L	L	Y

PAGE 126

123

2	3	1	2	3	1	3	1	2
3	1	2	3	2	3	1	2	1
1	2	3	1	3	1	2	3	2
2	3	1	2	1	2	3	1	3
1	2	3	1	2	3	2	3	1
3	1	2	3	1	2	1	2	3
2	3	1	2	3	1	3	1	2
3	1	2	3	1	2	1	2	3
1	2	3	1	2	3	2	3	1

SUDOKU SUM

$5 1 9 + 3 0 7 = 8 2 6$

PAGE 127

Fences

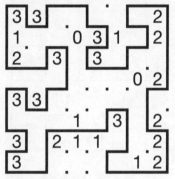

ADDITION SWITCH

$4 9 5 + 2 1 8 = 7 1 3$

PAGE 128

Join the Club

H	A	M		S	A	H	I	B		C	A	D	E	T
A	B	E		A	N	I	S	E		A	M	A	N	A
B	O	W	W	I	N	D	O	W		V	E	R	S	E
I	D	E	A	L			L	A	M	E	N	T		
T	E	D	S		S	P	A	R	E		S	M	U	G
			B	O	A	T	E	R	S		O	N	A	
E	N	S	C	O	N	C	E		L	A	U	D	S	
M	A	L	A	I	S	E		S	T	A	R	T	U	P
O	M	I	T	S			S	T	I	T	C	H	E	S
T	E	N		E	T	C	H	E	R	S				
E	D	G	E		O	R	A	T	E		V	A	S	E
		B	L	O	W	E	R			A	I	K	E	N
A	W	A	I	T		S	P	E	A	R	M	I	N	T
C	A	C	T	I		T	E	R	S	E		T	O	E
T	Y	K	E	S		S	N	A	P	S		E	R	R

PAGE 129

Go With the Flow

SAY IT AGAIN

CLOSE

PAGE 131

Coin Boxes

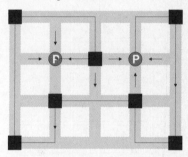

WHO'S WHAT WHERE?

Oslovian

PAGE 132

Hyper-Sudoku

2	1	7	4	6	8	9	3	5
9	6	5	2	7	3	8	4	1
4	8	3	1	5	9	6	7	2
8	4	9	7	3	1	5	2	6
3	5	2	6	9	4	7	1	8
6	7	1	8	2	5	4	9	3
5	2	6	3	4	7	1	8	9
1	9	4	5	8	2	3	6	7
7	3	8	9	1	6	2	5	4

MIXAGRAMS

A N T I C   C A S H
S W I S H   H A T E
R A D I O   O N Y X
A L L O W   W H E N

PAGE 133

By Degrees

S	L	A	W		C	R	U	Z		T	R	O	U	T
L	I	S	A		H	O	S	E		O	O	M	P	H
A	L	P	S		A	B	E	D		Q	U	I	T	E
B	A	C	H	E	L	O	R	S	B	U	T	T	O	N
S	C	A	R	L	E	T			L	E	E			
			O	F	T			T	C	U		D	R	O	P
I	D	I	O	M		O	H	A	R	A		U	N	I
H	I	S	M	A	S	T	E	R	S	V	O	I	C	E
A	O	L		N	A	T	T	Y		A	B	N	E	R
D	R	A	B		B	O	A		E	T	S			
		L	E	O			P	R	A	I	R	I	E	
O	N	D	O	C	T	O	R	S	O	R	D	E	R	S
S	E	O	U	L		J	O	A	D		I	T	A	T
L	O	T	S	A		A	B	L	E		A	R	N	E
O	N	S	E	T		I	S	M	S		N	O	I	R

PAGE 134

One-Way Streets

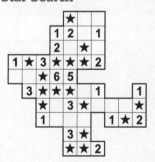

SOUND THINKING

RACEWAY

PAGE 135

Star Search

		★				
		1	2		1	
		2		★		
1	★	3	★	★	★	2
	★	6	5			
	3	★	★	★	1	1
★		3	★		★
1			1	★	2
	3	★			
★	★	2			

TELEPHONE TRIOS

ABSCOND, SHIP OUT, VAMOOSE

PAGE 136
Musical Notes

I	M	A	C		F	A	V	R	E		A	R	T	S
N	O	W	I		O	R	O	U	T		J	E	R	K
J	O	H	N	N	Y	C	A	S	H		S	P	A	Y
E	L	I	C	I	T			H	A	N		L	M	N
C	A	L	I	X		A	D	A	N	O		I	M	Y
T	H	E	N		S	T	A	T		N	I	C	E	R
		N	A	T	T	Y			R	O	N	A	L	D
	G	A	R	Y	U	S	B	O	N	D	S			
G	A	S	T	A	X		I	S	T	O	O			
A	S	T	I	R		G	N	M	A		O	L	E	S
L	T	R		A	M	I	N	T		D	R	O	I	T
L	A	I		T	E	L		C	O	P	U	L	A	
E	I	N	E		E	D	D	I	E	M	O	N	E	Y
O	R	G	S		S	E	I	K	O		O	G	E	E
N	E	S	S		E	D	G	E	S		L	E	N	D

PAGE 137
Sets of Three

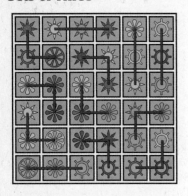

THREE AT A RHYME
BY, LIE, THIGH

PAGE 138
Sudoku

1	7	4	9	6	2	8	5	3
8	6	2	4	3	5	7	9	1
9	3	5	7	8	1	2	4	6
6	4	3	1	2	8	9	7	5
2	1	8	5	9	7	6	3	4
5	9	7	3	4	6	1	2	8
7	2	1	6	5	4	3	8	9
3	5	6	8	7	9	4	1	2
4	8	9	2	1	3	5	6	7

COUNT UP
12+3+4-5+6+7+8+9 = 44

PAGE 139
Hard Stuff

PAGE 140
Split Decisions

TRANSDELETION
TRACK SHOE

PAGE 141
Number-Out

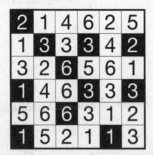

OPPOSITE ATTRACTION
TRUE, FALSE

PAGE 142
Spelling Bees

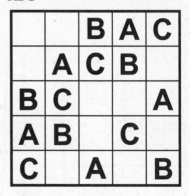

PAGE 143
ABC

		B	A	C
	A	C	B	
B	C			A
A	B		C	
C		A		B

CLUELESS CROSSWORD

C	U	S	T	A	R	D
A		Q		F		R
T	R	U	F	F	L	E
E		A		I		S
R	E	L	A	X	E	S
E		L		E		E
R	E	S	I	D	E	S

PAGE 144
Set In Stone
A: #10, B: #6, C: #5

BETWEENER
EASY

PAGE 145

Line Drawing

The words in each region have the same middle letter.

THREE OF A KIND

THE <u>MY</u>STERY NOVEL'S HERO MAY <u>BE STRONG</u>, BUT THE OUTLA<u>W IS HESI</u>TANT.

PAGE 146

Digital Display

A	L	A	N	A	L	D	A		E	X	P	O	S	T
P	A	R	A	S	A	I	L		Y	O	O	H	O	O
T	O	M	T	H	U	M	B		E	X	T	A	N	T
			T	E	D		A	R	L	O		R	A	E
G	A	R	Y		I	N	D	E	X	C	A	R	D	
O	P	E		S	I	S		S	T	O	A			
T	R	A	I	N	C	A	R				I	N	G	A
M	I	D	D	L	E	O	F	T	H	E	R	O	A	D
E	L	S	A			K	E	E	L	O	V	E	R	
		H	E	C	K		N	E	O		A	L	E	
O	N	I	O	N	R	I	N	G		Y	E	S	M	
C	O	D		C	O	D	A		A	S	A			
C	O	L	M	A	N		P	I	N	K	Y	L	E	E
U	N	E	A	S	Y		E	S	T	I	M	A	T	E
R	E	D	D	E	N		S	T	A	T	E	B	A	R

PAGE 147

Find the Ships

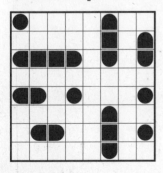

TWO-BY-FOUR

VERY, POUR

PAGE 148

Hyper-Sudoku

6	3	5	9	1	4	8	7	2
8	2	4	5	6	7	1	3	9
1	9	7	3	2	8	6	4	5
3	8	6	1	4	5	2	9	7
5	4	2	6	7	9	3	1	8
9	7	1	8	3	2	4	5	6
2	5	9	4	8	3	7	6	1
7	6	3	2	5	1	9	8	4
4	1	8	7	9	6	5	2	3

MIXAGRAMS

O U G H T	R O O M
S A L A D	T O G A
W R I T E	S A R I
C O V E T	H O W L

PAGE 149

All Those In Favor...

F	O	G	G		M	A	R	C	H		I	R	A	Q
I	K	E	A		O	C	A	L	A		M	E	N	U
F	A	R	R		T	O	M	E	S		M	A	T	E
E	Y	E	B	R	O	W	P	E	N	C	I	L	S	
			O	E	R			S	T	A	G			
C	A	B		C	H	O	K	E		P	R	M	A	N
H	U	E	D		O	N	A		P	R	A	I	S	E
I	D	R	E	A	M	O	F	J	E	A	N	N	I	E
L	I	T	T	L	E		K	I	D		T	O	D	D
E	T	H	E	L		S	A	B	E	R		R	E	Y
			C	A	R	T		S	A	X				
	A	Y	T	H	E	R	E	S	T	H	E	R	U	B
D	R	E	I		V	I	L	L	A		R	O	L	E
U	N	L	V		E	D	S	E	L		O	V	A	L
D	O	L	E		L	E	E	D	S		X	E	N	A

PAGE 150

Fences

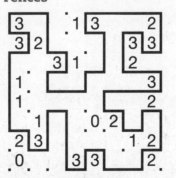

ADDITION SWITCH

1 2 3 + 5 8 6 = 7 0 9

PAGE 151

Tri-Color Maze

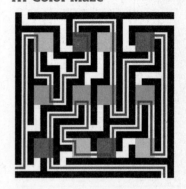

SAY IT AGAIN

MOPED

PAGE 152

Number-Out

1	2	4	2	5	4
3	2	3	6	1	4
4	1	3	4	2	4
1	5	3	4	6	3
6	4	2	4	3	6
5	6	6	1	4	2

OPPOSITE ATTRACTION

OPEN, CLOSE

PAGE 153

Something Wick-ed

S	T	O	P		S	H	O	O	T		V	E	N	I
W	A	V	E		H	A	R	P	Y		I	R	A	Q
A	X	E	S		A	D	L	E	R		D	A	B	S
B	I	R	T	H	D	A	Y	C	A	K	E			
			Y	E	T				I	O	T	A	S	
M	O	S	S	E	S		P	I	N	T	S	I	Z	E
O	C	E	A	N		G	E	N	E		M	A	V	
R	E	S	T	A	U	R	A	N	T	T	A	B	L	E
A	L	A		F	I	R	S		H	I	R	E	R	
S	O	M	E	B	O	D	Y		K	O	R	E	A	N
S	T	E	N	O		B	R	R						
			J	A	C	K	O	L	A	N	T	E	R	N
F	I	D	O		H	I	R	A	M		I	D	E	A
O	K	A	Y		A	W	A	R	E		E	N	D	S
G	E	M	S		T	I	L	E	R		D	A	S	H

PAGE 154

123

1	2	3	2	1	3	2	1	3
2	3	1	3	2	1	3	2	1
3	1	3	2	1	3	2	1	2
1	3	2	1	3	2	1	2	3
2	1	3	2	1	3	2	3	1
3	2	1	3	2	1	3	1	2
2	3	2	1	3	2	1	3	1
1	2	1	3	2	1	3	2	3
3	1	2	1	3	2	1	3	2

SUDOKU SUM

126 + 709 = 835

PAGE 155

Find the Ships

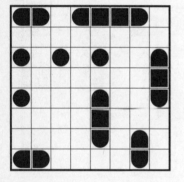

TWO-BY-FOUR

DOVE, TOUT

PAGE 156

I Love L.A.

C	A	M	P		A	A	R	P		A	T	L	A	S
A	S	I	A		V	S	O	P		L	A	I	N	E
L	H	A	S	A	A	P	S	O		O	X	B	O	W
		Y	U	L	E	S		C	H	E	E	S	E	
H	A	L	S	T	O	N		C	H	A	R	R	E	D
O	N	E	T	O	N		L	A	R	O	S	A		
L	O	W	E	S		F	A	C	I	E		L	A	H
E	D	A	M		T	O	R	T	S		P	A	T	A
D	E	L		M	E	R	C	I		F	E	R	R	Y
		C	L	I	N	C	H		T	O	T	T	E	D
A	L	I	E	N	E	E		D	I	N	E	S	E	N
B	O	N	N	E	T		R	A	N	D	R			
E	N	D	O	R		L	O	V	E	A	P	P	L	E
A	G	O	R	A		S	O	Y	A		A	H	O	Y
M	O	R	E	L		U	S	S	R		N	I	L	E

PAGE 157

Ship Spirals

IN OTHER WORDS

PIGPEN

PAGE 158

Stagecoach Maze

THREE AT A RHYME

ACED, HASTE, WAIST

PAGE 159

Star Search

TELEPHONE TRIOS

CELLIST, DRUMMER, PIANIST

PAGE 160

Say What?

C	A	W	S		L	A	R	A		J	U	L	E	P
A	B	I	T		O	L	A	V		E	N	I	A	C
J	A	D	E		A	I	D	A		E	B	E	R	T
U	T	T	E	R	F	A	I	L	U	R	E			
N	E	H	R	U		S	O	A	K		A	R	I	A
			S	S	E		N	E	A	T	E	N	S	
C	A	D		S	T	O	I	C		S	E	T	T	O
S	T	A	T	E	O	F	T	H	E	U	N	I	O	N
P	A	N	E	L		F	E	E	L	S		E	W	E
A	L	K	A	L	I	S			M	U	G			
N	E	E	R		S	P	C	A		A	R	U	B	A
			E	X	P	R	E	S	S	L	A	N	E	S
B	L	A	D	E		I	S	I	T		V	I	E	S
L	E	M	U	R		N	A	D	A		E	T	T	E
T	O	P	P	S		G	R	E	G		L	E	S	T

PAGE 161

Sudoku

6	1	8	4	5	7	3	2	9
3	7	4	6	9	2	8	5	1
9	5	2	8	3	1	4	7	6
8	9	3	2	1	5	7	6	4
2	6	1	7	4	8	9	3	5
7	4	5	3	6	9	1	8	2
4	2	6	1	8	3	5	9	7
1	3	9	5	7	6	2	4	8
5	8	7	9	2	4	6	1	3

MIXAGRAMS

```
S C E N T    N O D E
P L A I N    A J A R
D R O N E    B U Y S
U N F E D    L A S T
```

PAGE 162

One-Way Streets

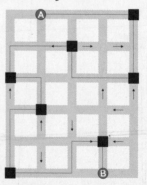

SOUND THINKING

UNEASY

PAGE 163

ABC

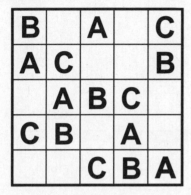

NATIONAL TREASURE
HAUNT, LANAI, NATAL, UNLIT, UNTIL

PAGE 164

Kid-Lit King

| L O O P | ■ | C B E R S | ■ | M O O D |
| P U R R | ■ | R U N A T | ■ | U S D A |
| G R E E N E G G S A N D H A M |
A S O C I A L	■	P R E P A Y S
■	I N K E D	■	R B I	■	■
T E N N	■	D R Y	■	B E T A S
E P O C H S	■	S E M I	■	A S P
H O R T O N H E A R S A W H O
E X T	■	B L E U	■	S H I N E R
E Y E O N	■	S S N	■	R Y N E
■	R A D	■	S I N G S	■	■
A S T A I R E	■	C O N T E S T
Y E R T L E T H E T U R T L E
E R I E	■	G R A S S	■	I C E D
S A G S	■	S E T T O	■	P H D S

PAGE 165

Glass Act
#7

BETWEENER
MODEL

PAGE 166

Find the Ships

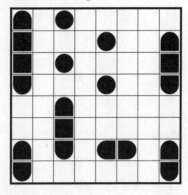

TWO-BY-FOUR
RANT, ROAR

PAGE 167

123

3	1	2	1	2	3	1	3	2
2	3	1	3	1	2	3	2	1
1	2	3	2	3	1	2	1	3
2	3	1	3	1	2	3	2	1
3	1	2	1	2	3	1	3	2
1	2	3	2	3	1	2	1	3
2	3	1	3	1	2	3	2	1
3	1	2	1	2	3	1	3	2
1	2	3	2	3	1	2	1	3

SUDOKU SUM
$5 2 8 + 1 0 9 = 6 3 7$

PAGE 169

Around the Bend

PAGE 170

Fences

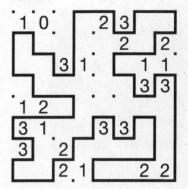

ADDITION SWITCH
$4 6 8 + 1 0 3 = 5 7 1$

PAGE 171

Number-Out

5	3	2	1	1	4
5	2	6	1	4	1
6	2	5	2	3	4
1	4	3	3	3	5
3	3	1	1	2	6
2	1	3	4	5	2

OPPOSITE ATTRACTION
BACK, FRONT

PAGE 172

Manual Operation

F E A T	■	A K I S S	■	I S M S
A N N O	■	R A D I I	■	N L E R
T I E D	■	T H I N G S T O D O
H A N D L I N G C H A R G E	■
A C T S A S	■	■	E T T U
■	■	H T T P	■	S E D A K A
A N G S T	■	A L I A	■	E L I A
F E E L I N G O F W A R M T H
E T N A	■	E S T S	■	L S A T S
W H A M M O	■	Z O L A	■	■
■	D I P L	■	I M A G E S
■	T O U C H I N G M O M E N T
K I D N E Y B E A N	■	E T U I
E R I K	■	T R I P E	■	B O R N
Y E N S	■	E E L E D	■	A N E T

PAGE 173
No Three in a Row

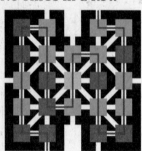

BETWEENER
WATER

PAGE 174
Hyper-Sudoku

6	1	4	2	5	9	3	7	8
9	3	2	8	4	7	6	1	5
8	5	7	6	1	3	4	9	2
3	4	9	1	6	5	2	8	7
7	6	5	9	2	8	1	4	3
2	8	1	7	3	4	9	5	6
1	9	3	5	8	6	7	2	4
5	2	6	4	7	1	8	3	9
4	7	8	3	9	2	5	6	1

MIXAGRAMS
SWEAT AGES
TOTEM LAVA
TRUST AMID
ADIEU RENT

PAGE 175
"D" As in Geography

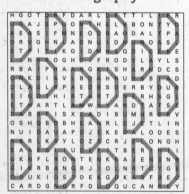

INITIAL REACTION
Two Heads Are Better Than One

PAGE 176
Keep Quiet

PAGE 177
Triad Split Decisions

TRANSDELETION
FORECAST

PAGE 178
One-Way Streets

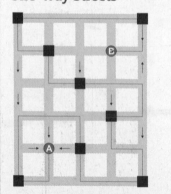

SOUND THINKING
IMMENSE and OMINOUS

PAGE 179
Sense of Yuma

PAGE 180
Solitaire Poker

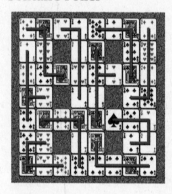

SAY IT AGAIN
MINUTE

PAGE 181
Star Search

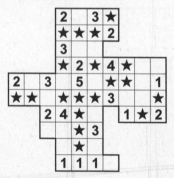

TELEPHONE TRIOS
AVOCADO, LETTUCE, PUMPKIN

PAGE 182

Sudoku

8	4	1	7	3	2	5	6	9
2	5	7	1	6	9	8	3	4
6	9	3	8	4	5	1	2	7
4	7	2	5	1	6	9	8	3
3	8	5	9	7	4	2	1	6
9	1	6	2	8	3	7	4	5
7	2	4	6	5	1	3	9	8
1	3	8	4	9	7	6	5	2
5	6	9	3	2	8	4	7	1

COUNT UP
1+234-5-67-89 = 74

PAGE 183

Praiseworthy Comment

M	E	S	H		P	A	T	H	S		A	L	M	S
U	C	L	A		S	T	O	O	L		T	E	A	L
I	H	A	V	E	Y	E	T	T	O		L	A	Z	E
R	O	M	A	N	C	E		T	W	E	A	K	E	D
		N	T	H		D	U	D	E	S				
S	M	E	A	R		B	E	B	O	R	E	D	B	Y
C	A	B	S		L	A	M		W	I	S	E	U	P
A	N	O		S	O	M	E	O	N	E		C	T	R
L	I	N	D	E	N		T	V	S		R	A	T	E
P	A	Y	I	N	G	M	E	A		J	U	L	E	S
		S	A	F	E	R		N	U	N				
E	I	G	H	T	A	M		S	O	D	A	P	O	P
L	I	M	O		C	O	M	P	L	I	M	E	N	T
L	I	E	U		E	R	I	C	A		O	K	L	A
A	I	N	T		D	Y	L	A	N		K	E	Y	S

PAGE 184

ABC

C			B	A
	A	B	C	
	C	A		B
B		C	A	
A	B			C

CLUELESS CROSSWORD

M	E	M	E	N	T	O
I		A		U		V
S	C	R	U	P	L	E
A		I		T		R
D	O	M	A	I	N	S
D		B		A		A
S	W	A	L	L	O	W

PAGE 185

Find the Ships

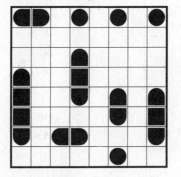

TWO-BY-FOUR
PITY, MULL

PAGE 186

Sport Play

B	E	L	G		C	L	A	D		C	C	C	L
I	L	I	E		H	I	R	E	D		L	U	R	E
B	A	L	L	P	A	R	K	F	I	G	U	R	E	S
	N	I	C	O	L	E		E	N	A	B	L	E	S
		A	L	I			R	I	M					
I	C	E	P	I	C	K	S		N	E	S	T	L	E
V	E	X		S	E	E	I	N	G		P	O	O	R
A	L	E	P	H		N	E	A		B	A	R	O	N
N	L	C	S		T	O	N	I	E	R		I	F	S
A	S	S	I	S	I		A	L	L	E	Y	C	A	T
			L	E	A			T	W	A				
I	N	S	P	O	T	S		B	R	E	M	E	N	
C	O	U	R	T	A	P	P	E	A	R	A	N	C	E
O	D	I	E		C	I	R	R	I		H	O	O	D
N	E	T	S			C	O	N	N		A	S	S	T

PAGE 187

Cut That Out
#8

THREE AT A RHYME
CHIC, MEEK, PIQUE

PAGE 188

123

1	3	1	2	3	2	3	2	1
3	2	3	1	2	1	2	1	3
2	1	2	3	1	3	1	3	2
3	2	1	2	3	1	3	2	1
2	1	2	3	1	3	2	1	3
1	3	1	2	3	2	1	3	2
3	2	3	1	2	1	3	2	1
1	3	2	3	1	2	1	3	2
2	1	3	1	2	3	2	1	3

SUDOKU SUM
7 0 9 + 1 2 5 = 8 3 4

PAGE 189

Fences

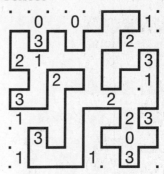

ADDITION SWITCH
7 3 5 + 2 1 6 = 9 5 1

PAGE 190

Playing Politics

C	L	A	N	G		B	A	R	B		T	B	S	P
C	O	C	O	A		O	P	E	R		W	A	I	L
V	O	I	D	S		R	E	N	O		I	N	T	O
I	N	D	E	P	E	N	D	E	N	T	S	D	A	Y
			S	A	L			T	U	T	O	R	S	
P	B	S		R	E	V	I	S	E	R				
I	O	T	A		C	O	R	E		O	L	D	I	E
E	X	E	C	U	T	I	V	E	S	W	E	E	T	S
T	Y	P	E	B		L	I	M	A		I	N	C	A
			O	P	E	N	S	U	P		T	H	U	
S	H	O	F	A	R			D	O	O				
C	A	P	I	T	O	L	G	A	I	N	S	T	A	X
A	G	E	S		M	E	A	L		C	H	A	R	M
P	A	R	T		P	A	L	E		H	E	N	N	A
E	R	A	S		T	R	E	X		O	A	S	E	S

PAGE 191
Hyper-Sudoku

9	3	5	7	1	8	2	6	4
8	4	1	3	2	6	7	9	5
6	7	2	5	9	4	3	8	1
3	9	6	8	4	2	1	5	7
2	8	4	1	7	5	9	3	6
1	5	7	9	6	3	8	4	2
7	1	3	4	5	9	6	2	8
4	6	8	2	3	1	5	7	9
5	2	9	6	8	7	4	1	3

MIXAGRAMS

```
I C I N G     C L U E
R O B I N     O G R E
F R I E D     B A K E
I N E P T     S U E T
```

PAGE 192
Split Decisions

TRANSDELETION
AFTERNOON

PAGE 193
By the Numbers

PAGE 194
Turn Maze

BETWEENER
STONE

PAGE 195
Number-Out

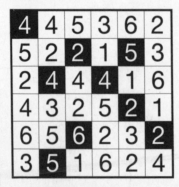

OPPOSITE ATTRACTION
THICK, THIN

PAGE 196
One-Way Streets

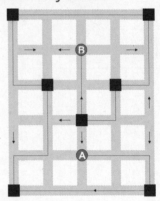

SOUND THINKING
LIGHTHOUSE

PAGE 197
Pardon My French

S	H	A	W		M	I	A	M	I		G	M	A	N
L	A	L	A		O	R	L	O	N		I	O	W	A
A	N	O	N		N	A	I	L	S		S	N	A	P
M	O	N	I	C	A	S	E	L	E	S		U	K	E
S	I	G	N	A	L			S	C	H	E	M	E	S
			G	R	I	M	E		T	O	R	E		
M	O	M		P	S	A	L	M		P	A	N	D	A
I	R	O	N		A	T	E	A	M		S	T	I	R
T	O	N	E	S		S	C	R	O	D		S	E	C
		A	W	L	S		T	E	N	O	R			
G	O	S	S	I	P	S		G	O	O	D	I	E	
A	C	T		M	O	N	E	Y	O	R	D	E	R	S
I	T	E	M		R	O	D	E	O		E	T	A	S
N	E	R	O		T	U	N	A	S		N	O	T	E
S	T	Y	E		S	T	A	R	E		T	O	E	S

PAGE 198
Sudoku

1	3	6	2	8	5	4	7	9
5	2	8	7	4	9	1	3	6
9	7	4	6	1	3	2	8	5
4	1	7	5	3	8	9	6	2
2	8	5	9	7	6	3	1	4
6	9	3	4	2	1	7	5	8
7	5	9	1	6	2	8	4	3
3	4	2	8	5	7	6	9	1
8	6	1	3	9	4	5	2	7

MIXAGRAMS

```
T H U M B     B A R E
B U G L E     A R I D
U M B E R     C R A G
A P P L E     K N O B
```

PAGE 199

Star Search

TELEPHONE TRIOS
BINDING, CHAPTER, FLYLEAF

PAGE 200

Wild and Woolly

T	O	R	S	O		T	A	M	E	D		S	H	A
A	B	I	E	S		A	L	O	N	E		H	O	W
G	O	O	N	T	H	E	L	A	M	B		E	V	A
S	E	T	T	E	E		S	T	I	R		E	E	K
		R	O	S	S		S	T	I	P	P	L	E
O	B	E	Y		T	I	P		Y	E	L	L
L	A	W		O	M	I	T		F	E	A	R	S
D	R	E	W		N	O	N	O	S		A	B	I	T
S	I	D	E	S		N	O	U	N		O	L	A
	O	P	T	S		N	C	O		T	R	E	Y
C	E	N	T	R	E	S		H	O	P	I
H	I	T		O	C	T	O		P	L	E	D	G	E
A	D	S		B	U	E	N	O	S	A	R	I	E	S
N	E	A		E	R	E	C	T		T	R	E	N	T
T	R	Y		S	E	L	E	S		H	A	T	E	D

PAGE 201

Minuteman Maze

SAY IT AGAIN
REFUSE

PAGE 202

Musical Trail

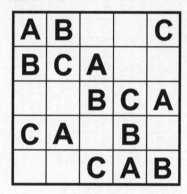

WHO'S WHAT WHERE?
Islander

PAGE 203

ABC

A	B			C
B	C	A		
		B	C	A
C	A		B	
		C	A	B

CLUELESS CROSSWORD

B	O	L	O	G	N	A
E		E		R		S
M	I	D	W	E	E	K
U		G		A		A
S	W	E	E	T	E	N
E		R		E		C
D	E	S	E	R	V	E

PAGE 204

Themeless Toughie

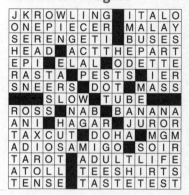

J	K	R	O	W	L	I	N	G		I	T	A	L	O
O	N	E	P	I	E	C	E	R		M	A	L	A	Y
S	E	R	E	N	G	E	T	I		B	U	S	E	S
H	E	A	D		A	C	T	T	H	E	P	A	R	T
E	P	I		E	L	A	L		O	D	E	T	T	E
R	A	S	T	A		P	E	S	T	S		I	E	R
S	N	E	E	R	S		D	O	T		M	A	S	S
		S	L	O	W		T	U	B	E	
R	O	S	S		N	A	B		B	A	N	A	N	A
A	N	I		H	A	G	A	R		J	U	R	O	R
T	A	X	C	U	T		D	O	H	A		M	G	M
A	D	I	O	S	A	M	I	G	O		S	O	I	R
T	A	R	O	T		A	D	U	L	T	L	I	F	E
A	T	O	L	L		T	E	E	S	H	I	R	T	S
T	E	N	S	E		T	A	S	T	E	T	E	S	T

PAGE 206

Find the Ships

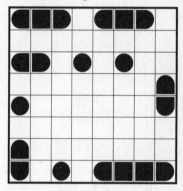

TWO-BY-FOUR
TIDY, FINE

PAGE 207

Hyper-Sudoku

6	4	2	8	5	7	9	1	3
3	7	1	9	4	6	5	8	2
9	5	8	3	1	2	7	4	6
7	6	4	2	8	1	3	9	5
8	1	3	7	9	5	6	2	4
5	2	9	6	3	4	1	7	8
4	8	7	1	6	3	2	5	9
2	3	5	4	7	9	8	6	1
1	9	6	5	2	8	4	3	7

BETWEENER
BOARD

PAGE 208
Themeless Toughie

```
T R I D E N T ■ L A T C H E D
R E M O T E R ■ O P E R A T E
A P P R O V E ■ G E N E R A L
P L A I N ■ M A G ■ S E D G E
P E N S ■ A B L E R ■ D I E T
E T E ■ C U L P R I T ■ E R E
R E L E A S E S ■ V E E R E D
■ ■ ■ A R T S ■ D U A L ■ ■ ■
G R A T E R ■ T O L L F R E E
N O N ■ T I S S U E S ■ I S M
A M O S ■ A P A R T ■ L O S E
R A I T T ■ E R N ■ P A T E R
L I N E A G E ■ E R O D I N G
E N T E R E D ■ S I L E N C E
D E S P O T S ■ S P O N G E D
```

PAGE 209
What's Next?

Square 4 (corner circles move 90 degrees counterclockwise each time, newly added circles are black each time), Square 4, Square 1 (+3, +4, +5, +6)

THREE AT A RHYME
MINE, SIGN, STEIN

PAGE 210
Fences

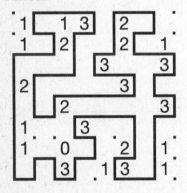

ADDITION SWITCH
3 0 2 + 4 5 9 = 7 6 1

PAGE 211
Themeless Toughie

```
H A D A S E A T ■ P A M P A S
A M O R E T T I ■ S C O R C H
R E N T A C O P ■ H A V E T O
K N E L L S ■ S H A P E S U P
E R I E S ■ S T O W ■ S O A P
R A T S ■ J O H N ■ N O R T E
T H I ■ S P A D E ■ M E N T O R
T H I ■ I N A S T E W ■ S R S
R O S I N S ■ C B S T V ■ ■ ■
A M O N G ■ M A S H ■ A P T S
M E G S ■ G U L P ■ F R O O T
P R O T R U D E ■ B E M I N E
L U N A T E ■ S A R D I N I A
E L I T E S ■ A M O U N T E D
R E C E S S ■ T E M P T E R S
```

PAGE 212
123

```
2 1 3 1 3 2 3 2 1
3 2 1 3 1 3 2 1 2
2 1 3 2 3 2 1 3 1
1 3 2 1 2 1 3 2 3
3 1 3 2 1 2 1 3 2
1 2 1 3 2 3 2 1 3
2 3 2 3 1 3 1 3 2 1
3 2 1 2 3 1 3 2 2
1 3 2 3 2 1 2 1 3
```

SUDOKU SUM
4 3 8 + 2 1 9 = 6 5 7

PAGE 213
Number-Out

```
1 5 4 2 3 2
1 3 6 1 4 5
5 5 1 6 2 2
6 2 6 5 6 4
1 1 3 1 6 2
2 6 4 3 1 6
```

OPPOSITE ATTRACTION
RIGHT, WRONG

PAGE 214
Themeless Toughie

```
A B R I D G E D ■ M O W E R S
L E O N A R D O ■ E N A M E L
L A Y A N E G G ■ D E R I V E
I R A N ■ W E S ■ D I N G E D
E E L E R ■ T E L L ■ R A D
D R E ■ O N S A L E ■ P A L E
■ ■ A B O A R D ■ P E T E R
C A V E R N ■ E A R N E D ■ ■
R A N I S ■ T U R N I N ■ ■
U R N S ■ K A N S A S ■ I S T
F O O ■ V I S E ■ M A N O R
F L U T E S ■ A W E ■ E D I E
L I N E R S ■ T A C I T U R N
E N C A S E ■ E N H A N C E D
D E E M E D ■ N E O N A T E S
```

PAGE 215
Shakespearean Jigsaw

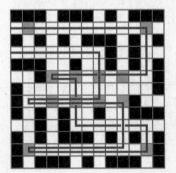

IN OTHER WORDS
EMCEE

PAGE 216
Straight Ahead

SAY IT AGAIN
RESIGN

PAGE 217
Themeless Toughie

R	E	C	E	S	S		A	R	R	E	S	T	E	D
A	D	R	O	I	T		B	E	A	N	P	O	L	E
K	W	A	N	Z	A		L	E	S	G	I	R	L	S
E	A	T	S	A	T		E	D	H	A	R	R	I	S
S	R	I		B	U	R			R	E	E	S	E
I	D	O		L	E	E	W	A	R	D		N	O	R
N	I	N		E	S	C	A	P	E	E		T	N	T
			Q	U	I	L	T
B	I	P		C	U	R	S	O	R	S		M	P	S
E	T	A		B	E	S	T	M	A	N		O	R	E
A	S	T	O	R		B	I	O		D	E	N
T	O	R	I	A	M	O	S		N	O	T	I	M	E
S	K	I	N	D	I	V	E		I	P	E	C	A	C
M	A	C	K	I	N	A	C		N	E	R	U	D	A
E	Y	E	S	O	N	L	Y		G	R	I	M	E	S

PAGE 218
ABCD

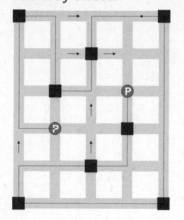

C		D	A	B
A	B		D	C
	C	A		D	B
B	D			A	C
	A	B	C		D
D		C	B		A

NATIONAL TREASURE
INMATE, NATIVE

PAGE 219
Sudoku

8	7	1	2	6	5	9	4	3
3	2	5	1	4	9	7	8	6
9	4	6	8	3	7	2	1	5
7	9	3	4	2	6	1	5	8
6	5	8	3	9	1	4	2	7
4	1	2	5	7	8	6	3	9
5	8	7	9	1	4	3	6	2
1	3	9	6	5	2	8	7	4
2	6	4	7	8	3	5	9	1

MIXAGRAMS

S	P	O	O	F		A	N	T	E
R	A	I	S	E		N	O	N	E
L	U	C	R	E		K	I	L	N
F	L	A	M	E		A	T	O	P

PAGE 220
Themeless Toughie

S	A	F	A	R	I		M	A	R	I	N	A	R	A
P	R	O	B	E	D		A	G	O	N	I	Z	E	D
A	M	O	E	B	A		S	A	M	S	P	A	D	E
T	A	L	L	A	H	A	S	S	E	E		L	I	P
U	M	A		R	O	U	E	S		T	R	E	A	T
L	E	W		R	U	I	N		H	A	L	S
A	N	A		A	F	A	R		E	M	O
S	T	Y	M	I	E	S		G	L	A	S	G	O	W
	U	R	N		B	A	L	D		O	R	R
P	A	W	S		G	I	R	L		A	D	A
O	S	A	K	A		M	O	A	T	S		L	A	P
P	S	I		D	E	P	O	S	I	T	S	L	I	P
O	U	T	M	O	D	E	D		M	O	L	I	N	E
F	R	E	E	R	I	D	E		E	V	E	N	E	R
F	E	R	R	E	T	E	D		R	E	W	E	D	S

PAGE 221
One-Way Streets

SOUND THINKING
CASSEROLE

PAGE 222
Split Decisions

TRANSDELETION
SEAT BELT

PAGE 223
Themeless Toughie

C	A	C	K	L	E	S		A	E	R	O	B	I	C
E	M	A	N	A	T	E		D	I	O	R	A	M	A
R	E	N	E	W	A	L		A	N	A	G	R	A	M
A	R	I	A	S		V	E	G		M	A	R	G	E
M	I	N	D		M	A	N	I	A		N	O	I	R
I	C	E		L	E	G	I	O	N	S		O	N	O
C	A	S	C	A	D	E	D		S	T	A	M	E	N
			O	D	D	S		S	W	I	M
T	U	N	N	E	L		S	H	E	R	I	F	F	S
I	T	A		S	E	N	I	O	R	S		L	I	P
R	I	T	A		D	O	T	E	S		L	E	N	O
A	L	I	V	E		V	E	T		P	A	E	A	N
D	I	V	E	R	G	E		R	I	O	T	I	N	G
E	T	E	R	N	A	L		E	S	S	E	N	C	E
S	Y	S	T	E	M	S		E	M	E	R	G	E	D

PAGE 224
Looped Path

SAY IT AGAIN
PRODUCE

PAGE 225
Star Search

		2	★	1		
1		★				
2	2	★	4	★	2	★	1
★	★			★		2
		2		3		★	2
		3	★	★	★		★
★	★		★	5	3	★	3
3		3	★			2	★
★				3		
2	★	2	★	2	★	

TELEPHONE TRIOS
CURTAIN, SHUTTER, VALANCE

PAGE 226
Themeless Toughie

S	C	A	N	D	A	L		S	A	N	T	A	N	A
C	A	L	O	R	I	E		A	D	O	R	N	E	D
R	I	O	T	E	R	S		D	I	V	I	N	E	D
A	N	N	E	X	E	S		D	E	I	C	E	R	S
P	E	E	R	E	D		P	L	U	C	K			
			L	O	R	R	E		E	S	S	E	X	
H	A	J	J		U	H	O	H		S	T	O	R	E
I	D	E	A		T	A	C	O	S		E	L	A	N
R	E	A	C	T		P	E	R	U		R	O	S	A
T	E	N	O	R		S	E	N	S	E			
			B	I	P	O	D		H	A	V	E	A	T
F	L	I	R	T	E	D		G	I	S	E	L	L	E
R	A	V	I	O	L	I		O	B	E	R	L	I	N
A	N	O	I	N	T	S		N	A	I	V	E	S	T
T	E	R	S	E	S	T		E	R	N	E	S	T	O

PAGE 227
Number-Out

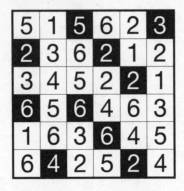

OPPOSITE ATTRACTION
DEEP, SHALLOW

PAGE 228
Line Drawing

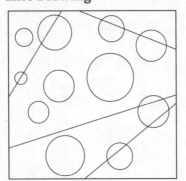

TWO- BY-FOUR
EDGY, HORN

PAGE 229
Themeless Toughie

I	C	O	N	F	E	S	S		W	E	B	C	A	M
M	R	P	E	A	N	U	T		O	R	I	O	L	E
B	A	T	T	L	E	R	S		M	U	L	D	E	R
E	V	I	T	A		F	I	R	E	P	L	A	C	E
D	E	N	Y		M	E	M	E	N	T	O			
			F	E	D	O	N			W	O	R	M	
S	N	A	P	A	T		N	E	A	T	I	D	E	A
C	O	T	E	D	O	R		E	T	O	N	I	A	N
T	R	O	T	S	O	U	T		S	A	G	E	L	Y
V	A	N	E		N	Y	M	E	T					
		R	E	G	A	L	I	A		B	A	L	M	
U	P	A	N	D	A	T	E	M		H	O	N	E	Y
S	A	N	E	S	T		N	O	S	E	R	I	N	G
E	N	T	R	E	E		O	S	O	L	E	M	I	O
R	E	S	O	L	D		L	A	N	D	S	E	N	D

PAGE 230
Triad Split Decisions

TRANSDELETION
MINESTRONE

PAGE 231
Space Holders
A: #9, B: #8, C: #3

THREE AT A RHYME
HUES, LOSE, BRUISE

PAGE 232
Themeless Toughie

T	R	A	C	E	R	S		C	L	I	M	B	E	D
H	O	N	O	R	E	E		L	I	S	S	O	M	E
E	X	T	R	E	M	E	M	E	A	S	U	R	E	S
L	A	I		S	U	K	A	R	N	O		R	R	S
E	N	C	S		S	E	L	I	G		D	O	G	E
A	N	O	M	Y		R	O	C		P	A	W	E	R
D	E	M	E	A	N	S		S	P	R	Y	E	S	T
		P	A	S	E			G	I	R	D			
F	A	E	R	I	E	S		L	A	M	O	T	T	A
E	A	T	E	R		A	G	E		P	O	R	E	D
E	M	I	R		E	T	O	N	S		M	O	N	O
L	I	T		A	L	I	A	S	E	S		U	S	P
F	L	I	B	B	E	R	T	I	G	I	B	B	E	T
I	N	V	O	L	V	E		N	A	C	E	L	L	E
T	E	E	P	E	E	S		G	L	A	D	E	Y	E